AF531385

NGOs AS PRIME MOVERS
Sectoral Action for Social Development

NGOs as Prime Movers
Sectoral Action for Social Development

SHIVANI DHARMARAJAN

KANISHKA PUBLISHERS, DISTRIBUTORS
NEW DELHI-110 002

KANISHKA PUBLISHERS, DISTRIBUTORS
4697/5-21 A, Ansari Road, Daryaganj
New Delhi-110 002
Phones : 2327 0497, 2328 8285
Fax : 011-2328 8285
e-mail: kanishka_publishing@yahoo.co.in

First Published 2001
Second Edition 2007

ISBN 81-7391-405-2

PRINTED IN INDIA

Published by Madan Sachdeva for Kanishka Publishers, Distributors, 4697/5-21A, Ansari Road, Daryaganj, New Delhi-110 002, Typeset by Sunshine Graphics, Delhi, and Printed at Nice Printing Press, Delhi.

Preface

This book titled "NGOs As Prime Movers: Sectoral Action for Social Development" mainly focuses on the roles and responsibilities bestowed upon modern-age NGOs in terms of social development, human capacity building, poverty alleviation, health-care initiatives, environmental and human rights' protection.

"Social Development", today, has emerged as the prime area of concern in contemporary society. Most of the parameters of social development are being given attention, more the ever before. The success of the "World Summit on Social Development" is a proof that economic upliftment without social emancipation is no more considered to be a genuine development paradigm. Similarly the other facts which has been realised worldwide is that without NGOs' active involvement, the required level of social development is impossible to be attained. Today, NGOs' role has become the key factor in people-centred development. That is why, arguments in favour of and against the ability of NGOs to raise the confidence and competence of people through their activities, have become a matter of serious debate. The role of NGOs in poverty alleviation, delivery of healthcare, spread of education, development of human resource, restoration and conservation of environment, and above all, in protection of human rights, has attained much significance. Government-NGO relationship, as antagonistic cooperation framework, also needs to be understood both in sectoral and cross-sectoral perspectives. Practical experiences and suggestions need to be put forward to enable the NGO-Government relationship to be more positive and productive.

No doubt, today, people are at the heart of development. The promotion of individual, family and community well-being provides a human-development agenda around the global, in particular, when more than 1 billion of human population still live much below the poverty live. The role of NGOs in human resource development and in mobilizing resources for the same, has attained considerable significance. Also, the fact remains that by working with and through such non-profit voluntary institutions and individuals/activists, governments, in particular, in Third World nations, will rather empower community organisations. Citizens, themselves will play a larger role in the leadership of society and in their own self-development. Whatever the precise formulation, appropriate to individual countries, there is a set of critical and related elements which could be considered as core constituents in any integrated view of Human Resource Development (HRD). These include, education and training; primary health care; population and poverty; healthy environment; and basic human rights. The fact that NGOs have close interpersonal interaction with people in the communities they work with, is extremely useful for implementing required interventions for attaining the said goals. Similarly, NGOs often work in areas and regions which are not generally covered by the governmental programmes. Besides, NGOs do have greater flexibility to accommodate changing programmes and public needs and are tuned to innovate and implement new initiatives without major hindrances. Therefore, NGOs can be more efficient and effective in the use of resources and can provide support directly to people and communities. Above all, NGOs have an important collaborative role in planning, implementation, and evaluation of national social development programmes. Therefore, a healthy growth of the NGO led social movement is rather a national necessity. Besides other established factors, it requires trained personnel, adequate funding support and specific rules for establishing accountability. Then only, NGOs can play distinctive roles towards creation of a just, sustainable and inclusive global society.

In general, NGOs commonly refer themselves as voluntary agencies. Yet, in light of the aforesaid roles, the pressure to "professionalize" NGOs generally lead towards assigning more of the control and responsibility to full-time staff who function much as the paid staff of a business or a government agency. The role of "volunteers" may become limited mainly to make financial contributions for supporting the work of paid staff, resulting in a loss of the ability to mobilize voluntary energy that is one of the distinctive qualities of a true NGO.

Many NGOs, especially in the Third World, argue the need for an alternative development vision. This vision encourages modernization in physical consumption, financial self-reliance, and the conservation and recycling of resources. It focuses on local ownership and use of local resources of meet local needs. It calls for economic and political democratization as the cornerstone of economic and political justice. In India too, like in many other countries, NGOs have become most important agents of change and social development. In light of the aforementioned facts, this book with serve the purpose of an eye-opener, not only for existing NGOs but also for them who want to be the part of this evolving global movement.

Shivani Dharmarajan

Abbreviations

ACP	Africa, Caribbean and the Pacific
ADLI	Agrarian Development Led Industrialization
AI	Amnesty International
ARI	Acute Respiratory Insufficiency
BCR	Central Bank of the Republic (Peru)
BE	Basic Education
CAS	Country Assistance Strategy
CCFCL	Egypian NGO
CCPA	Canadian Centre for Policy Alternatives
CDRN	Community Development Resources Net
CPR	Contraceptive Prevalence Rate
CSW	Commission on the Status of Women
CTUWS	Centre of Trade Union and Workers Services
CWCC	Concern for Working Children Centre
CYSD	Centre for Youth and Social Development
DGAP	Development GAP for Alternative Policies
DWCRA	Development for Women and Children of Rural Areas
EAP	Economically Active Population
EAP	Employment Assistance Programme, Egypt.
EAS	Employment Assurance Agency
EGP	Employment Guarantee Programme
ECLAC	Economic Commission for Latin America and Caribbean
EEC	European Economic Community
ENDES	National survey of Health (Peru)
ENNIV	National survey of living standards (Peru)
EP	Equipo PUEBLO
ERDA	Ethiopian Resources for Developing Agriculture
ERRP	Emergency Project of Recuperation and Reconstruction

ESC	Economic Social and Cultural
EU	European Union
FAM	Mutual Support Forum (Mexico)
FFEP	Food For Education Programme
FWCW	Fourth World Conference on Women
GNP	Gross National Programme
GOI	Government of India
GSP	Growth Support Programme
HDI	Human Development Index
HDR	Human Development Report
IAG	Inter Africa Group
ICPD	International Conference on Population
IDB	Interamerican Development Bank
IDS	Institute for Development Studies
IJRY	Intensified Jawahar Rojgar Yojna
IMR	Infant Mortality Rate
INEI	National Statistics Institute (Peru)
IPS	Inter Press Service
IPS	Institute for Policy Studies
IRB	Indian Reserve Bank
IYEP	International Year for the Erradication of Poverty
JRY	Jawahar Rojgar Yojna
LE	Egyptian pounds
MERCOSUR	Common Market of the South (Argentina-Brasil-Paraguay-Uruguay)
MRD	Ministry of Rural Development
MWS	Millions Wells Scheme
NAFTA	North American Foreign Trade Agreement
NFE	Non Formal Education
NIP	National Indicative Program
NREP	National Rural Employment Programme
NWRC	New Woman Research Centre
OCU	Overseas Contract Workers
ODA	Official Development Aid
PAPSCA	Prog. to Alleviate Poverty & Social Costs of Adjustment
PMRY	Programme for micro enterprises, India
PoA	Program of Action
PPA	Participatory Poverty Assessment
RAC	Region Autonoma Cordillera

RAMM	Region Autonoma Mindanao Musulmana
RLEGP	Rural Landless Employment Guarantee Programme
RMALC	Mexican Network for Action on Free Trade
RMK	Rastriya Mahila Kosh
SAP	Structural Adjustment Policy
SAS	Structural Adjustment Support
SUNS	South-North Development Monitor
TGE	Transitory Government of Etiopia
TRYSE	Training of Rural Youth for Self Employment
TWN	Third World Network
UBNI	Unsatisfied Basic Needs Index
UNCED	United Nations Conference on Environment & Development
UNCTAD	United Nations Conference on Trade And Development
UNFPA	United Nations Population Fund
WB	World Bank
WCHR	World Conference on Human Rights
WEDO	Women's Environment and Development Organization
WHO	World Health Organization
WIDE	Women in Development Europe
WSC	World Summit on Children
WSSD	World Summit on Social Development

Contents

1

NGOs, Social Development and HRD

The NGO world is complex. There are national and international NGOs. There are product-oriented and process-oriented NGOs. There is a complexity of interaction within the world of NGOs; within government, and between the two. NGOs can contribute to human resource development by their very existence, and through the development and introduction of new technologies.

COMMITMENTS THAT MIGHT MAKE HISTORY

In 1995, the governments of the world committed themselves solemnly and publicly, to eradicate poverty and to achieve equality between women and men. Now it is no longer acceptable as a "face of life" that half of humanity is denied the full enjoyment of their rights because of its gender or that one out of five human beings is condemned to a life of deprivation.

The decision to end poverty and inequity has been compared with last century's historic decision to end slavery. The heads of state and government stated in Copenhagen that in committing themselves to these goals as an "ethical, social, political and economic imperative of humankind" they were not putting forth an idea originated in bureaus and meeting rooms, but reacting to what their constituencies were pressing them to do: "We acknowledge that the people of the world have shown in different ways an urgent need to address profound social problems, especially poverty, unemployment and social exclusion". And at the same time they recognized that the achievement of these goals requires the commitment and concerted action of governments, international organizations and civil society.

Thousands of Non-Governmental Organizations (NGOs) accredited to the World Summit on Social Development and the Fourth World Conference of Women brought to the international negotiating process the voices of the citizens and communities that the world leaders were already hearing from at home. Tens of thousands organizations not officially accredited to the conferences gathered in Copenhagen and Beijing in "parallel" NGO forums.

For many decades NGOs have been active in implementing development projects in their own countries and their own communities. The 1993 UNDP Human Development Report (1993), estimates that NGOs manage to reach 250 million of the poorest people. According to the World Bank, NGOs in India spend US $ 520 million a year, a figure representing a full quarter of the foreign aid India receives annually. The 'Grameen Bank' has succeeded in setting up small-scale credit programmes for landless farmers in at least 23,000 villages in Bangladesh alone.

Social development, full employment and the well-being of humanity are objectives included in the UN Charter since the creation of the organization half a century ago and NGOs have also had "consultative status" with the UN since then. But this participation was limited during the first decades of the UN to a handful of large international organizations and the UN itself was not very successful in leading a worldwide coherent social development effort. The Cold War between East and West and the decision by the Reagan administration in 1982 to stop the North and South dialogue (transferring all major macro-economic decisions to Northern-dominated fora) were some of the main factors that stood in the way of effective international co-operation.

In the nineties, the UN organized a series of high level international conferences to redefine the strategies of the international community on several key issues. The series started in 1990 with the UN World Summit on Children (WSC), which was followed by the UN Conference on Environment and Development (UNCED) in Rio, 1992; the World Conference on Human Rights (WCHR) in Vienna, 1993; the International Conference on Population Development (ICPD) in Cairo 1994; the

World Summit for Social Development (WSSD) in Copenhagen and the Fourth World Conference on Women (FWCW) in Beijing, both in 1995.

NGOs were invited to attend those conferences, and they did so in large numbers and with enthusiasm, drawing public attention to the meetings, contributing to the discussion process and committing public support to the implementation of each conference agreement. The NGO participation was not restricted any more to large international federations or to "development NGOs"—Northern and Southern institutions implementing projects channeling international co-operation funds—but now included representatives of local communities, indigenous peoples, national citizen organizations, researchers and many others. "Agenda 21", the sustainable development blueprint agreed in Rio reacted to the challenge of participation by recognizing a key role in its implementation to what it called "major groups": women, farmers, indigenous peoples, unions and entrepreneurs, organizations of the youth, scholars, local authorities and NGOs. In the Social Summit documents a similar role was requested from organizations of "civil society".

The introduction of these concepts clearly reflects the notion that the achievement of the common agreed international goals: environmental sustainability, gender equity, poverty eradication, respect for human rights, full employment and social integration is not a linear operation, where a plan is agreed upon, budgeted and implemented according to a blueprint; but a rather complex process, involving conflict and co-operation at local, national and global levels, involving a variety of actors: governments, international institutions, business and citizen organizations.

An increasing number of NGOs are therefore widening their scope of activities, no longer restricted only to the implementation of projects, but also concerned with mobilizing public opinion and influencing the decision makers and governments at a national and international level.

During 1994 and 1995 many NGOs were also involved in the preparations for the World Summit for Social Development in Copenhagen and the Fourth UN World Conference on Women in Beijing. They contributed to the discussions with hundreds of written and oral interventions, position papers, documents, publications and leaflets. An unprecedented number of countries from all regions of the world recognized their expertise and included NGO representatives in the official delegations. National coalitions were built, international networks were created or strengthened and the participants at the meetings of the preparatory committees organized themselves in several caucuses.

The World Summit on Social Development

Placing "people at the centre of our concerns" was the major achievement of WSSD. The conference recognized that the market by itself does not solve social problems and that economic growth will not by itself provide full employment, education, health care and other social services. Therefore, among other things, the policies of the IMF (International Monetary Fund) and the World Bank will have to be adjusted. The loans granted to poor countries under Structural Adjustment Programmes (SAPs) have put a heavy burden on social expenditure in many countries of the South. Poor countries need to be supported in striving for social development. This can be done, among other things, by forgiving their external debts and by increasing the levels of external aid.

It is disappointing that the Social Summit, while acknowledging these principles, did not yield concrete measures to increase aid or reduce debts. The meeting did encourage countries to spend 20 per cent of ODA and 20 per cent of the budget of the recipient country on social provisions. However, this plan is not binding as it only refers to 'interested' countries. It does however mean that capital needed for social development can be found by making changes in the existing budgets of both the donor and the recipient country.

In their single most important concrete commitment, the governments promised "as a matter of urgency" to formulate "preferably by 1996" and "in partnership with all actors of civil society (...) national policies and strategies geared to substantially reducing overall poverty in the shortest possible time, reducing inequalities and eradicating absolute poverty by a target date to be specified by each country in its national context".

The Fourth World Conference on Women

The Fourth World Conference on Women held at Beijing, on 4-15 September 1995 produced concrete measures to make the "empowerment and advancement of women" possible, and clearly stated that "women's rights are human rights".

The negative effects of structural adjustment programmes on women and great emphasis on social development of women, such as access to the decision-making process and economic structures, education, health care and credit were recognized.

The causes and effects of the increase in women among the world's poor—i.e. the 'feminisation of poverty'—have been acknowledged by the Beijing conference with firm statements against this trend.

The role played by autonomous, non-governmental organisations and civil society in bringing attention to women's rights, problems and concerns has been strongly confirmed. Such organisations were identified as having an essential role of carrying out the actions called for in the Platform of Action.

Other important achievements include: making visible unremunerated work in statistics; confirming the Social Summit standpoint on bilateral and multilateral debt and on the 20/20 compact: spending 0.7 per cent of GNP on development co-operation, in which the quality and effectiveness of aid must be enhanced by integrating a gender approach; and finally providing additional and adequate financing for the advancement of women.

It was further agreed that national governments must have developed, by the end of 1996, strategic plans on how they will implement the results of this conference.

Social Development

According to UN Secretary-general Boutros Boutros-Ghali: "Social Development should be understood in a broad sense implying progress towards higher living standards, greater equality of opportunity and securing of certain basic human rights... enhancing the abilities of individuals to control their own lives through economic, social and political actions...".

In development thinking, social, economic, political and cultural aspects are often described as separate fields. Economic development problems are often referred to as "hard" issues, whereas social subjects are designated as "soft" issues.

In reality, however, the division between policy fields is not so obvious. They are strongly interrelated. The most recent World Development Report of the World Bank attributes the success of rising employment, decreasing poverty and decreasing income inequality in East Asia to a combination of export-oriented economic growth and high investments in education, health care and nutrition of the population.

Social Watch understands that the struggle against poverty is basically about empowering the people living in poverty. This is not a definition to be found in those words in the Social Summit documents, but the governments clearly stated in Beijing that "women's empowerment and their full participation on the basis of equality in all spheres of society, including participation in the decision-making process and access to power, are fundamental for the achievement of equality, development and peace" (Beijing: 13). If this is true for the "half of the heaven" disempowered because of their gender, it should also apply to the fourth (or third, depending on counts) of humanity excluded by poverty.

Poor people should not be seen only as victims; they are part of the solution. They must be given the chance to participate actively in social development. The following measures are usually considered as the basis of a social development policy:

- Providing basic health care (including family planning), primary education, food security, clean drinking water and sanitation;
- Income-generating and income-supporting activities for the poor (especially women): small-scale credit facilities, work-guarantee programmes, agricultural extension programmes and support to small-scale agricultural production;
- Strengthening social organisations; e.g. farmers' associations, women's organisations, co-operatives, trade unions, human rights organisations.

Social development is primarily the responsibility of national governments and, in economic terms, it is ultimately a problem of distribution. Income distribution can be measured in many different ways. One of the most simple income distribution indicators is obtained by comparing the share of national wealth perceived by the top fifth of the population with the lower fifth. Brazil heads the list of countries with most inequitable distribution according to this ratio (among the countries for which data are available). Thus, even when the national income *average* of Brazil places the country among the world middle-class, the number of

Brazilians living in poverty is of several dozens of millions. On the other end of the scale, very poor countries like India or Bangladesh distribute better their national income.

National social development policy in those cases can certainly improve the fate of the poor, but those countries cannot be expected to produce dramatic changes in the poverty front unless they experience fast economic growth. National policy cannot be seen apart from international policy, since major constraints to the economic growth of those countries derive from the way the international economy works. Social Watch will therefore address both the national, and the international levels.

Some of the fields where NGOs have demanded policy changes are:

- *Official Development Aid (ODA):* In lobbying the Social Summit and the Women's Conference NGOs advocated spending 50 per cent of ODA on social development. At least half of this should be allocated to projects aimed specifically at women.
- *National policies of governments:* Governments should give higher priority to social development in their national budgets. Currently those national priorities are often on national security and the military expenditure related thereto. In addition, many developing countries are struggling under a heavy external debt burden and repayment obligations. Social expenditure is often the closing entry on national budgets.
- *Structural Adjustment Programmes (SAPs):* Social development, with poverty eradication as its main objective, should not be frustrated by economic measures taken in the framework of SAPs.

  In their present form SAPs hit the poor, and especially poor women, especially hard.

  The Social Summit and the Women Conference asked for a substantial revision of the structural adjustment programmes of the World Bank and the IMF, better assessments of their impacts and policy co-ordination among the Bretton Woods Institutions and the UN (see article in this report). Social Watch will report about developments in this field.
- *The debt problem:* Structural measures on debt relief need to be taken to enable countries to set free the financial

resources required for social development. There are many countries in which the debt burden weighs so heavily on the national budget that there is hardly any room left for poverty alleviation. The creditor countries will be reminded by Social Watch of their commitments and responsibilities in this regard.

In Asia as in other parts of the so-called Third World, social and voluntary action have been most powerfully influenced by the idea of revolution. Inspired by the struggles of Asian peoples against colonialism, explicitly revolutionary mass movements have swept across the region for a great part of the twentieth century. Their ideological roots are western and predominantly Marxist or socialist.

If the collapse of socialism in Eastern Europe and the former Soviet Union has weakened orthodox revolutionary projects, the idea of socialism has not ceased to inspire revolution. The reason is simple: social reforms continue to fall short of expectations, and problems of rights, development, and environment continue to increase while the means to solve them remain inadequate.

Both successful and failed revolutions in the Asia-Pacific region have been based on alliances of peasants, workers, and youth, usually led by a proletarian party. Peasants produced the mass membership and most of the guerillas who together mobilized the rural masses. Workers, considered by revolutionary orthodoxy as the advanced forces of production, were the leading class. Youth and students, because of their special position in society, sparked the revolutionary prairie fire.

The paradigm holds sway to this day. Even the more recent form of voluntary organization, the NGO, cannot quite part from tradition, and continues to support grassroots movements of peasants, workers, and communities.

Peasant movements include organizations of farmers, fishers, indigenous peoples, rural women, and peoples' co-operatives, all generated and sustained endogenously or by urban-based institutions. The movements address a wide range of issues, including land tenure, inequalities in income and income distribution, public policy biases against the rural sector, social service delivery, trading and marketing, usury, and deterioration of the environment.

The most potent peasant movements have been those

associated with revolutionary projects, as in China and Indochina. In both, failed and still-thriving revolutions—for example in Indonesia, Thailand, Malaysia, the Philippines—peasant movements have been the base of national movements. Even in countries where national revolution is nowhere on the horizon, peasant movements still constitute the largest movements of the oppressed.

In the more industrialized countries like Japan and the newly industrializing countries (NICs) of South Korea and Taiwan, farmers' movements continue to be a significant although gradually diminishing force. Japan's 3 million farmers, represented by major farmers federations, linked to mainstream political parties, still greatly influence government policy formation.

In South Korea, the *Saemul Undong* or New Village movement was created by the authoritarian elite to serve as its rural base for industrial takeoff. In Taiwan, the Kuomintang formed tbe Farmers' Associations, patterned after Mao's peasant movement, to link the government to the countryside. In both cases, the farmers' movements were the most powerful of the forces that shaped agricultural development.

In the Philippines, a major part of the peasant movement is communist-led and constitutes the main rural base of the New People's Army. There are many independent peasant organizations that are influenced by other ideologies. Independent peasant organizing in the country has also been assisted by many rural development NGOs. To counter both types of peasant movements, former President Marcos rapidly formed more than 20,000 farmers' co-operatives by using subsidized credit from the World Bank.

In South Asia, peasant movements and rural cooperativism are the single biggest force in the local economy and self-governance. South Asian NGOs, which are the largest in the world, are mostly rural development-oriented and benefit mainly peasants and the rural poor. Together, the peasant movements and the NGOs form the basis of grassroots democracy.

Fishers' organizations are organically linked to peasant movements because they also address agricultural problems. They are also linked to trade unionism by big commercial fishing, large-scale aquaculture, and fishery-based industries. However, they are emerging as a distinct grassroots movement. Fisherfolk have long fought for control over coastal and marine resources, and against over exploitative fishing giants, illegal fishing methods, industrial and human pollution, and the destruction of fish habitats.

Fishers' groups lead in advocating aquatic reform and in negotiating the Law of the Sea Treaty. Migratory fishstocks straddling territorial boundaries in the high seas is also an outstanding issue.

Ethnicity is a stranger to the traditional revolutionary paradigm, where indigenous peoples are no more than a mass of diminishing tribes to be won over lest they become enemies of the revolution. But now, indigenous peoples, oppressed by centuries of colonialism and marginalized by modernization, are central to the environment versus development debate.

Today, indigenous peoples are high on governments' and NGOs' list of priorities. They are held to have the same rights as the enfranchised lowland citizens. They are the main protectors of the forests and upland eco-systems and other primary resources that are relentlessly over exploited by corporate interests. Their disappearing cultures seem to harbour the solution to the enviornment and development crisis confronting humanity.

Indigenous peoples have a long tradition of asserting their right to self-determination and of resistance against domination. Beyond the issue of sovereignty is the question of sustainable development itself. Advocates of sustainable development claim that we need to re-examine our view of what makes an enduring society and that we must become ecocentric, as opposed to anthropo-centric. Our new world view should include the key role of indigenous cultures and beliefs in social transformation.

The struggles for the rights of indigenous peoples strike at the heart of globalization from above, a process that concentrates resources and decisions in the hands of the major powers. The aboriginal movements in Australia, the Maori peoples struggle in Aotearoa (New Zealand), the nuclear-free and independence movements in the South Pacific island states, and the struggle for nationhood of the Kanaks and the East Timorese are all examples of movements for self-determination. Like the American Indians, indigenous peoples in Asia-Pacific have been pushed to near extinction by genocide, colonization, resettlement, population control, and destruction of their homelands and cultures.

Through years of resistance, indigenous peoples have preserved their tradition, culture, language, religion—their way of life—against relentless attempts to assimilate them and other oppressive policies of settlers and states. Their resistance teaches useful lessons in protecting diversity of cultures in face of homogenization and massive violation of human rights. In the mid-1970s, for example, the Cordillera peoples of northern Philippines showed how a united struggle could stop construction of a multimillion-dollar dam project funded by the World Bank.

The role of trade unions is also being rethought. Workers have always been a major force in modern history and in the most significant transformations in the Asia-Pacific region. Agenda 21 cites them and trade unions as one of the nine groups with a major role in implementing the global plan.

Industrial workers are but a small fraction of the nearly 3 billion people in Asia, but they wield power disproportionate to their number. They are the main builders of the industrial societies of Japan, Australia, and New Zealand. They helped to realize the economic miracles of the NICs. They are the principal modernizing sector of the emerging economies of the basically agrarian countries of the Asia-Pacific region.

Workers' movements, found in most Asian-Pacific countries, are the most highly organized and, as a rule, a major part of social movements. In the traditional revolutionary model, they lead other mass movements. But they are also more subject than others to the influences of political parties and their state agenda. Their inclination towards self-governance stops at the factory premises. Outside the factory lies the world of politics and the struggle for state power. Here, trade unions tend to be adjuncts of political parties, whether in power or waiting for electoral victory.

Following the Euorpean socialist tradition, many Asian trade unions started as co-operative societies before plunging into the politics of collective bargaining, first at the factory and then at the industry level. Factory unions grew into federations and then into trade-union centers that linked Asian labour movements to each other and to global unions.

Trade unions and workers' parties in the Asia-Pacific have always led movements for social and national change. They were at the vanguard of revolutions in China, North Korea, Vietnam, Laos, and Cambodia. They forced regimes out of power in Japan, Australia, New Zealand, and parts of India. Worker-based citizens' movements felled dictators in the Philippines, Bangladesh, and Nepal. Even where less successful, they continue to challenge the state and corporate systems.

The biggest resistance to the authoritarian elite of South Korea was initiated by workers, thousands of whom confronted the power structures beginning in 1987 and led the long drawn-out strike in the strategic Hyundai shipyard in April 1989. The middle class joined the struggle, forming a powerful national movement that toppled the Chun dictatorship.

But times are changing fast, more so since the collapse of socialism in Central Europe and the former Soviet Union. The historic changes have a far-reaching and profound impact on the role of workers and the trade union movements in social and national transformation. Social movements are now thoroughly re-examining, if not rejecting completely, the revolutionary model that revered workers.

Three other trends might explain the dwindling influence of workers, trade unions, and their political parties:

One, key countries that still adhere to the socialist vision, like China and Vietnam, are rapidly turning from the state-dominated economy to the free-market system, undermining constitutionally guaranteed wages and benefits that workers have enjoyed for decades. The role and position of workers and trade unions have been downgraded and subordinated to that of the emergent entrepreneurial class.

Two, many now see industrialism, which gave the workers their honoured role, as responsible for many of the troubles confronting humanity. While the economic miracles of the NICs have not lost their allure for governments and big business, their viability and desirability are being questioned by citizens' movements.

Three, the regime changes and challenges to dominant paradigms have given birth to a new type of social movement that is no longer worker-dominated but that cuts across social classes. In these emergent broad citizens' movements, hegemony belongs to those who can challenge and offer alternatives to orthodoxies. Working-class vanguardism is out; dynamic plurality is in.

Environmental issues were of marginal interest to Asia-Pacific social movements until the 1980s. Perhaps this is because the ecological space in the region remains wide; its source and sink capacity have yet to be exhausted. Human rights and development were the focus of voluntary action from the 1960s to the 1980s, the decades of authoritarian development that saw many countries, led by South Korea and Taiwan, fall under dictatorships.

Human rights were propelled mainly by the middle classes. In the 1980s, human rights movements took on development and environmental concerns. The meeting of 202 Asian human rights organizations in 1993, in advance of the June World Conference on Human Rights in Vienna, attested not only to the comprehensive nature of human rights advocacy but also to the strength of human rights organizations in the region.

Environmentalism in Asia has been greatly influenced by western ecological movements. The "hippie" generation of the 1960s inspired similar back-to-nature movements in Asia, which drew many young people towards greater concern for environmental protection and traditional cultures and religion, especially Indian spiritualism.

Asian social movements linked environment and development only in the late 1980s. Earlier, citizen action on environmental issues was sporadic and isolated. There was little public awareness of the extent and potential threat of rainforest destruction, chemical agriculture, overfishing, and industrial pollution until just before the U.N. Conference on Environment and Development (UNCED) meetings, after which environmentalism took giant strides forward.

Meanwhile, the consumers movement has gained headway, especially in Malaysia, the Philippines, and Japan. Where it once focused on prices and product quality, it has now taken up environmental safety and consumption patterns that stress eco-systems. Since colonial times, the region has seen major conflicts among the global powers. Now citizens' movements against militarization and nuclear proliferation are part of the broad movement whose long-term goals are peace and security.

The Involvement of Civil Society

The final Declaration of the WSSD made strong recommendations to strengthen civil society:

> "Effective implementation of the Copenhagen Declaration on Social development and the Programme of Action of the Summit requires strengthening community organisations and non-profit non-governmental organisations in the spheres of education, health, poverty, social integration, human rights, improvement of the quality of life, and relief and rehabilitation, enabling them to participate constructively in policy-making and implementation."

"The support and participation of major groups as defined in Agenda 21 are essential to the success of the implementation of the Programme of Action. To ensure the commitment of these groups, they must be involved in planning, elaboration, implementation and evaluation at both the national and the international levels. To this end, mechanisms are needed to support, promote and allow their effective participation in all relevant United Nations bodies, including the mechanisms responsible for reviewing the implementation of the Programme of Action." *(WSSD: 100)*

The WCW adopted the following paragraphs:

"Non-governmental and grassroots organisations have a specific role to play in creating a social, economic, political and intellectual climate based on equality between women and men.

Women should be actively involved in the implementation and monitoring of the Platform for action.

"Non-governmental organisations should be encouraged to contribute to the design and implementation of the strategies or national plans of action. They should also be encouraged to develop their own programmes to complement government efforts.

Women's organisations and feminist groups, in collaboration with other non-governmental organisations, should be encouraged to organise networks, as necessary, and to advocate for and support the implementation of the Platform for Action by Governments and regional and international bodies." *(Programme for Action Chap. V, p. 298)*

Economic, Social and Cultural Rights

The "Benchmark Document" signed by hundreds of NGOs during the preparation of the Social Summit criticized the draft declaration because "within it 'poor' people are still seen merely as victims. We feel it is regretable that persons living in poverty are viewed as people in need of aid, instead of as citizens universally entitled to development and civil, political, economic, social and cultural rights."

While this view still prevailed in many sections of the Copenhagen and Beijing Declarations, both conferences recognized the importance of the International Covenant on Economic, Social and Cultural Rights in monitoring (certain) aspects of the Declaration and Programme of Action."

The Covenant that enshrined the so-called ESC rights entered into force in 1976 and has been ratified by 129 countries (December 1994), i.e., by more countries than most other human rights conventions.

By ratifying the Covenant, governments commit themselves, *inter alia,* to progressively achieve the full realization of the rights recognized in the Covenant, such as food, clothing, housing, health care, education, and the right to work and join unions "...to the maximum of available resources". This does not necessarily mean that the government as such always provides these goods (which corresponds to the governmental 'obligation to fulfill'), but it does imply that it creates a climate in which people are able to provide for these resources, (which corresponds to the governmental 'obligation to respect') in freedom and in keeping with their capabilities, without interference by third parties (which corresponds to the governmental 'obligation to protect').

Contrary to conference declarations, the Covenant IS a binding document, which overrules national law when a country ratifies it. This is often overlooked. ESC rights are not just arbitrary policy objectives that may be pursued at will. They impose obligations on such governments. The Committee on Economic, Social and Cultural Rights, which monitors States' compliance with the Covenant would seem to be capable of immediate application by judicial and other organs in many legal systems. Some of these rights are directly enforceable, e.g., article 3 (equal rights of men and women), article 7 (equal remuneration for work of equal value), article 8 (trade union rights), article 10 (protecting children from economic and social exploitation).

Citizens' Movements

Civic responses to the endemic crisis of participation cross-class boundaries. Traditional categories are proving inadequate for identifying friend and enemies who, many now realize, can come from any class or institution and may switch roles so unexpectedly that the fixed lines of old are blurred.

Although rooted in the earlier conventional mode of social mobilization, citizens' movements that rose in the 1970s and 1980s were multi-class or supra-class in membership and leadership. Previous revolutions were also multi-class, but the mass of participants came mainly from peasants and workers, and leadership was usually assumed by workers' political parties. In contrast, the citizen uprisings in Iran in 1979, in the Philippines in 1986, and in South Korea in 1990, plus the democratic upsurge in China in 1989 and the citizen revolutions in Eastern Europe and former Soviet Union that began in 1989, drew mass support from the entire citizenry and a leadership not distinctly proletarian.

The struggles for participation are common to both capitalist and socialist systems. Indeed, citizen responses are not particularly motivated by the ideological basis of either system but by the elite's monopoly of power. The endemic crisis of poverty and environment has closed the traditional ideological divide. Rights, development, and environment have ceased to be class issues and are now issues for every citizen demanding a more equitable and sustainable society.

Although peasants and workers continue to provide the base of voluntary movements, women's emancipation movements have recently emerged as a powerful force. The strongest feminist organizations are found in Australia, India and the Philippines. Their numbers are difficult to ascertain, but their collective voice and influence penetrate all classes and sectors of society. There are women's organizations among the workers, peasants, and indigenous people, in the urban poor communities, among consumers, in the so-called NGO community, in the academic and professional community, in government and business, and among the middle class and the rich.

Co-operativism among poor women is strong. In South Asia, savings and credit organizations of peasant women are the best example of how the poor can mobilize resources and build and manage alternative systems for financing their own development projects. Indigenous women's groups are among the most outspoken critics of the model of development that they believe undermines their rights and destroys their fragile habitats.

Women are prominent in some Asian trade unions. In South Korea, for example, women workers, who account for more than half the labour force, were in the forefront of thousands of strikes and street marches from 1987 to 1990. Organizations of women workers have also been formed in the Philippines and other countries.

Women are in the thick of other citizens' movements for consumerism, environmentalism, peace and security, population, and health. Women's emancipation movements might even one day replace workers' parties as the vanguard and lead other social movements with a new perspective and vision of development.

Youth and children are also gradually taking responsibility for the future of the region., Thousands of associations of youth and children are found in schools, workplaces, cities, and villages. Most NGOs are run by people who were once involved in youth and student movements.

Feared by elites and governments, youth movements have always added fire and spirit to mass movements and great social upheavals all over the world. Youth associations mobilized massively during the Vietnam war. More recently, they led the Tiananmen uprising. Idealism and dynamism—and, negatively, the prospect of an uncertain future—drive the youth to voluntary action.

The citizens' movements that have brought about some of the most dramatic changes in twentieth-century Asia-Pacific are yet to be fully understood. Explanations from purely social, economic, political, and cultural perspectives are inadequate.

One missing link is the spiritual and ethical dimension of struggle. The issues around which millions of citizens mobilize and risk their lives have a moral value. These people see their struggles as a moral cause, a fight between good and evil. Being on the side of the good gives people spiritual strength. This invisible inspiring element also serves to cement the solidarity among the actors.

The spiritual dimension is an integral part of the struggles of indigenous people and minorities in Asia-Pacific. They invoke the power of the spirits whenever they defend a tree against commercial loggers or a river against a dam project. This holds true for the Australian aborigines, the Maoris of New Zealand, the Polynesians, and all indigenous peoples and tribes in Asia-Pacific.

The influence of Islam, Hinduism, Buddhism, Christianity, and other religions also runs deep. It affects rulers and ruled alike. Religions can be a stabilizing or destabilizing force. Their intervention or non-intervention makes and unmakes political regimes or, at the very least, influences social changes.

The Iranian peoples' revolution that overthrew the Shah in 1979 is an outstanding example of the power of religion. Islamic values inspired the revolution from its beginning until the climactic fall of the government and after.

In South Korea, an August 1993 mobilization called the South-North Human Chain for Peace and Reunification Rally was initiated and organized by the Korean churches. Some 60,000 men and women linked arms to form a 50-kilometer-long human chain to symbolize their long-standing desire for reunification of their divided country. The human chain started from the Independence Park in Seoul and went up to the dividing line at Panmunjom. It was a modern form of *Kang-kang-su-wul-le,* which is derived from a traditional Korean play where women held hands forming a circle, singing, dancing, and wishing upon the moon. It has been adopted by peace and environmental movements in other parts of the world.

Since 1945, reunification has been a running theme in the activities of various citizens' groups and churches in South Korea. Although muffled for a long time, the aspiration for reunification has resonated in recent years, following the successes of citizens' mobilizations against the authoritarian order. Many Korean churches have consistently supported people empowerment activites, ranging from organizing trade unions and campaigns for democratic constitution and elections to environmental protection and national reunification. Fortynine denominations are now involved in the reunification movement led by the National Council of Churches of Korea, which itself has only six member churches.

In the Philippines, the citizens' revolution that toppled the Marcos regime drew support from the churches, both spiritually and materially. Church-inspired social action has long been part of the social movement in the country; words of support from church heirarchies even lent legitimacy to extra-legal initiatives of the citizens.

Democratization of information is another big factor in the growth and success of citizens' movements. Although the ownership and modes for using information continue to be monopolized by a few, modern communication technologies have made information more accessible to a great number of people.

Grassroots organizations and NGOs in Asia-Pacific relate to each other face to face and indirectly through a variety of communications media. Telephones, faxes, modems, VCRs, radios, and printed media complement and sometimes substitute for direct communication.

Suppression of information always accompanies authoritarian regimes. Yet even under the strictest of conditions, people are able to find ways to get the information flowing. The authorities themselves, whose legitimacy is under question, help create the forces that one day will topple them. They have to provide better education to produce a highly educated work force needed for economic takeoff. In the process, they produce educated citizens who demand more freedoms. This irony was vividly illustrated in the case of the Asian economic miracles. In South Korea and Taiwan, for example, the citizens' movements that challenged authoritarian governments included highly educated individuals.

The value and impact of the media may be difficult to determine. But it is safe to say that television, radio, newspapers, and other forms of media have been important in shaping mass behaviour and in deciding the outcomes of dramatic social changes in Asia-Pacific. Certainly, media played a role in galvanizing people's responses, in deterring dictators from engaging in mass slaughters in the Philippines, South Korea, Nepal, Bangladesh, Thailand, and elsewhere, and even in just letting people know what is happening in a faraway forest.

THE NGOs AND HUMAN RESOURCE DEVELOPMENT

What contribution, then, can the vast and diverse array of NGOs make to human resource development? In addressing this question a fundamental distinction is made between what contribution NGOs make through their work-programme, that is what they actually do on the ground, and what contribution they make in themselves, by, as it were, their very existence. These are examined in the reverse order. Out of these discussions will emerge the strengths and weaknesses of the NGO sector, enabling a return more specifically to a review of relations between NGOs and governments.

What do NGOs contribute to human resource development in their own right, by their very existence, apart from what they achieve on the ground? Is it the case, for example, that NGOs compete for scarce high-level or technical personnel, starving other institutions: government; the health services; the schools system; rural development agencies, of one of their scarest resources? This is a charge sometimes made against the NGO sector, especially in those countries in which shortage of particular skills or levels of experience are acknowledged as major constraints on development.

In situations of extreme skill shortage, the NGOs compete along with other would-be employers for scarce skills. Here the importance of the definitional discussion becomes clear. National NGOs (whether they operate on the national or local level) are far less likely to bid up the price of such labour than are international operational NGOs. Indeed, an examination of the cases where there have been complaints of NGOs poaching scarce people from government (and paying them highly in the process), shows that it has usually been the international operational NGOs that are the subjects of such criticism. They can afford to pay; and there is a sense in which they cannot afford to run the risk of their projects collapsing because of poor recruitment and personnel policies. Most of the big international operational agencies are under irregular but intense public scrutiny and failure makes poor publicity. They tend to seek to insure against that by attracting the very best people they can find and paying them enough to retain them.

Such is, or was, the basic market position. It needs to be moderated in at least three directions:

1. International agencies can afford to bring in expatriates, and tend to do so if local skills are in short supply. This can bring them into conflict with national indigenisation policies.
2. Like other international agencies (especially the World Bank and some of the more enlightened bilaterals) and at about the same speed, NGOs have learnt the indispensable contribution sound management can make to a programme of work. They therefore tend to plan and budget for senior staff development, even if in the interim they have to employ expatriates.
3. The international operational agencies have learnt a great deal, often by making mistakes, over the last 20 years. They have learnt the centrality of good management locally, but they have also begun to learn that the old, post-colonial contrast between 'local' and 'expat' is too crude. Some of the best practice in the international

operational NGOs now is to rotate senior appointees of all nationalities, giving a Kenyan, say, experience working with an expatriate in Kenya; then a spell working in London or New York or Paris; then a spell in Tanzania or Ghana; then back, perhaps to a very senior or even the senior position in Kenya.

This process of senior staff development reflects not only the increasing size and sophistication of many of the larger organisations; it also reflects something of what they have learnt about the processes of development itself: that no one country, no one project, has all the answers (nor all the questions); and that the fundamental processes of impoverishment, marginalisation and victimisation recur in different guises throughout the developing world.

While it may well be irritating for government and public services to find a steady but rather modest leaching of talent to the NGOs, the loss has to be seen in a wider context of what conduces to good development practice in the country as a whole. There is, however, a more delicate point to be made. It is sometimes said that the NGOs not only poach good, or even the best, people from government; they offer a heaven for the malcontents, the antagonised, the irreversibly critical, and give them a powerful platform from which to speak. The author has heard such complaints from senior government figures in Ghana, Bangladesh, India, Sri Lanka and Kenya. In Mali it is notorious that many of the civil servants purged as a result of an IMF administered structural adjustment loan set up a vast and highly integrated 'shadow' civil service in the NGO sector.

There is clearly truth in this. A senior civil servant who falls foul of his or her minister may well find life in a well-financed and active NGO a more pleasing prospect, especially if he or she can achieve there things that he or she was prevented from achieving while in government employ. There is little doubt that in at least some countries, of which Bangladesh and Kenya are the two most vivid examples, the strained relations between the government and atleast some of the bigger international (or internationally-financed) NGOs stems from the sense that both politicians and civil servants have that they are being constantly sniped at by people who have power but no (official, publicly accountable) responsibility. The solution does not lie in trying to silence the critics, a policy that has backfired badly in countries (like Malaysia, Zimbabwe and, somewhat earlier, Malawi) that tried it. Rather it lies in fashioning channels of communication and genuine hearing where both sides can speak honestly, fearlessly, but with a proper understanding of the constraints of the other. Some recent authors have argued that NGOs have a duty to challenge government officials to serious, well-informed debate on key issues on which they have specialist knowledge and first-hand experience. That is not necessarily comfortable for the officials concerned; and too often such challenges are resented or shrugged aside as irrelevant or misguided.

What of the more modest levels of skills? Do NGOs make a positive net contribution or are they parasites on the rest of the community? Most NGOs are far too small and fragile to mount the sophisticated training and career development programmes that are a feature of some of the best large private sector concerns. One of the prevailing weaknesses of the NGOs, is their relatively short time horizons. this is partly the result of their project orientation: it is also a fact of their own lives as publicly (voluntarily) funded bodies. The funds might dry up, as they spectacularly have in a number of UK and US agencies over the last seven years. It is also the case that there tends to be a more rapid turnover of staff in the NGO sector than comparable government or industrial bodies. This is partly a result of the insecurity that is the flip side of short planning horizons; partly the result of relatively low pay (and sometimes of esteem); partly the result, especially in the Indian sub-continent where government and private sector provision is more advanced, of lower fringe benefits (especially pensions).

The net effect of this is to give NGOs little incentive to train middle-level employees in a sustained and planned way that will bring out all their potential. That is one side of reality. The other side, no less important, is that many NGOs, especially national NGOs, have an ideological commitment to their staff that extends far down the hierarchy of skill and responsibility. Again one needs to disentangle: some NGOs are unimaginative and hidebound with respect to the potential locked up in their employees, reflecting some of the worst hidden assumptions of neo-colonialism; others are the reverse. Some indeed see sharing training capacity with government employees as a natural extension of their work. Thus Action Aid Vietnam selected people with responsibility for agricultural extension from provincial and district government for training in improved agricultural techniques for environmental protection and enhanced production.

To the author it appears to be generally true that the more 'process'-oriented the NGO, the more concerned it is to secure whatever training or experience it can afford for its own staff; and, less usually, for government collaborators. 'Process' agencies tend to be less hierarchical, less impermeable, less rigid. They also tend to be smaller and poorer. They tend thus to be more willing but less able to develop their own staff to the full.

A final topic in this general area is the provision by NGOs of volunteers to fill gaps in the manpower supplies of particular sectors, usually but by no means always, of government service. Teachers are the classic example. The NGO sector is deeply divided about the wisdom of making good deficiencies of personnel in countries with high unemployment: should not governments, it is argued, be encouraged to establish sufficient training capacity to make good whatever shortfalls there are rather than becoming dependent on inexperienced expatriates? However, training needs trainers, and some of the best volunteer programmes are offering training rather than chronic gap filling. Whether volunteers are in fact used as short-term solutions to training needs or as near-permanent and cheap substitutes for indigenous skills is a matter for governments to decide. Whether they decide wisely is a question to be answered by the conditions prevailing at that time.

Skills and Technology

To see the NGO sector as a whole as parasitic is as misguided as to see it as rich source of new skills. Where new skills are imparted, are they the right skills? Whereas the rhetoric of many (especially international) NGOs is that they develop the right technologies, their critics argue that the NGO sector is as insensitive to the appropriateness of the technologies it introduces as are the multinational corporations. Again one can find examples where that is undoubtedly the case. The author visited the offices of an international operational agency in Bangladesh in the wake of a hurricane and found the sole topic of conversation among the senior (and mostly expatriate) executives to be the difficulties that surging electric current was causing for the computer-based project recording system. Although no doubt there is a place for computer skills in Bangladesh, it is open to question whether the imparting of such skills by an NGO is entirely 'appropriate'. Set against that is the remarkable work done in many primary health care projects. In the best of these, medical and para-medical staff are 'untaught' many of the assumptions and approaches they have acquired in curative and pseudo-high-technology medicine (often in western medical schools) and re-equipped with relevant health-promotion and illness-prevention techniques that make them more able to contribute valuably to their country's health. The integration of western skills with traditional curative practices, as in a project run by the Comissao pela Criaco do Parque Yanomami in Brazil and funded by a consortium of international donors takes that logic a step further.

Somewhat similar arguments can be applied across a wide range of developmental disciplines. In many, from engineering to education, there are reasons for thinking that the best of the NGOs have developed techniques, approaches, ways of doing things that are an improvement on 'best (western) practice'.

It is not always easy, however, for professionals in government service, many of them with years of experience, to learn from tiny, fragile, foreign semi-professional organisations dominated by expatriates, or their young employees.

A remarkable institution in India, run by an expatriate but now almost exclusively funded in India and staffed entirely by Indians, has shown how much can be achieved, using relatively simple aids, to enable the severely handicapped to become self-sufficient. The institutions has become widely recognised as a training ground for special needs teachers from all over India and its staff have established 'daughter' programmes in a number of cities.

In both these cases, the NGO sector has provided a new technology, technique or approach and has taught that to enough of its own staff to make a much wider impact. In this sense, the very existence of the NGOs adds a source of innovation or adaptation which is more likely to be successful because the NGOs are typically short of funds and, as they constantly claim, closely in touch with the real needs of their clientele. This raises a set of questions for government, only some of which can be touched on here.

It is of course an open question whether the innovations pioneered by the NGO sector in the field of human resource development are then applied more widely. There may be valid reasons why public sector programmes do not adopt them: there may be doubts about replicability; about the need for additional training; about the cost of recurrent expenditures; about the long-term quality or viability of the output. These are all serious issues that have to be investigated carefully on a case by case basis, by government departments already short of resources and skilled manpower in relation to the tasks imposed on them. Sometimes, government departments do indeed adopt technologies developed by the NGOs, and even hand over part of the work of the ministry to be carried out, under contract, by the NGO concerned. For example, the Government of Uganda has decided to use the model of teacher training developed by the Mubende Integrated Teacher Education Project run by Action Aid Uganda in ten of its northern regions.

However, there is too often a certain bias in the public service against innovations, either technical or incorporated in particular NGO trainees, that come from the voluntary sector. In part this is the result of the wider problem to which this paper will return; in part it is the result of pressure of time on senior public servants; in part it is ignorance of what could be achieved; and in part it is a public service *amour propre* that too readily discounts ideas, often very simple ideas, that come from outside. More often it comes from two related issues that the public sector finds hard to handle. The first is the integration of elements from different ministries; the second is the recruitment and retention of dedicated people who will work in unattractive locations for sustained periods.

Many governments would find it hard to replicate the pattern of work illustrated in Burkina Faso. Moreover, when government is slow to react, the NGO sector sometimes finds itself caught in an unenviable trap. If the public services are slow to adopt the technology that has been developed, the private sector may be anxious to do so, but at a cost that will exclude the poorest sections of the community, the very people the NGO sector is usually proclaiming itself as most anxious to protect and serve.

Officials sometimes complain that NGOs do, or seek to, distort the priorities of the department. The resources that the NGO can bring makes compliance with their priorities a real temptation to the hard-pressed, resource-poor department concerned. Some departments, for example agriculture in both Zambia and Tanzania at various times in the last 15 years, have developed quite sophisticated negotiating strategies to deal with this situation, recognising that though they have little in the way of resources, they are nonetheless the vital gate through which the NGOs must pass if they are to work in the rural areas at all. This enables the ministry to extract a price; and the price can be higher if two NGOs are in competition to work in the same area or in the same technical field. If part of the price is to put resources into something that the department does recognise as a high priority (even though the NGO may not share that view), it is possible that both sides can benefit. It hardly needs adding that this negotiating approach needs delicacy, skill and sensitivity. Most NGOs have more claims on their resources than they have capacity to meet, and so too tough a negotiating stance on behalf of the ministry can have the effect of frightening the NGO off altogether.

Peoples' Participation

As has already been seen, there is a type of NGO, more commonly national rather than international, that emphasises process above project or product. It is false to make too rigid a distinction, however, and many product-oriented agencies have learnt much about process in the last ten years and now seek to take it seriously. Inevitably some are more successful in doing so than others. Nonetheless 'peoples' participation' has for long been part of the argot of the NGO sector, implying that it is more democratic, more participative and, so the argument goes, more likely to be effective than 'top-down' development. Aspects of this argument will be referred to later; for the moment the bare outlines of the case suggest that NGOs give a higher priority to a participative style than do typical government development schemes. Does it then follow that the implementation of NGO schemes therefore raises the competence or confidence of participants in a way that would be consistent with conventional notions of human resource development?

The NGO community itself certainly believes that to be the case. It can cite a large number of case-histories that make the general point that a participative approach, consistent with but not quite identical to what an earlier generation called 'felt needs', is both more humane and more effective than normative planning from a government agency, however well intentioned and democratic that government might be. More specifically the argument is made that such an approach identifies the latent talents of the people and puts them to use. Invidious as it is to choose one exemplar, a regional peasant farmers' organisation in Chimborazo, Equador, has shown how a community facing extinction through environmental breakdown can be revitalised by mobilising the resources, skills and enthusiasm of the people. In that sense the process is the very best type of human resource development, for it discovers the resources available in the community and sets them to work.

It is not part of the present argument to call that into question nor to impugn the quite astonishing results that some of the best agencies using these 'animation' techniques have achieved. However it is worth sketching in the other side of the coin. While process-development can be extra-ordinarily effective, it cannot be assumed of itself to solve all the familiar problems of grassroots development. For it is too often true that the more process-oriented NGOs are weak on the management of increases in production. As in the case of the Tanzanian grapes, all the process in the world is in the end no substitute for more income, more resources. Yet the NGO sector, partly because of a degree of ideological rigidity, is sometimes slow to recognise the centrality of the need to raise income. Process-oriented NGOs tend to respond to that charge by making the point that to raise income without enabling people to preserve or adapt their institutions and ways of relating to each other is only to open the gates to the network of exploitative relationships that surround the poor in general and perhaps especially the rural poor. Governments and politicians need to take that argument seriously; but NGOs have to learn to recognise that it should never be allowed to stand in the way of the primacy of production and income generation. At the moment there is too often a dialogue of the deaf on this, and related issues. It is worth pausing to ask why.

In most of the developing countries of the Commonwealth, projects are seen as sources of patronage to local politicians. They offer the chance of jobs for clients and potential clients; and the politician can usually claim to have been instrumental in securing the benefits of the project for the people. Process-based work offers no job opportunities and no immediately tangible benefits. Indeed the more radical process-based work will encourage the peasantry to ask searching questions about the legitimacy and role of the local politicians, often encouraging them to expose the self-serving quality of many politicians' supposed service to the community. To put it crudely, then, politicians want 'real' projects which offer lots of potential patronage. (Some) NGOs, aware of the dangers of having benefits hijacked by politicians, will only offer process. In the Australian project at Magarini among the Giriama, the NGOs actually refused to do anything but process-type work for three years, thus attracting the wrath both of the Government of Kenya and of the Australian International Development and Aid Board. Both wanted to see results, but the former also wanted to buy clients in an area that has for long been deeply contested politically.

This general issue becomes the more germane as NGOs tend to target the very poorest (and often the most marginalised) groups, of which, as it happens, the Giriama are a good example. The justification for such targeting hardly needs spelling out here, though it is worth emphasising that the NGOs often claim that it is their intention to reach groups, often with very considerable hidden or undeveloped capacities, that are almost by definition excluded, whether deliberately or by oversight, from government programmes. These may range from groups discriminated against by reason of gender, ethnicity, physical or mental handicap, age, remoteness, political loyalty or illiteracy to groups which for no apparent or easily identifiable reason simply fall through the net of government services. For most of those categories there is little problem from the standpoint of government. These are groups that are, by definition, hard and expensive to reach with services; let the NGOs do what they can. The case is different, though, with groups that are thought to be hostile to the government. The Northern peoples of Uganda under Obote; the Turkana for a time under Kenyatta in Kenya; the Indian peoples of the Amazon basin in present-day Brazil, immigrants from the Sahel in the Ivory Coast and to a lesser degree in Ghana; these are some examples. Government is not especially keen that these peoples be brought benefits, especially if those benefits could be deployed in areas where the government has a chance of attracting support. Least of all does government want these people being 'conscientised' with the support of foreign NGOs.

Governments may be too anxious on this score. It has to be asked whether NGOs can actually overcome the structural marginalisation of these groups to enable them to participate first in their own immediate economic, social and political environment; and then in the wider environment of the region and the nation? Some NGOs certainly use rhetoric that suggests that such is their aim. Some, of which the Bangladesh Association for Rural Development is perhaps pre-eminent, succeed, sometimes brilliantly.

The great majority, even of the well-financed international organisations, however, lack the resources first thoroughly to understand the sources of structural marginalisation; and second the institutional patience to stay with the marginalised groups for long enough fundamentally to change their self-understanding and capacity for action.

There will always be tension between NGOs and governments about potential beneficiaries. The tension could be reduced if governments did not allow themselves to be the victims of the NGOs' own propaganda. this is part of a wider issue of information flows, which will be returned to later.

Local Development and Self-Governance

Democracy from below has two key elements: voluntary action and the organized participation of citizens, and community-centeredness and horizontal spread of popular centers of power.

Voluntary action involving masses of people democratizes society. The more inclusive the participation, the more democratic the outcome. the spread of decision-making power across sectors countervails the monopoly of power by government and corporations.

But plurality in decision-making does not necessarily lead to local development and self-governance. Social movements, especially workers and trade union movements and trade union-influenced sectoral movements, for example, have followed a vertical path of organization.

Local development and self-governance require deliberate reorientation of voluntary action. Creating a favourable national climate is essential to expand the space for local initiatives. But for democratization to be thoroughgoing, decision-making has to be pulled down to the lowest possible level at which small groups and even individuals can exercise control.

Democratization at the sub-national level is happening not only in isolated communities; NGO-supported grassroots movements are working everywhere to transform local communities and their environments through a holistic area development strategy.

The concept of integrated area development has evolved over time. In the 1970s, it was promoted by bilateral and multilateral agencies such as the U.S. Agency for International Development and the World Bank. The integrated area development strategy required concentration of development assistance in areas such as agricultural basins to build a geophysical framework for local government development efforts directed by a central authority.

Integrated area development varies from country to country. Where the ecosystem is the defining factor in development, as it is in the upland indigenous communities or lowland agricultural basins, the area is designed around the watershed. Where geopolitics is the prime consideration, the area follows political boundaries.

Area scope likewise varies greatly, depending on geophysical, demographic, political, and economic factors and, most important, the scale of an area. In some countries, areas are only as big as a district or province. In others, they are no less than a bioregion spanning several districts or provinces, such as the desert of Rajasthan in India.

The challenge of making an impact on the local economy and micro-eco-systems has been taken up by many NGOs and grassroots organizations across Asia-Pacific.

A sustainable area-development process hinges on the regaining of sovereignty by local communities, which must dictate the substance and direction of their own development and end the net resource outflow. Thousands of grassroots and development support organizations are striving to regain their sovereignty by promoting integrated area development. Their activities include awareness raising, organization and leadership building, land and asset reform, management training, natural resources management, livelihood systems development, savings and credit and alternative development financing, sustainable agriculture, micro-enterprises, alternative trading and marketing, and improved service delivery systems.

Through consciousness-raising programmes, local communities become aware of their own realities as well as of greater society's, of the development-versus-environment debate and of the imperative of voluntary action. NGOs help local communities acquire skills in scale management and organisation. Primary peoples' institutions, such as sectoral associations, co-operatives, and community organizations, eventually grow into area-level structures of self-governance. They also launch local and national campaigns against poverty and for welfare, reform, and environmental protection.

These local communities engage in livelihood activities designed to build a community-centered economy attuned to the carrying capacity of the environment and based on sustainable agriculture and rural development. Alternative financial systems, from micro-savings and credit schemes to people's banks, mobilize the funds.

The poor, indeed the poorest among them, have demonstrated often and in many parts of Asia that they can set up, own, and run their own banks to finance their livelihood projects and other activities. The most oustanding example so far is the world-renowned Grameen Bank in Bangladesh. It is one of the most successful experiments in extending credit to the landless poor.

Alternative trading and marketing reduce and eventually eliminate the exploitative monopoly traders and directly link rural producers to urban consumers. The more successful communities now trade globally. A new experiment, the local exchange and trading system in Australia and other countries, seeks to cut the local economy off from the global system by localizing currencies. Patterned after Robert Owen's labour exchange in England in the nineteenth century and similar efforts in Austria, the United States, and Canada, the system is successful only in small areas. Whether it will work elsewhere on a large scale remains to be seen.

Restoring damaged eco-systems is a tall order. Activities and funding for environmental protection, restoration, and management have increased visibly. Local communities and NGOs are mobilizing massively for conservation and development of the integrated protected areas systems, community-based agroforestry, watershed protection and management, and coastal and marine resources management.

The most popular campaigns to save the forests have been mounted by indigenous peoples and local communities in Sarawak, Thailand, Indonesia, the Philippines, and India. These campaigns target governments, the multilateral development banks, and the timber companies.

Despite significant advances in environmental protection,

controversies remain: the subordination of indigenous peoples and local communities to external profit-seeking groups in the conservation and management of the forests; persistent logging; inadequate state policies and laws; poor enforcement of laws; intervention by foreign NGOs; and funding by the World Bank and the Asian Development Bank of projects that undermine conservation, such as the construction of big dams in forests. High consumption in rich countries such as Japan also sets back environmental protection because it is one of the causes of poverty and misery in less-developed countries.

Official development assistance for area development is sorely inadequate. Not only does it fail to reverse the net outflow of resources from communities, it has been used to promote globalization that undermines local autonomous development. In contrast, donor NGOs in the North, such as NOVIB (Netherlands), support local efforts at integrated area development in different parts of Asia, although the impact of funds and other forms of assistance on local self-reliance is yet to be fully evaluated.

Because local development and self-governance need a supportive national policy, grassroots movements and NGOs lobby to influence public policy. Advocacy themes vary from country to country. The concerns of citizens' movements in industrial countries, such as Japan, Australia, New Zealand and the NICs, differ from those in poor countries, such as Bangladesh. Issues also differ from one country to another. China, for example, confronts problems different from those of India. But no matter how different priorities are, these countries have much in common. Every issue they address is linked to the environment-versus-development debate, to disparities in and among countries, and to the right of citizens to demand public accountability and respect for human rights.

Equity is the most prominent policy advocacy theme. Central to sustainable development, the resolution of inequality between and within nations, betwen men and women, and between the present and future generations will remove the main stumbling block that divides societies.

Two out of 10 Asians are members of the elite. Nationality matters little. Twenty per cent of the population earns more than US $20,000 a year and produces over 20,000 kilograms of waste annually. In contrast, five to seven of 10 Asians, depending on their country, are poor and powerless. They live on US $2 a day at most. They probably produce less than 1,500 kilograms of waste per person annually—a level that U.N. scientists say will enable humanity to sustain itself through to the twenty-first century, assuming constant population and no deforestation.

Progressive citizens are aware of the dangers of ignoring equity for the sake of growth. Land reform, as part of asset reform, is a popular cause in poor as well as middle-income countries of Asia because skewed landownership symbolizes the great disparities in resource and power distribution. Citizens' movements also address problems of foreign debt, trade and investment, and aid, seeking debt relief, fairer trade terms, and the reversal of resource flows.

Citizens' movements work for the basic right of every person to demand good and responsive governance, inclusive participation, and equal electoral opportunities. Citizens' electoral movements have a long tradition in countries such as the Philippines—back to the 1950s and earlier. The National Movement for Free Elections (NAMFREL) was the first to mobilize thousands of volunteers around nonpartisan activities, such as voters' education, campaigns for clean and fair elections, poll watching, and ballot counting.

The tradition continues to this day as even more groups take part in protecting the ballot. The 1984 and 1986 elections called by former President Marcos saw tens of thousands of citizens risk their lives and limbs to ensure that voters could exercise their free choice and that every vote was counted. Those events are captured by photographs of ordinary citizens on 24-hour vigils and of nuns, priests, and high-society women in a tug-of-war with armed men and escorting ballot boxes to their destinations. In Thailand, Myanmar (Burma), Cambodia, South Korea, Nepal, and other countries that have recently undergone transitions to democracy, citizens banded together into movements to press for new constitutions and free elections.

Policy advocacy and integrated area development are complementary dimensions of a holistic strategy for transforming the substance and process of development. Policy advocacy creates the climate for expanding area development, and area development shapes policy advocacy. Lack of appreciation of this dynamic can create tension within the voluntary sector. True enough, policy advocacy that is not well-rooted in local community-based initiatives lacks substance and will most likely run out of steam in the long haul.

But to reduce everything to local empowerment and community development is one type of fundamentalism; it may be called area determinism or eco-anarchism. It can foster the illusion that area development can be sealed off from external influences and mature entirely on its own.

Local areas are the ultimate site of development projects—state, corporate, or otherwise—although the benefits may be destined for someone else. There are centers and institutions of decision-making detached from but affecting the local communities. The local area is but one of the arenas or spaces of engagement for development activists and voluntary organizations. The others are the nation-state; inter-state systems at the sub-regional, Asian, and global levels; multilateral institutions; and global corporate structures.

To be effective, voluntary action should take place in all these arenas. Some voluntary organizations operate at all levels simultaneously. Others confine themselves to one arena. But if all voluntary organizations share the same development vision and values, their efforts will converge and achieve their common goals.

SERVICE DELIVERY AND NGOs

There is a need to review some of the services typically delivered by the NGO sector in the general area of human resource development. The following are some of the issues around which tension between governments and NGOs tend to emerge.

Health Care

The part played by international and national NGOs in health care, especially the delivery of primary care to the poor and remote, needs little emphasis here. The Churches and other religious groups gave the provision of healthcare an early priority, and inevitably given the chronology, that took the form of building and staffing hospitals. In Malawi, for example, the Private Health Association of Malawi (PHAM) was for many years the sole provider of hospital care, co-ordinating the efforts of a wide variety of mission agencies in this area. Although, interestingly, the first major experiments in primary health care (PHC) were introduced through the government health service (again in Malawi), the NGO sector was quick to learn the arguments for switching resources from hospitals to PHC. Although some notable rearguard actions were fought, especially by German and French church-based agencies, by the mid-1970s PHC had become the focus of the vast majority of new expenditures by NGOs in the health sector. Again with some notable exceptions, most governments sought, not always successfully, to follow the same track.

With the emphasis on PHC went concentration on mother and child health (MCH) and largely out of that grew an awareness that even MCH had to be seen in the wider context of community health. This in turn demanded a radical new approach to training the doctors who were to deliver this type of health care. Two of the most challenging experiments in training this new generation came from the NGO sector in the Indian sub-continent: from Vellore in southern India and from the Aga Khan Medical School in Karachi. It is a matter of regret that in these two countries, and in others which have not had the living testimony of these institutions, even more so, bitter opposition from the medical establishment, well ensconced politically, has made the dissemination of this type of training much slower and more attenuated than concern for the delivery of health care to the mass of the people would warrant.

If the NGOs have played an honourable and sometimes distinguished role in making the intellectual and practical case for the revolution in health care, they are, in most countries, only a small proportion of the total health system if measured in terms of personnel or patients seen. They are, however, far better resourced than the local equivalent unit of the government health service, so that the proportion of the total health expenditures accounted for by the NGO sector can be very considerable. If this is broken down further and account is taken of, say, the vehicles dedicated to healthcare delivery, it is often found, especially in sub-Saharan Africa, that it is the NGOs (including in this category UNICEF) that far outweigh the government health service.

That this leads to a number of frictions is inevitable, for example, the discrepancy that often follows in the quality of care between the NGO sector and the government health service, especially in remote rural areas. It is not (or not necessarily) that the government health professionals are under-motivated and under-trained; it is rather that they have no vehicle to visit the community; they have few drugs to prescribe; they have the minimum of support staff; they have no adequate laboratory facilities and, very often, having no functioning autoclaves, cannot safely perform even minor surgery. For all its limitations the nearest NGO clinic or PHC unit compares favourably. For the truth is that if the NGO was not able to offer a higher standard of service, it would have to quit. Its constituency would not tolerate the conditions under which many health professionals are obliged to work by the extreme scarcity of resources at the command of the government.

If the NGOs are typically better resourced than government services, they are not necessarily better organised or integrated. Family planning is a difficult but desperately important case in point, raised to a higher power by the onset of AIDS in much of Africa. In their original conception, both PHC and MCH were supposed to include proper emphasis on family planning, the argument being that take-up rates were much higher when family planning was put in the context of the health of the family as a whole. For a number of reasons, not excluding lack of enthusiasm by some governments for family planning on the grounds that their countries were under rather than over-populated, the proper integration of family planning has often proved remarkably awkward. The NGO sector has often been to blame; with family planning and MCH organised vertically (often back to international organisations like the IPPF and UNFPA) with inadequate local co-ordination and too much protection of areas of responsibility. The result has often been, not only unnecessary duplication and cost-raising, but also lower take-up rates, quicker rejection and lack of confidence in the technology. It is debatable whether the NGO sector can tackle these problems by itself. The evidence from India suggests probably not. It may prove to need very determined political leadership to ensure that health strategies that rightly emphasise the survival of the child are routinely accompanied by strategies that maximise parents' control over their own family building.

This points to a wider issue, which can be touched on only briefly here. As exemplified by UNICEF (and the WHO, not, of course, an NGO), the NGO sector has a penchant for vertical programmes. A problem is identified, and resources are mobilised to deal with it. Family planning is one example; but the Expanded Programme of Immunisation of WHO; the Child Survival Package of UNICEF; the safe drinking water projects or latrine construction projects of a large number of agencies are others. This raises much wider questions than co-ordination of delivery services. It raises questions of priority; of sequencing; of maintenance; of supervision; of community participation and of coverage. These are critical issues in terms of the long-term success of any intervention and to ask whether the vertical approach takes them sufficiently seriously is neither to prejudge the issue, nor, much less, to argue that a more horizontal approach would necessarily produce better solutions. What is clear is that intensive vertical 'drives' are not especially efficient in the long run as the evaluative literature on water supply has long pointed out. They may be the easiest way for the NGO sector to mobilise, but to make the criterion is to put the cart before the horse.

To this extent, the way in which many Commonwealth governments have sought to integrate development administration at the regional or district level should be a means by which the NGO sector can be persuaded to co-ordinate and integrate their services better with both other NGO efforts in the area and with government services at large. That is the hope. The experience so far in many countries is that regional development administration too easily falls victim to two diseases; inefficient management; and constant misappropriation of funds by politicians. As long as that is true, the NGO sector will not wholly unreasonably fight shy of becoming bogged down in regional administration, in healthcare or any other activity.

Education

Next to health care, the major historical focus of the NGO sector in most Commonwealth countries has been education, again led by the missions. At independence, governments tended to take all formal educational provision into their own hands, sometimes leaving a handful of religious foundations in the private sector. From that it does not follow, however, that the NGO sector has made no further contribution to education. There very different types of involvement are highlighted here.

As early as the mid-1960s it had become clear that the formal educational sector in many Commonwealth countries was in deep trouble. Voters demanded universal primary education and as much secondary education as possible, but governments did not have the resources to meet those demands, and even in trying to do so, often put quality seriously at risk. Further it quickly became apparent that for many graduates of the school system, there were no jobs that used their educational attainments. How did the NGO sector react to these problems?

Community-based Schools

First, the NGO sector became a significant additional supplier of education. The most obvious example of this are to be found in Kenya and, outside the Commonwealth, in the Ivory Coast. In both countries, government encouraged schools to be constructed and maintained by voluntary associations of would-be parents and their allies in the community. In slightly different ways, government covered recurrent costs (especially teachers and their salaries) to staff schools for which local associations took responsibility. In the vast majority of cases, these were entirely local efforts with no support from abroad and little enough from the capital. In some ways they illustrate precisely what can be done when the community becomes aware of its own capacity to meet its real needs.

That such community-based schools, by no means limited to Kenya and the Ivory Coast, bring their own problems is well known. Management is sometimes poor. Continuity of policy can be short-lived. Maintenance of the physical plant (and of the teachers' houses) may be slipshod. The community may be dissatisfied with the quality of the teachers provided, and the teachers can resent the control exercised by the community. Such difficulties are common, but need not be fatal. Perhaps more serious is the finding that it is the more successful, more economically integrated and more ambitious communities that have the resources, confidence and local leadership to provide this type of school for their own young people. This implies that the kind of communities increasingly targeted by national and international NGOs are precisely those who are least likely to be able to meet their own educational needs. Governments tend to resist such NGOs (except occasionally religious groups) founding schools to serve such poor communities, with the result that regional income and welfare differences become the more marked.

Skill Training Schemes

The second way in which the NGO sector has responded to the difficulties that beset formal education in many Commonwealth countries is to try to equip the unschooled or the early drop-out with marketable skills. For understandable, but with hindsight, regrettable reasons some African countries demanded the closure of many such programmes at the time of independence on the grounds that they were a relic of colonialism, preparing the people for a life time of servitude. It took between ten and twenty years for that mistake to be reversed, and perhaps for the last shreds of paternalism or racism to disappear from vocational projects.

One of the foremost examples of the new approach, very popular in Kenya in the early 1970s, was the Village Polytechnic. The idea behind this approach, spearheaded by the development department of the National Council of Churches of Kenya (NCCK), was to give a range of skills to young people in one locality so that each trades person would be a customer for the others and, by providing complementary services, extend the range of contracts the group as a whole could credibly compete for. Although it attracted wide international support and enthusiasm at the time, the Village Polytechnic movement was relatively short-lived, and that for a reason that has bedevilled many parallel ideas in skill training in the rural areas. The market is simply too narrow.

Inevitably, the graduates of the Village Polytechnics either reverted to subsistence agriculture, thus allowing their skills to degenerate through neglect; or they went to the towns in search of work. There they encountered as competitors graduates from urban skill training programmes, some funded by the private sector, some by government, but the great majority funded by national or international NGOs. Whatever the source of funding and management, these projects run into much the same problems: at the end of the course, the newly qualified worker cannot find a job that will enable him (and less usually her) to use the newly acquired skill.

It is this constant problem that has led many NGOs into starting income-generating projects annexed to or growing out of training schemes. Gonoshashthaya Kendra in Bangladesh is one well-know example; work sponsored by the NCCK in Mombasa and by the Christian Service Committee in Malawi are fair parallels. By and large, governments have not been willing or able to follow the NGO down this track. There are good reasons for that. The rate of return on many income-generating schemes tends to be low, especially if the products are not designed for a niche export market or do not have the support of an NGO marketing organisation. The schemes take a great deal of managing and often require disproportionate amounts of scarce and expensive accountancy and book-keeping input. Nor very often do they successfully achieve what they set out to achieve: supplying outlets for middle-grade technical skills. Too often they quickly degenerate into low-skill, routinised production jobs, for rates of pay that, for the scheme to be even remotely self-financing, have to be fixed below the legal minimum. Thus Shree Seva Mnadii, an Indian NGO based in Madras, found itself faced with a strike by its workers, poor women from some of the worst slums, because the workers discovered that they were being paid less than the law demanded.

That there is a near-insoluble problem here is beyond doubt. May be a more carefully planned and integrated approach to skill-formation by both the NGO and government departments involved could play a role, most probably quite a modest one, in atleast ensuring that the supply side of skills more roughly approximates the demand side. The sad reality, however, is that many people, especially the more able, energetic young people, want to have a skill so that they can atleast compete in the job-market. Without any skill, they have no chance of a job. With skill, they have a fighting chance. They will do all in their power to acquire that chance; and the NGO sector cannot and probably should not be prevented from giving them one. A more radical proposal would be for government to actually reduce its role in this area, leaving the NGO sector to meet as much of the demand as it is able. Politically that may pose problems, but the pressures that would be felt could be somewhat sidetracked if the closer collaboration of the NGO sector and government, which is one of the main points of this chapter, could be achieved.

Literacy Work

A third type of educational enterprise that has seen major NGO involvement in a wide range of countries is literacy work. Fashions have come and gone on both the priority to be accorded literacy and the techniques by which it is to be achieved. Those fashions have affected multilateral official funding rather more than NGO activity, especially perhaps that associated with religious work where ability to read the scriptures and the hymnal has long had great emphasis. Some of this work has grown and been secularised until it forms an important part of the whole national effort. For example, in Sierra Leone, the Provincial Literature Bureau and the Bunumbu Press were originally founded in 1946 by the United Christian Council of Sierra Leone and the Sierra Leone Government. The latter has continued to fund it and it now produces adult literacy materials and carries out literacy programmes for the government.

Where literacy work has been fundamental to 'conscientisation' or 'empowerment', two terms much used by NGOs that are process-oriented, governments have been somewhat, and occasionally, especially in Latin America, very, hostile to it. Unfortunately some of this hostility has too often washed over on to all literacy work. The reluctance with which the Government of Bangladesh sanctioned the work of LISA is one example. Anxieties have been expressed by the Governments of Kenya, Sri Lanka (especially in the face of the threat from the Tamils with which some Church-related literacy groups were associated) and the Philippines.

However understandable, the evidence suggests that this hostility is somewhat misplaced. It is hard to find any examples of regimes which have been seriously threatened, much less toppled, by the work of literacy or conscientisation groups. The only credible candidate might be thought to be Somoza's Nicaragua, but even then most independent and objective observers would now agree that it was the disaffection of the urban middle classes that was far more important in bringing the regime down than the opposition of newly-literate peasants. Even in North Brazil, the home and proving ground of conscientisation, the organisational and empowerment skills of the 'base communities' are directed much more against the illegal seizures of land by 'possessors' than against the state or federal governments as such. In the Philippines 'people power' was in fact much more an urban, middle class phenomenon than a peasant's movement. Certainly some groups from the urban slums who had been 'conscientised' by NGOs and radical church groups joined in demonstrations that helped to displace Ferdinand Marcos, but their earlier attempts to persuade the government to address their own grievances, e.g.

lack of water supply or harassment by the police, had been unfruitful. To put it perhaps cynically, governments have very little to fear from literate, even 'radicalised', peasants and slum dwellers as long as the urban middle class is not in open revolt. Arguably they have much more to fear from an illiterate and confused peasantry who can more easily be misled by demagogic rabble rousers.

Co-operation and Credit Unions

There is one further area of service delivery that merits some exploration in the context of human resource development, though it may seem to fit awkwardly with some of the more traditional activities usually considered under that head. The enabling of people to trust one another sufficiently to work together; to share resources; to share labour and its product; to plan together; that enablement is central to the whole undertaking of co-operatives and credit unions. In most countries, NGO involvement in co-operatives or credit unions actually predates that of governments; indeed many people argue that it is essential to the very nature of co-operation that it be spontaneously generated from the bottom rather than imposed or encouraged (or bribed) from the top.

Especially in the years immediately after independence many African Commonwealth countries sought to use co-operatives as a way of accelerating the rate of agricultural progress without giving rise to a capitalist rural economy and the emergence of a class of landless labourers. There thus followed the superimposition on the often small and fragile NGO-related co-operative movement, a huge raft of officially sponsored co-ops. In some cases, as in Tanzania, Uganda and Zambia, the results were tragic; in others merely wasteful.

Naturally one needs to recognise the political dynamics that lay behind this history. Nonetheless, it is an object lesson in how the rapid and insensitive scaling-up, and simultaneously the political co-option, of a voluntary form of organisation can break it. While it is true that in some countries, Zambia for example, the NGO-related co-operatives were too small and too few to give much of a guide as to the nature of the problems that would be encountered and their possible solutions, in others, like Ghana and Kenya, that was less true. Even in Zambia the NGO and churches sought to warn the government (and the President directly) that the ambitious plans for producer or credit co-operatives were likely to come seriously awry. As happens too often, government was unready to hear bad news, especially from the voluntary sector which was too quickly dismissed as amateur or idealistic.

Partly as a result of the mistakes that were made in the 1960s and 1970s, there is now much more understanding of how delicate and demanding even the simplest co-operative is in terms of the human relations that make it work; and in terms of the skills and aptitudes required of its members. More governments have either launched or thoroughly overhauled their co-operative training programmes, but in many countries, again especially in Africa, these remain seriously underfunded with inevitably negative impacts on the quality of training given. Rather few countries have seen the possible benefit of a coalition approach to co-operative training with the NGOs nor the possibilities for tapping the resources of the bigger international funding NGOs that this could bring. Through the Mindolo Ecumenical Foundation in Kitwe, Zambia has explored these possibilities with some success.

While many Commonwealth governments have sought to encourage agricultural producer and marketing co-operatives, the ultra-small scale credit union movement, especially among women, has been typically largely left to the NGOs. Occasionally, as in India, these have been so successful that they have become national institutions, and have then attracted government interest. For the most part, the tiny revolving funds, or variations on the theme of credit unions (sometimes, as in the *shomitis* in Bangladesh, incorporating a community-improvement element) have been left to the NGOs for the obvious reason that they are too small, too fragile and too demanding of managerial inputs to be worth government effort. That does not, however, prevent hard questions being asked: is it the case that the savings thus mobilised, tiny in individual amounts but sometimes significant in aggregate, are used with maximum effect in the micro-economies from which they come or in the macro-economy at large?

It is clearly the case that some NGO-inspired savings are not effectively applied, but that is true of every saving institution in every Commonwealth country, large commercial banks included. The central question is whether small credit unions and co-operatives with surplus funds have access to high-yielding (that is abnormally profitable) investment opportunities; and if they do so have access, are they inclined to finance those opportunities? The evidence on this is very confused. Academic research on the informal sector has shown that some very small-scale investments can be immensely profitable; but that is not inconsistent with the more usual argument that returns to capital, like returns to labour, are on average low at the bottom of the income distribution. It is, however, hard to see what follows from that. Poor peoples' savings may not indeed be ideally invested; and, the mirror image of that, excellent investment opportunities further up the income scale may go unfunded. From that it does not follow either that the credit unions waste capital; nor that NGOs are performing a disservice by encouraging poor people to save.

World in Need, a British international funding agency, plays an innovative role in Indonesia in this respect, by acting as a mini-investment bank, channelling savings from projects, co-operatives and credit unions in its portfolio to carefully researched and supervised projects in need of capital. Because of its own wider funding base and financial strength, it is able to guarantee the lenders against loss, while giving them a stake in potentially highly profitable investments. It might be thought that this is a role for an official agency, perhaps an offshoot of an agricultural bank or other source of official credit. Without ruling that out altogether, it is worth pointing out that such an involvement would imply the government in three obligations it would be well advised to weigh very carefully: guaranteeing the performance of small, high-risk enterprises; supervising those enterprises, sometimes on an almost day to day basis; and, third, finding the resources to make good the savings of depositors in case of the financial collapse of the investing enterprises. One only has to reflect on the nature of these risks (and costs) to see that this activity is much better left to (a rather rare quality of) international NGOs. If governments are really concerned about the efficiency with which the savings of the poor are invested, they should consider encouraging financially strong NGOs, or consortia of them, to provide this intermediary function, rather than trying to do it themselves.

Transnational Democracy

Over the last three decades, democratization from below has crossed local and national frontiers and spread throughout Asia-

Pacific. Peoples' movements and other voluntary organizations are now linked regionally by structures and processes they have created over the years.

Before, Asian peoples were linked mainly through structures and mechanisms created from above. People-to-people linkages, mediated by states and interstate systems, were centered on trade, education, culture, and sports. They were, and still are, largely bilateral or subregional, such as the South-east Asia Treaty Organisation and its successor, the Association of South-east Asian Nations. Except for the Asian Games, Asia-wide state-mandated people-to-people contacts are almost non-existent.

Citizens' groups and movements are more closely linked to their Northern counterparts than they are to one another. One reason is globalization that accompanied colonialism and modernization. Another is the vastness of the region, with distances between countries magnified by poor communication technology. For instance, it is much easier to communicate or travel between the Philippines and Europe than between the Philippines and India, even though English is widely used in these two countries in official as well as personal communication.

Colonialism, imperialism, and wars have a way of bringing people closer to one another. They have triggered the feeling of "Asian-ness" among Asians. Unfortunately for the Japanese people. World War II moved Asians towards solidarity against them and their country. The Indo-china War gave birth to powerful anti-U.S. peoples' solidarity movements across the Asia-Pacific. The wounds of war take time to heal and the healing has not been hastened by the behaviour of either the United States or Japan, whose continuing hegemony brings Asian peoples closer together.

The consensus among Asian elites that economic growth should be pursued at any cost has been consolidated by the success of the NICs. Governmens and big business justify their position by pointing to the economic stagnation and the endemic and rising poverty in the region. The elites' idea of growth will likely be the dominant influence in the development processes that will take Asia-Pacific into the next century.

Grassroots movements and voluntary organizations are challenging the new growth orthodoxy with their own vision and strategies. They are not anti-growth; their alternative development agenda promotes equitable and eco-logically sound development for the whole region.

In 1988, a Japanese peoples' alliance proposed a brilliant, forward-looking and innovative idea: People's Plan for the 21st Century. The idea is now an Asia-Pacific, if not global, citizens' movement. It was originally proposed by the Pacific-Asia Resource Center, an action-oriented research, education, and documentation center established in 1973 to promote people-to-people solidarity mainly in Asia-Pacific. The movement is now known as PP21.

PP21 grew out of the need to "produce a vision of the future society which is worth winning together." It counterposes a people-based, people-centered vision of an alternative Asian future to regional economic, political, and cultural integration by transnational corporations and international power elites. It proposes a model of development that measures social progress by the degree of equality, justice, dignity, and conviviality with nature.

By 1989, PP21 had linked largely autonomous activities of grassroots and citizens' movements throughout Japan and Asia-Pacific. Farmers and fishers, indigenous peoples and ethnic minorities, workers, women working outside the home, housewives, consumers, and activists in the co-operative, alternative trade, alternative aid, anti-nuclear, peace, human rights, environmental, and NGO movements all began to go beyond criticism of society to the assertion of a positive vision of the future. In 1992, Thai groups replicated PP21. Some groups in the Philippines are doing the same.

From 1989 to 1992, several gatherings of Asian voluntary organizations took place. Women, indigenous peoples, NGOs, and adult and popular educators were the most active. They forged sectoral, national, and sub-regional positions on development and environment, but no common Asian position.

During the last three decades, events that had transboundary impact or that affected large masses of people brought citizens' organizations together. War, war-related famine, gross violation of human rights, massive rainforest destruction, and large-scale natural disasters were caused or worsened by states, multi-lateral institutions (such as the World Bank and the Asian Development Bank), and transnational corporations.

Peace movements born during the vietnam war, far from being exhausted, continue to fuel voluntary citizen action despite the end of the so-called Cold War era. Citizens are mobilizing and pressuring governments to establish a nuclear-weapons-free and demilitarized zone of peace and security. They are particularly worried by the remilitarization of Japan, the continuing military presence of the United States in South Korea and elsewhere in the Pacific, and the rising tension resulting from intense economic competition between the United States and Japan.

The 1971 war in Bangladesh was another important transboundary issue. It inspired a sense of common humanity and gave rise to citizens' movements inside and outside the country in support of war victims. Most of the big NGOs in Bangladesh were born during this period. International assistance created a great sense of people-to-people solidarity.

Transnational democracy movements in the Asia-Pacific region are fuelled by massive human rights violations in countries that follow the path of authoritarian development. Asians have been moved by atrocities in Indonesia in the 1960s and, more recently, in the Philippines, Thailand, South Korea, Taiwan, Singapore, Kampuchea under the Pol Pot regime, Bangladesh, Nepal, Myanmar (Burma), and Tiananmen.

Human rights movements are also at the vanguard of struggles for democracy because development and environment are fundamentally issues of rights and, therefore, linked to almost every human concern that moves every citizen to voluntary action.

The 1993 U.N. World Conference on Human Rights in Vienna brought human rights groups from all over Asia together. Before the meeting they agreed on a common position. In Vienna, they engaged Asian government delegations in sharp debates, indicating that they can pressure governments into changing their policies. Later, human rights groups made their presence felt at the meeting of government ministers hosted by the Singapore government, a clear sign that states are forced to respond to pressures from below.

A Permanent Peoples Tribunal established in Rome by the International League for the Rights of Peoples has responded to 17 complaints. The Asian cases it has taken up include self-determination for Tibet, gross violations of human rights during martial rule in the Philippines, Soviet aggression against Afghanistan, and industrial disasters, such as the massive chemical poisoning in Bhopal and mercury poisoning in Minamata.

In July 1993, Japanese citizens' groups organized the Tokyo Tribunal to judge the Group of Seven. It was modelled after the

1988 Berlin Permanent Peoples Tribunal, which charged the International Monetary Fund and World Bank with acting as agents of global capital and with imposing a variety of intolerable economic burdens on countries of the South. The Tokyo Tribunal charged the United States, Japan, Germany, Canada, the United Kingdom, France, and Italy with causing poverty and inequality and with destroying the environment.

In keeping with the spirit of transnational democracy from below, the Tokyo Tribunal deliberately refrained from rendering a judgment. Asserting that the privilege was reserved for the peoples of the world, it indicated the G-7 countries based on oral and written testimonies and the knowledge and experience of its panelists.

Citizens' environmental movement strengthen regional democratization from below. Some of the best recent examples are the campaigns to save the Sarawak rainforests and to stop the Narmada dam project in India, the Pak Mun dam in Thailand, the Three Gorges Dam in China, and the nuclear testing and dumping of hazardous, toxic, and nuclear wastes in the South Pacific. The considerable impact of these campaigns evokes in citizens' movements across and beyond the Asia-Pacific a sense of urgency to act and to demonstrate their solidarity with the millions of people affected.

Broad movements found that they needed institutional structures to link their activities. Different groups formed a string of Asia-wide coalitions, networks, forums, and co-ordinating committees.

The nature of the structures depends on the reasons for forming them, the kind of groups that gravitate toward each other, and the groups' goals, activity cycle, resource requirements, and resource availability. Some structures are permanent; many last only as long as the project.

Long-term groups include the Asian Coalition for Agrarian Reform and Rural Development (ANGOC), the Third World Network, the Asia-Pacific Bureau on Adult Education (ASPBAE), Asia-Pacific Peoples Environmental Network, Asian Alliance of Human Rights Organizations, and the Asian Students Associations. Examples of temporary and more fluid groups include the UNCED coordinating committees, the Asian Development Bank lobby group, the South-North Project for Sustainable Development in Asia, and Sustainable Agriculture Network.

ASPBAE stands out among NGOs because its main focus is education. Founded in 1964 in Sydney, Australia, following a UNESCO seminar, ASPBAE is recognized internationally for its contribution to non-formal adult education. Its membership base includes national associations of adult education, individuals, and institutions. By 1988, it counted among its members 14 national associations, 35 institutions, and 75 individuals. At its First General Assembly in 1991, hundreds of delegates came representing around 35 countries. ASPBAE is also affiliated to the International Council of Adult Education (ICAE).

Regional and national activities of ASPBAE and its members cover a wide range of concerns: peace and human rights, trade union education, environment, women, youth education, education of indigenous peoples, social awareness, curriculum and pedagogy development, participatory methodologies, and many others, including health and drug abuse.

Many other groups in the Asia-Pacific are training and developing an increasing number of popular educators who can galvanize citizen action around development, environment, and human rights issues. Not only do they deliver a basic service to the millions who continue to suffer government neglect, they use education as a means to people empowerment.

In many cases, centralized structures are not necessary to establish Asia-wide links among organizations and movements. Bilateral relationships are sometimes favoured over multilateral. Multiple bilateral arrangements and flexible multilateral structures avoid bureaucratization and promote a wider latitude for direct voluntary action.

Supranational integration of economic and political power is the biggest impediment to democratization from below. As markets and ecological space diminish, resources and decisions are concentrated in fewer and fewer institutions dominated by the most powerful states and transnational corporations. The result is regionalization. While regionalization can move power away from the traditional international elite, it can also mean hegemony of Japan or more intense Japanese competition with the United States, which is not about to give up its hold on Asia-Pacific.

The elite consensus that growth should be achieved at any cost means that the social and ecological problems of this century will be magnified severalfold in the next. Rapid economic growth will undermine the commitment of Asia-Pacific states to carry out

UNCED agreements. NIC-type industrialization, together with Japanese-type modernization, will further stress the ecological capacity of the region. Asia is still rich in biodiversity and minable resources but will not be able to sustain high-speed growth for long. The region's sink capacity, which remains comparatively large, will not last long either once industrialization goes full stream ahead.

The international power elites have a decided edge over grassroots and citizens' movements in the battle for Asian hearts and minds. The media and all instruments of educating and informing the masses are under elite control. The superhyping campaigns for NIC development in schools, newspapers, television, and radio—not to mention the voluminous literature churned out by official development institutions—highlight the citizens' movements disadvantage.

Citizens' movements, especially at the grassroots, are handicapped by channels for information exchange that are not only limited but expensive. As noted earlier, access to information has improved a great deal in the past few years due to electronic technology and computer-based communication systems. But while some voluntary organizations are already hooked up to these systems, many more are not, especially grassroots groups that cannot afford installation fees or whose remote location does not allow them easy access to the systems.

The feverish pace of globalization of development and environment problems underlines the need for more effective communication in order to pool together and organize the scattered responses of different citizens' groups. The policies and activities of regional institutions, such as the Asian Development Bank (ADB), the World Bank, transnational corporations, and interstate bodies must be monitored.

As a major development institution, the ADB has become a focus of lobby activities of a growing number of NGOs and peoples' organizations within and outside the Asia-Pacific region. Since its founding in 1966, the bank has financed development investments in its developing member countries (DMCs) amounting to US $43 billion—a total of 1,180 projects in agriculture and agro-industry, energy, industry, transport and communications, social infrastructure, finance, and the private sector. Its annual lending increased from US $1.7 billion in 1981 to US $5.3 billion in1993.

An ADB NGO lobby began in 1989 through the initiative of two U.S. NGOs—Friends of the Earth and Environmental Policy Institute—and ANGOC. All three have also been involved in the World Bank NGO lobby network. Since then, there has been a dramatic increase in the number of lobby groups demanding reforms in ADB policies and activities.

The twenty-fifth ADB Annual Meeting in May 1992 in Hong Kong saw a significant expansion of the lobby network with the participation of the South-North Project for Sustainable Development in Asia. This was organized in 1990 to do research and lobbying around the themes of agriculture, forestry, and micro-ecosystems. It was originally composed of six Asian organizations—AWARE (India), Project for Ecological Recovery (Thailand), PRRM (Philippines), PROSHIKA (Bangladesh), SAM (Malaysia), WALHI (Indonesia)—and a donor-partner in the North, NOVIB (Netherlands). During the lobby phase, two more groups were enlisted into the network—Japan Tropical Forest Action Network and the Bank Information Center, USA—because of their track record in lobby work with multilateral development banks.

Participation in the lobby campaigns increased to over 30 organizations between the 1992 and 1993 ADB annual meetings. Aside from members of the major networks, these included AID Watch (Australia), Greenpeace International, Sustainable Agriculture Network, Philippine Development Forum (from the United States), Freedom from Debt Coalition (Philippines), Environmental Defense Fund (U.S.), and Thailand Rural Reconstruction Movement, among others.

The NGO lobby has raised a variety of issues and concerns over the social and environmental impacts of Bank policies and projects. These issues have been forcefully backed up by case studies conducted by the NGOs in partnership with affected local communities.

ADB has been responding positively to NGO pressure for changes. Apart from liberal use of trendy sustainable development rhetoric, ABD has recently issued new guidelines incorporating environment and social dimensions in policy formation and programme and project cycles. ADB has also opened some space for NGO and local community participation in project implementation, monitoring, and evaluation.

But these reforms are considered by NGOs and local communities as too little and too slow in coming. A budget analysis reveals that the bulk of ADB's money still goes to traditional growth projects that produce adverse social and ecological effects. Justifiably, the lobbyists continue to doubt if ADB is capable of making a fundamental shift in its strategic orientation, policies, and activities.

One problem confronting the voluntary sector is its dependence on development assistance from the North. Some grassroots movements and development support organizations are totally dependent on foreign funding. Their dependency gives rise to a number of problems, the most important of which is the loss of autonomy of the recipient organizations. Many donor organizations impose their own views on how development should proceed in the South. Local organizations' dependence draws them away from opportunities that are available within the country, limiting the possibilities for local resource mobilization. The decline or cutback of foreign assistance will surely magnify this problem.

Civil society flourishes in pluralism and diversity. Conflicts of agenda and multiple strategies and approaches add colour and fire to citizens' movements. As long as groups can demonstrate a fairly high threshold of tolerance for differences, they will overcome dependence and other problems, and eventually converge towards a common higher goal.

NGO-GOVERNMENT RELATIONS

That the relationships between governments and the NGO sector as a whole are too often unsatisfactory has emerged again and again in the foregoing pages. A recent writer has used the term 'antagonistic co-operation' to describe the relationship. In the all too common atmosphere of mutual distrust, contempt and misunderstanding, everyone involved loses, and no one loses more than the very people both NGOs and governments claim to serve.

Part of the difficulty arises from a tendency in the NGO sector to exaggerate its benefits and its achievements; and to deny its many difficulties and shortcomings. NGOs tend to attract the idealistic, the committed, the critics of the status quo. That is part of their strength and their genius. It tends to lead, however, to both an impatience with criticism of their activities: and an overreadiness to condemn the activities of others, including others in the NGO sector itself, that deviate from the purity of the line of a particular NGO. With this intellectual and emotional over-commitment, there goes a largely repressed anxiety about the actual effectiveness of what the NGO is doing. In private very many NGO leaders and employees will admit that their scale is too small to make any difference to 'the problem'; that they cannot deliver sustainability and replicability in the design and implementation of their projects; that once they withdraw their support, their cherished schemes will disappear as fast as the morning dew.

This anxiety makes them extraordinarily defensive or aggressive in their relations with those they see as their critics; with the NGO sector itself or outside it, and especially towards government officials, who too often are demonised as the protectors of the *status quo*, the paid agents of the rich, the powerful and the oppressive.

Government personnel, however, bring their own misperceptions to the relationships. At the political level, there is, as we have already seen at some length, a tendency to exaggerate the likely threat posed by groups with whom process-NGOs work. More widely, there is a fear that the NGOs will threaten existing power structures perhaps by direct political action; more likely by the generation of adverse publicity or ill-informed public comment. Now that the NGOs have much closer relationships with the World Bank (and even, through the Bank, with the International Monetary Fund), the perceived threat (almost certainly exaggerated) has taken on a new, more daunting, dimension, and certainly governments have sometimes over-reacted. Malaysia took draconian powers against environmentally related NGOs in 1981/82; and Kenya became increasingly hostile and suspicious as the demand for more open government took hold in the late 1980s.

If politicians tend to exaggerate the threat posed by NGOs, NGOs often under-estimate, and are therefore naive about, the patronage that attaches to their work. Of course politicians will seek to exploit them, both materially and rhetorically, and of course they will lean on civil servants, especially at the local or regional level, to ensure that the location, cost, structure and stream of benefits maximise the opportunities of patronage. This is one (but only one) reason why decisions from regional development committees or their analogues are slow, confused, subject to sudden reversal, sometimes unimplemented, and even unimplementable. To the NGO, especially one led by expatriates or accountable to a funding agency overseas, these characteristics are as frustrating as they are infuriating. In an extreme case, the NGO either pulls out or, in some ways much more dangerous in the long run, seeks to minimise its contacts with the government, doing as much as it can invisibly.

However, it is at the level of civil servants that the most abrasive relationships develop. That there is a degree of straight jealousy, especially in the upper echelons, had better be faced directly. Senior civil servants see some NGO leaders as better paid, better serviced, better travelled and far more independent and therefore deriving greater job satisfaction. In most countries, this is, however, true of only a tiny handful of NGO leaders; even in a country like Bangladesh that is well stocked with NGOs, perhaps only 30 Bangladeshis in the NGO sector have conditions of service that greatly exceed what they could aspire to command in government service. Most NGO employees are paid on government-related scales or less.

There are, however, countries where the problem is greater: and there are international NGOs that have shown themselves remarkably insensitive to the difficulties that can be caused by over-paying local employees. Oxfam, that in general has an enviable reputation in most of the countries in which it operates, has, surely unwisely, decided to pay its Ethiopian employees at the same rate as expatriates. That may deliver Oxfam from the familiar and uncomfortable hook of paying people with different skin pigmentation different rates for the same job, but it does nothing to allay the fears of government employees that they are being criticised by over-paid amateurs in the NGO sector.

Another source of irritation is the perceived mismatch between the styles of official and NGO agencies. Civil servants are quick to deride the lack of what they regard as professionalism among the NGOs. This can range from trivial issues like clothing and hair styles to much more substantive issues like accounting procedures; taxation returns; performance of immigration duties and filings to whatever department of government has oversight of the NGO sector as a whole. There is a culture clash, and the more determined the NGOs are (and some of the process-NGOs are very determined) to fashion alternatives to bureaucratic, hierarchical and formal styles of working, the more resonant is that clash.

Civil servants could helpfully look beyond style, however, to substance. The questions that need to be asked are not about ways of doing things; but about the long-term results that are achieved on the ground, and that of course poses another set of problems for the civil servants. They do not see, and usually cannot fairly be expected to see, what is going on the ground, which may be three days hard travelling from their desk. They are dependent upon the reports of the NGOs themselves, or on the reports of their local officials. The former they discount (sometimes but not always rightly); the latter have their own difficulties which will be examined now.

Many NGOs are unclear about how to relate to the government bureaucracy as a whole; and to its local manifestations in particular. They tend to have to deal directly with fairly senior people in the capital: the Ministry of Finance to get foreign exchange and import clearance; the Ministry of Labour or Foreign Affairs to get work permits; the Ministry of Agriculture to agree a programme of work in the rural areas; the Ministry of Local Government to get clearance to work in a particular area and so on. Having established, often with great difficulty, delay and frustration, this network of relationships, they tend to use them directly rather than go through the local bureaucracy. The Irish agency, 'Concern', for example has equipped its field officer in Wollaita, Ethiopia, with a field telephone so that he can call the relevant official in Addis Ababa and over-ride the local officials. Its operation in Tanzania worked in much the same way.

Understandable from the viewpoint of an overstretched field director (and his impatient overlord at HQ), this leads to friction, often disguised, denied or suppressed, with the local officials. When asked for their impression of the work of the agency by their own superiors in the capital, they are exaggeratedly negative. A report is an invitation to even the score.

That there will always be tensions between civil servants and the NGOs can be taken as axiomatic. The question is whether more formal machinery will help or hinder the relationship. Those countries that have established elaborate bureaucratic systems to liaise with the NGOs have often been accused, sometimes not without justification, of seeking to control the NGOs, and thus rob them of the feature they prize above all others, their independence.

A far better approach is to seek the assistance of the NGOs in establishing a liaison office, for which NGOs and government accept equal responsibility, and equal financing. This joint system should be seen first and foremost as a mutual listening post; a forum where ideas can be discussed; where experience (even in the form of formal evaluation reports, those most sacred of objects that are usually released to only the most inner quorum) can be shared; failure acknowledged; success appreciated; irritation expressed; difficulties and misunderstandings ironed out.

A few Commonwealth countries have something approaching this, usually in rather an embryonic, informal and above all sectoral stage e.g. the Voluntary Health Association of India. One of the major difficulties that has been experienced in countries where it has been tried, such as India and Bangladesh, is that the NGO sector itself is so disparate, disorganised, competitive and fiercely independent, to the point of mutual jealousy and deep distrust, that it has proved impossible to put together a vehicle that will genuinely represent and serve all organisations, especially, paradoxically, if relations with government are to be a major part of the agenda. It is clearly unacceptable to have a multiplicity of such umbrella organisations, not least because the time of government personnel of a seniority that ought to be taking part is strictly limited. It would be sad if governments were tempted to impose such a structure as a price of continued access to the country, for such imposition would compromise the systems from the start.

If those are the difficulties, they should not blind us to the progress that is being made. For example, in Togo, the government invited the Conseil des Organismes non-Governmentaux en Activité au Togo (CONGAT) to play a role in co-ordinating NGO activity with government activity. Although the relationship has not always been easy, the very fact that the government felt able to take that initiative is a sign of a quality of co-operation that is rare in Africa and only marginally less so in Asia.

Yet without much more regular, honest and open communication, it is hard to see how relationships will improve. Much of the hostility is based on misinformation, misperceived threats or the misapprehension of propaganda for fact. The communication needs to be two-way. Many NGOs, particularly the 'radical' variety, are strong on ideology, but weak on practical experience, especially of larger undertakings. Their ideology is their prerogative and it would be an act of political barbarism to seek to repress it. It needs, however, to be checked against the reality; the reality as perceived by a large number of actors from a large number of perspectives. What stands up from the critical examination perhaps needs to be taken seriously by all the parties in the dialogue.

Communication alone is not enough. Out of it is likely to emerge a series of changes: some very trivial; some routinely administrative; some much more profound, that each side could make to accommodate the legitimate concens of the other. The question then arises how free each side is, or thinks itself to be, to make those changes. The degree of freedom are often very limited. The National NGOs are accountable to their constituents and their supporters (though, and this is a further complication in the relationship, some governments believe that they are accountable above all to them). More and more are, in one sense or another, accountable to the international funding agencies, whether voluntary or official. The international agencies are accountable to their donors, often alert to any breath of scandal or inefficiency assiduously relayed to them by the media.

By the same token, civil servants are accountable to their seniors and ultimately to their political masters, and the political masters are likely to want to bring their own agenda to this debate, not always in helpful ways.

While it is far too simplistic to conclude that without major political change nothing can be done, it is wise to acknowledge that the degrees of freedom are probably quite small. That makes it the more imperative that what can be done is done, that is:

- joint sectoral working parties for information exchange at quite senior levels of both NGO and government,
- so far as possible standardised administrative procedures that both sides thoroughly understand and accept,
- a small but powerful trouble shooting desk, perhaps in the office of the Prime Minister or President, which is both a first point of contact and buffer between NGO and government,
- above all an openness and mutual confidence that can set aside posturing in favour of an honest address to the crucial issues.

All that will only come out of sustained dialogue. That dialogue will, however, have to accept that the self-understandings; the motivations; the drives and ambitions of NGOs are neither identical among themselves; nor, much more, the same as those of government, whether in its administrative or its political persona. To expect perfect harmony or unity of purpose is therefore a triumph of hope over reality. That should not, however, deter all those involved from seeking mechanisms that improve on a situation that currently varies from the scandalous to the mildly inefficient. The poor of the world have the right to demand that.

2

NGOs and Poverty Alleviation: A Policy Initiative

It is widely assumed that NGOs are able to reach and improve the well-being of the poorest who are the subject of NGO assistance. Overall, the sixteen evaluations of NGO projects paint an encouraging picture. Twelve of the sixteen broadly achieved their objectives, and had a positive impact in alleviating poverty, even if only one was clearly successful in achieving all its objectives. In contrast, only two can be said to have failed both to meet their overall objectives and to make headway in reducing poverty. The final two achieved some of their objectives, but fell short in others, with the result that it was not possible to derive a firm assessment of their overall contribution to poverty alleviation.

This overall judgement of project success, while subject to a number of qualifications, appears to be consistent with the findings of other comparative studies : three-quarters of the sample appeared to meet objectives set, and had an impact in alleviating poverty. In the successful projects there was evidence that incomes had increased, in some cases quite substantially, consumption had improved, and there were ongoing investments in land, livestock, and assets. In addition, the social status and self-confidence of the poor were found to have been enhanced in the process, increasing their capacity to make use of locally available opportunities.

Successful project interventions were found to be related to a number of different factors, none of which in isolation was sufficient to achieve project objectives. Three, in particular, stand out: beneficiary participation, effective management, and skilled and committed staff. In addition to these factors, a favourable external environment was found to be conducive to project success: it was far easier for projects to succeed in their objectives when the local economy was expanding (or at least not contracting), resources were plentiful, and local élites were broadly supportive of their objectives. The evidence also suggested that those projects which had been prepared and designed more carefully were among the more successful performers.

The sixteen case-studies confirmed the importance of beneficiary participation in the planning, design, and implementation of projects. Projects were more likely to succeed where their objectives corresponded to the priorities of the poor, and where the intended beneficiaries were regularly consulted and involved in decision-making at all stages of the project cycle. Although there was some evidence of success in projects lacking in participation, the benefits derived were unlikely to be sustained over the longer term without more direct involvement. Most of the NGOs placed a high premium on the formation of new groups or the strengthening of existing groups as a means of raising awareness, fostering participation, and empowering the poor, although these were not always integral to successful interventions.

The sixteen projects highlighted the importance of a strong and competent leadership, skilled in management and possessing an overall vision of project goals. Strong leaders were able to maintain channels of communication with government officials, enabling them to lever additional resources or circumvent potential problems. At the same time, excessive centralization of decision-making in some projects undermined staff commitment and limited the potential impact of the intervention.

A third factor underlying project success was staffing. The calibre of project staff, their commitment to overall project objectives, and their degree of empathy with the intended beneficiaries all contributed to the more successful projects. Well-trained and educated staff motivated by a reasonable level of remuneration and decent working conditions played a critical role in this regard.

Not unexpectedly, while the overall judgement of project performance was favourable, the projects exhibited weaknesses in certain key respects.

1. *Reaching the poorest.* First, and most importantly, many of the projects failed to reach the very poorest, and even in cases where poverty alleviation occurred, improvement in economic status was modest. There was little evidence to suggest that many beneficiaries had managed to escape from poverty on a permanent basis. However, these results need to be seen within the wider context. Thus what appear to be marginal improvements to an outsider (even for those closely associated with the project) can be of major importance for the poorest themselves, especially when considered in a broader environment of marked economic decline. Equally, it would be unrealistic to expect rapid change to occur in a relatively short space of time. Some of these assisted are what are sometimes called 'borderline' poor—people who experience spells of seasonal poverty. For them, even small increases in income during the peak agricultural season can be enough to tide them over a lean patch. Similarly, the creation of new or, more commonly, additional periods of employment during the off-peak months was found to play an important role in reducing vulnerability to the fairly hostile external environment in which most poor people have to live.

2. *Cost-effectiveness.* Second, most of the studies revealed that these types of interventions are costly to implement and the benefits take time to mature. In five of the projects, the benefits clearly exceeded the costs of achieving them. In five others the objectives were achieved, but at a high cost in terms of staffing and resources. In the two projects which failed to meet their objectives the costs far exceeded the benefits. For the remaining four projects, it was difficult to make precise judgements, either because the project was relatively new or because the data were insufficient. In addition, the studies confirmed that cost-benefit analysis appears novel to some NGOs, and that overall costs are usually higher than NGOs believe them to be.

3. *Sustainability.* On the question of sustainability, relatively few of the projects demonstrated the potential to continue once the NGO ceased operating in the area. Some were heavily constrained in this respect by an adverse physical environment. In others, insufficient attention on the part of the NGO to cultivating the capacity of grass-roots organizations to manage economic programmes undermined their potential for self-reliance over the longer term.

Reaching the Poorest

Conventional wisdom asserts that NGOs are particularly good at reaching the poorest: the assertion that they are better at this than government and official aid agencies suggests both that they may be better at involving poorer or the poorest groups, and that they may be better at improving their lives. Thus an important aspect of project impact is the distribution of gains accruing to different groups of beneficiaries. The evidence from the sixteen evaluations shows—positively—that the projects were not set up for the rich, and that few direct and exclusive benefits were obtained by the non-poor. Equally, however, no projects were both set up for and exclusively benefited the poorest. Almost without exception, the poor benefited to a greater extent than the poorest, and men to a greater degree than women, by virtue of having prior access to land and other assets. In only four of the sixteen projects evaluated were the incomes of the poorest raised significantly; in eight they were either bypassed or the benefits that they received were limited in comparison to individuals who were less poor. These results lead to the important question of the characteristics of projects which did reach the poorest, and why even NGOs find it difficult to reach down to and improve the lives of the poorest.

One sub-group of the poorest are the chronically poor who lack the means to satisfy their basic food requirements. These include the sick, the elderly, and others who are not generally economically active, together with a small number of people who will be reluctant or unable to participate in projects due to suspicion, lack of motivation, or pressure from dominant social groups. Such people tend to constitute a minority of the rural population; they are usually beyond the reach of most economic interventions and stand to benefit more from improved social services, rather than through development projects designed to promote self-reliance.

But another—and larger—sub-group include landless labourers, marginal farmers, those with few durable assets and little or no education, and a high proportion of households headed by women. Part of the reason for NGOs failing to reach these people in larger numbers lies in the constraints of human and financial resources. Almost by definition the poorest tend to be scattered, disorganized, and living in resource-poor areas, or are heavily dependent on the non-poorest groups for employment and credit requirements. When NGOs attempt to design projects exclusively for these people they form functional groups to encourage their participation. Alternatively, they try to implement projects on the basis of direct contact. But even if NGOs follow the latter course of action, they are constrained in this: it is no easy task to devise programmes aimed at raising the incomes of individuals without land or other assets: unskilled workers with little capital tend to produce products that sophisticated consumers do not want to buy, while the poorest have no money to buy such goods. These problems were encountered both by the Action Aid Mityana Programme (AMP) in western Uganda and ActionAid Bangladesh.

However, four of the sixteen projects where the poorest did benefit directly offer some insights into the types of NGO interventions which stand a higher chance of success: the CASA Phase III programme in coastal Andhra Pradesh, the ActionAid credit programme in southern Bangladesh, the Simukai collective farming co-operative and the Campfire project in Zimbabwe. The CASA and ActionAid Bangladesh projects both used rigorous targeting of beneficiaries, and worked hard to ensure that the poorest were well represented in beneficiary groups. Beyond that, a concentration on the disbursement of small loans directed towards activities selected by the beneficiaries in consultation with, and subject to careful monitoring by, project staff helped to ensure both that the poorest could cope with the (small amount of) assistance provided and that the money loaned was likely to go into productive uses of value to the poorest even though the loans were not always sufficient to meet their needs. In Zimbabwe, the Simukai co-operative benefited the poorest, as co-operative members were largely young unskilled, uneducated, and assetless ex-combatants, but the numbers involved were very small (less than forty). In the case of the Campfire project, the poorest gained because the project embraced everyone living in the designated area. In both instances, however, the administrative costs were high in relation to the numbers of people benefiting and the extent to which positive benefits were generated.

In some of the other projects, the poorest clearly gained as the benefits trickled down to them even though they were not actively participating. Small farmers assisted by crop loans provided by RDT in India expanded the area they cultivated, increased their share of cash-crops, and in some cases started to cultivate several crops a year: all these activities led to expanded employment opportunities for the poorest. Similar employment expansion is evident from the UWFCT and ActionAid projects in Uganda generated by small businesses set up by individuals who received credit and skills training. However, few of the NGOs participating in the study realized the extent to which some types of intervention had a multiplier effect manifest in increased local demand for goods and services and employment.

Alleviating poverty is, of course, concerned with far more than raising income levels or attempting to increase short-term financial security (although it is often linked with these): a point recognized in the usually broad set of objectives of the projects examined. These include a range of social benefits which are less amenable to quantification but can be of great significance to the poor, especially in the South Asian context: for example, reduced dependence on money-lenders and local political élites, greater independence in decision-making, lower seasonal out-migration, improved ability to cope with contingencies such as illness and natural disasters, greater political participation and awareness, reduced social discrimination, and increased self-respect and mobility for women. Thus in Uganda, the Women's Finance and Credit Trust not only provides examples of increasing income, for instance from developing a small business, but in addition the income gains enhanced the status of the poor (especially those previously without land or assets) within the wider community, providing the conditions for widening of opportunities for subsequent gain in the medium term. Or again, people from the scheduled-caste community in coastal Andhra Pradesh report that the practice of untouchability has declined as a result of their being able to sell goods and provide services valued by higher castes, as a result of the NGO intervention.

Most of the evaluations revealed few major, new social tensions arising from successfully enhancing the social and economic status of the poor, either with local (male) élites or other poor non-beneficiaries. This is a notable achievement for, as the evaluations make clear, attempts to raise the incomes of the poor usually take place in a social and political environment which is at best difficult, and often hostile to the objectives of the projects. However, it could also signify that the projects failed to challenge the prevailing balance of power or existing patterns of gender discrimination.

The relative absence of tension between rich and poor was

usually related to the type of projects executed. Four factors appeared to play a role here: the economic benefits were perceived by the rich to be too insignificant to be of interest to them, or the project was completely self-contained (ActionAid, Bangladesh; CASA, India; and the Simukai co-operative, Zimbabwe); the particular technological innovation (homestead-based tree planting) introduced primarily benefited only the poor (e.g. Caritas Bangladesh); the rich also gained as the benefits accrued to the entire community (natural-resource management or investments in the village infrastructure as in India and Bangladesh and under the Zimbabwe Trust); and the NGO was able to persuade the rich to co-operate because the increased income for the poor also led to increased income for the rich (e.g. the fisheries programme in Bangladesh). In some projects, the NGO was able to exploit differences between rival dominant groups and successfully avoid polarization, or else to eliminate the exploitation of politically weak middlemen (CASA and fishermen's federations in India). But the lack of tension in most of the projects reflects the fact that they focused less on mobilizing the poor to challenge the structural causes of poverty (unequal landholdings, low wages, etc.) and more on enhancing their incomes and material status.

However, social tensions did arise in some projects, sometimes spilling over into violence, especially when richer groups felt that their interests were under potential or actual threat. In India especially, dominant social groups (landlords, money-lenders, and high castes) sometimes reacted violently to a loss of patronage and income (from high-interest loans for example) by resorting to coercion, smear campaigns, exploiting factional divisions, and physical attacks on project participants or staff members. In the Zimbabwe Trust project, the comparatively powerful district council appeared to try to control the significant income gains acquired from wildlife management which ought to have been channelled down to the ward participants.

The Involvement of Women

Since the early 1980s, NGOs have been highlighting discrimination against women and the relative disadvantages that women suffer in many societies in the developing world. This is probably why their interventions are believed to be effective in reaching poor rural women. While this study's selection of projects indicated a commitment to gender issues, their involvement and impact upon poor women was generally limited. With the notable exception of the Uganda Women's Finance and Credit Trust, set up exclusively for women, there was little evidence to suggest that the projects selected effectively challenged prevailing patterns of gender discrimination. Men dominated the agricultural credit schemes studied—Christian Care in Zimbabwe, RDT in India—even if these included special programmes for women. Women were also usually under-represented both in committees of beneficiaries set up to liaise with the NGO and among the project staff of the NGO, unless there was a positive attempt to expand their involvement.

In only six of the sixteen projects did women benefit to any significant extent, either through their direct participation and involvement, or in terms of a perceptible improvement in their economic and social status. Equally, however, it needs to be said that improving the economic status of women in male-dominated societies is both a complex and delicate issue and one which is bound up with the wider problem of poverty. In the face of women's difficulties, it is highly unlikely that significant advances can be made in short space of time; indeed, it would be naive to expect NGO projects, especially over a short period, to transform their role and status. In some projects, pressure from the men forbidding their wives to take on new income-enhancing activities was often outweighed by the extent of family poverty, and the chance to obtain more cash or food.

This was evident in the GKT horticulture and agriculture programme and the ActionAid programme in Bangladesh. In both cases, the rise in income contributed towards increasing women's confidence in the prospects of an improved quality of life. As the UWFCT project in Uganda and the CASA project in India demonstrate, in the short term at least, increased self-respect and even limited financial independence can be very important for poor women in a male-dominated society. Nevertheless, there are frequently limits to the extent that disadvantaged women can gain increased independence from such interventions. For example, the ActionAid credit programme in Bangladesh indicated that male family members used loans secured by women to finance their own economic activities.

Where efforts were made to involve women and promote their economic well-being, the projects revealed a tendency to emphasize more traditional occupations for women, characterized by relatively low economic return and market potential. The reason is understandable: it reflects existing economic and domestic commitments which place severe restrictions, especially time restrictions, on the ability of women to take on new tasks. The result, however, is that gender divisions tend to be reinforced rather than resolved by such interventions. Yet there were examples of projects where NGOs were able to help women identify opportunities for deriving new sources of income include tree cultivation and backyard nurseries on household plots, in the Caritas social forestry programme in Bangladesh, and tailoring, poultry-raising, and dairying, in the CASA Phase III programme in India. In such cases it was apparent that increased income for women brought wider benefits in the form of improved food intake for children and higher expenditure on health and education.

The Role of Groups

The sixteen case-studies broadly confirm that view the most NGOs place a high premium on the formation of new groups, or the strengthening of existing groups, as a means of raising awareness, empowering the poor, and promoting self-reliance. However, not all the NGOs operated through full-fledged groups. In Uganda, for instance, in two of the four projects (UWFCT and the Busoga diocese health programme) beneficiaries interacted with NGO personnel largely on an individual basis. For the remainder, groups have differed in their origins, size, and function. In some instances, groups were already in existence prior to the NGO intervention; these included self-help groups (such as the farmers' groups in Christian Care and Silveira House) and membership organizations (the ASM farmer's co-operatives and the fishermen's associations in India). For the most part, groups were established by the NGO at the outset of the project.

In some of the projects, the groups functioned little differently from groups set up or utilized in non-NGO projects. Their main function was to facilitate the distribution and collection of credit, or to provide a mechanism to channel inputs to the beneficiaries. In others, however, the groups performed a rather different, or at least additional, role, best captured in the notion of 'empowerment'. In Uganda the NGOs usually worked with groups formed prior to project commencement, or with very loosely structured associations. In Zimbabwe individuals with similar backgrounds, especially common church membership, were brought together to facilitate the allocation of small-scale credit and agricultural inputs to farmers. But in neither country was there much evidence of NGOs spending time forming new groups, or explicitly attempting to involve the poorest. To some extent, this appeared to reflect a wish to reduce risk and to maximize the anticipated impact of particular interventions.

In contrast, in Bangladesh and India seven of the eight projects began with the explicit task of forming groups which were established with the objective of bringing together the poor, on the basis of class, gender, and locality. Here groups were formed for two purposes:

First, to promote participation in the design and organization of economic programmes, and to provide a channel through which credit and other inputs could be directed; and

Secondly, in order to achieve a range of specific social and political objectives.

In India, in particular, the case-studies provide evidence of the groups formed playing an effective role in empowering their members. The results are manifested in various ways. In some cases, groups provide the basis for collective social action, enabling communities to seek redress over legal wrangles, to mediate in conflicts over land rights, or to challenge government legislation. The fishermen's associations in Tamilnadu illustrate not only the way in which the exploitative mark-ups of middlemen and money-lenders were successfully circumvented, but also how substantial political leverage was acquired by the associations, which enabled them to influence government policy on fishing rights. Likewise, the CASA project provided the structure for poor people not only to gain confidence to approach officials, and to interact with people from outside their own community, but also to secure access to resources from government institutions and banks.

The positive gains from NGOs working with and through groups, however, needs to be put into broader perspective. Five of the sixteen projects lacked community participation but were, none the less, clearly successful in raising incomes. Groups only appeared to play a significant role when they genuinely represented the interests of the poor (rather than acting as a front for élite groups) and where they provided effective channels of communication with the NGO. In projects where groups were characterized by unstable membership or internal conflicts, performance was adversely affected. Equally, even with projects which resulted in higher incomes or increased status for the beneficiaries, fear of losing the gains achieved often pushed group members towards exclusivity and a reluctance to open up membership to the poorest. Thus, in some projects where members were self-selected (such as the Silveira House farmers' groups in Zimbabwe or the fishermen's associations in India), the beneficiaries introduced stringent entry requirements: membership became conditional on the ownership of land and assets, which resulted in the poorest automatically being excluded.

Projects are often designed so that, if individual members perform poorly, the project as a whole suffers. For example, some credit projects operate in such a way that when one member defaults it adversely affects the credit standing of others. Default or an inability to meet repayment obligations was the most common cause of group break-up in ActionAid Bangladesh and Silveira House in Zimbabwe (although an underlying factor was the vlunerability of the poor to domestic and environmental calamities). Furthermore, group pressure to repay loans to the project can result (as in the case of RDT) in some members of the credit scheme returning to the village money-lenders to borrow funds simply in order to remain in good standing with the NGO.

Another problem with functional groups is that, while they may be conducive to effective project management in the short term, longer-term sustainability can be more difficult to achieve. Certainly the small-scale credit programme of ActionAid Bangladesh, the crop loan programme of Arthik Samta Mandal and RDT in India, and the Silveira House credit programmes in Zimbabwe all appeared to have similar problems with the capacity of project members to take over administrative responsibility from project staff.

Another frequent objective in the NGO group approach is to try to develop effective leadership among the poor. Again, a number of the case-studies provide evidence of successes here, notably in the CASA project and the fishermen's associations in India, although strong leadership can adversely affect the nurturing of group democracy and in the long term heighten the risk of non-sustainability, since other group members can lose interest and fail to take an active part in group affairs, as the ASM case-study illustrates.

Clearly, therefore, the issue of groups and their role in NGO projects is more complicated than might initially be thought. Groups may not be a *sine qua non* for successful NGO interventions. During the life of the project, performance is related to a range of factors, only one of which is the way in which the beneficiaries are organized and their input into decision-making structured.

NGO Impact and the External Environment

The question of sustainability leads naturally to the contribution of the external (i.e. non-project) environment to project outcomes. For each of the sixteen projects, impact was usually contingent on local and, to some extent, on national and international factors. Yet most of the evaluations indicate that the NGOs underestimated or failed to take into account the wider environmental context in which they were operating: they repeatedly underplayed the significance of economic and social factors outside the immediate parameters of individual projects. In particular, any positive changes in the lives of the poor are primarily attributed to the development projects initiated by NGOs, even though they might result from external factors.

The West Acholi Engineering Workshop in Uganda provides the clearest example of this. The workshop was initially set up to produce ox-ploughs to service the needs of small farmers in the area. But demand dwindled due to a rapid depletion of cattle brought about the continuous bandit raids in the context of political insecurity. The workshop attempted to diversify production, but the quality of the products was poor and its economic viability was threatened. While it may not have been possible to anticipate a drastic fall-off in demand when the project was being initiated, there was clearly a need to build in an element of flexibility to allow a range of products to be manufactured in the face of market uncertainties.

Crop prices and demand for products are clearly important determinants of success in projects which attempt to raise the income of farmers through cash cropping. In Zimbabwe, the case of Silveira House illustrates that the economic viability of maize production by small farmers supported by crop loans was conditional on the attractive prices set by the official Grain Marketing Board, while the Mzarabani case-study illustrates the weakness of the marketing system which the project simply failed to address. In India the Rural Development Trust provided credit to help farmers invest in crop inputs, which in turn encouraged a shift towards groundnut production. This was feasible in economic terms because increased national demand for groundnut oil had pushed up prices. Yet in both the Silveira House and the RDT projects, crop output was itself conditional on climatic variations: recurrent drought reduced yields, and farmers defaulted on their loans.

A rather different illustration is provided by the CASA project in India, where prawn cultivation was introduced by the NGO to provide new sources of income generation for the poor. The initiative succeeded despite the fact that it was located in a remote and relatively inaccessible area, because Japanese demand for prawns had escalated over the previous decade, driving up prices, creating a profitable activity, and making it worth while for private traders to arrange transportation and marketing. Similarly, sericulture in both the CASA and the ASM projects succeeded in part because national demand for silk was buoyant, and grants and subsidized credit were made available by the government. There is no guarantee, however, that favourable prices will continue to prevail, particularly if local production reaches saturation point as a result of competition from private investors, and this highlights the risk element in such ventures.

In other cases, however, the NGOs proved insensitive to the pattern of local demand and potential competition from the private sector when identifying opportunities for self-employment. For example, people who had received skills training from ActionAid in Uganda and went on to set up businesses found it difficult to compete with established artisans who could produce superior products which they sold at more attractive prices. Similarly, training programmes in RDT and ASM in India did not appear to be sensitive to the local opportunities for gainful employment, with the result that only a relatively small proportion of those who received training were applying the skills they had acquired. In contrast, Gono Kallyan Trust in Bangladesh was able to capitalize on its relatively close proximity to Dhaka by identifying market outlets for horticultural produce grown by poor farmers.

In several projects, the NGO insulated producers from local market forces by creating an artificial and temporary source of demand. ActionAid Uganda trained local unemployed youths in tile-making and purchased most of the tiles they produced for use in its own house-building programme. Women trained in printing and dyeing techniques by CASA went on to produce saris and other items of clothing, most of which were purchased by the NGO to augment its disaster relief stock. In neither case, however, was it certain that, once the NGO withdrew, the products would be competitive in the local market.

The distribution of land and other assets also conditions the options available to local NGOs. In Bangladesh a large landless population with minimal access to capital limits the prospects for rapid and enduring poverty alleviation. ActionAid Bangladesh provided credit for income-generation programmes but the degree of material improvement was relatively small, since demand was low and the investment was geared towards activities which, at best, supplemented earnings from casual labour. In such an environment, it would be unrealistic to expect substantial benefits to accrue to the poor in the absence of major structural reforms centred on the redistribution of land and capital assets. In India, by comparison, crop loans and grants for minor irrigation schemes provided by Arthik Samta Mandal were successful in raising farmers' incomes because some prior redistribution had taken place.

Another issue of importance for particular projects is the nature and extent of repression on the part of the local élites. Resistance to programmes designed to strengthen the poor, or appropriation of their benefits by the rich, can clearly limit the potential impact of NGO interventions. Several of the NGOs in India encountered opposition from local politicians and dominant groups, who tried to subvert their activities. This was especially evident in the case of the fishermen's co-operatives which attempted to market fish collectively and RDT's attempts to help farmers escape from the clutches of money-lenders who controlled rural credit. Project performance in such situations has to be assessed in the context of a political environment which is averse to NGO attempts to promote social and economic empowerment.

Perhaps the most dramatic example of external factors which undermine project impact is sporadic natural disasters, to which resource-poor environments are particularly prone. Severe flooding in Bangladesh destroyed the fish-ponds excavated with assistance from GUP, while a tornado devastated houses and crops belonging to those assisted by GKT. A cyclone which hit coastal Andhra Pradesh soon after the CASA and ASM evaluations were completed, resulted in widespread loss of livestock, assets, and crops. Despite these catastrophies, the people affected were able to rebuild their lives fairly quickly as a result of an immediate influx of disaster relief, and the reduction in vulnerability brought about by the NGO's interventions.

Anti-Poverty Programmes

Although still a mainstay of the economy, agriculture in India is of declining relative importance. Between 1965 and 1989 the share of GDP attributable to agriculture declined from 44 per cent to 32 per cent, with corresponding increases for industry (22 per cent to 30 per cent) and services (34 per cent to 38 per cent). Agriculture currently accounts for 39 per cent of exports, and provides livelihood for over 70 per cent of the population. Population growth in India averaged 1.93 per cent per year in 1985-90, some reduction from the 23 per cent average in 1965-80. Total population is expected to exceed 1 billion by 2000. India is the ninth most industrialized country in the world, yet, with 322 million from a total of 816 million estimated to be living in poverty in 1988, it contains more poor people in absolute terms than any other country. Although the Government of India (GoI) predicted a trend decline in poverty incidence in the 1980s and early 1990s, the data suggest that there has been no significant trend away from 40 per cent since the 1960s. This is reflected in India's poor performance in terms of social development. For example, the adult literacy rate in 1990 was 62 per cent for men and 34 per cent for women, and life expectancy at birth 59 years. Although the under-5 mortality rate has halved since 1960, it remains at 130 per 1,000 live births.

While rural-urban migration is swelling the numbers of the urban poor, poverty in India remains largely a rural phenomenon. It is strongly linked to access to land: while the number of operational holdings rose from 70.5 million in 1970-71 to 89.4 million in 1980-81, the number below .1 hectare grew from 36.2 million to 50.5 million over the same period. From 1973 to 1983, the proportion of casual labour (i.e. those generally without any access to land) rose from 22 per cent to 29 per cent of the total work-force, at a time when 55 per cent of casual worker households were below the poverty line.

There is a significant spatial and social dimension to poverty in India. Central (Madhya Pradesh, Gujarat, Karnataka) and eastern (Bihar, Eastern Uttar Pradesh, Orissa, West Bengal) states are 'characterized by higher concentration of poverty than the north-east (Punjab, Haryana, Western Uttar Pradesh). In 1986-87, for instance, 53 per cent of the population were below the poverty line in Bihar, against 15 per cent in the Punjab. These differences are attributable not only to the ineffectiveness of land reform in the central and eastern states, but also to previous government expenditure on irrigation, agro-chemical subsidies and research into Green Revolution varieties of rice and wheat, all of which are more relevant to the agro-ecological conditions of the north-west.

A large number of poverty alleviation programmes have been undertaken in India since the early 1950s. It is impossible in the present context to do more than review the main outcomes. Early efforts (the community development programme, the intensive agricultural district programme) did not distinguish clearly enough between interventions accessible to all, and those restricted to identifiable groups of rural poor. As a consequence, many of the benefits they brought were appropriated by the rich.

The integrated rural development programme, launched in 1978, is one of the largest efforts, aiming to reach 45 per cent of households living in poverty during the Eighth Plan period. Despite its ambitious objectives the programme has had some difficulty in reaching the specified target populations (especially women) and in identifying viable income-generating technologies lying within the management capabilities of the poor. Its impact has therefore been rather limited, even if it has proved popular politically.

Large-scale employment-generation programmes include those promoting the acquisition of artisanal skills (e.g. training of youth for self-employment through which almost 1 million individuals passed in 1980-85, and various schemes for the employment of unskilled labour in (largely) the construction of community assets. Both have had some impact on poverty, but the latter have been plagued by low involvement of women, low wages and delayed payments, and failure to generate a sense of 'ownership' among the communities of the assets created, and the former by the lack of demand in many of the agriculturally under-developed areas for the types of skills in which training is being given.

On the whole, while demonstrating some government commitment to poverty alleviation, the above programmes have been characterized by weak targeting, poor follow-up, low repayment levels and problems of asset retention. They have also been subject to local political pressures and petty corruption which has in turn undermined their potential appeal for the poor. Access to credit from banks on a recurrent basis in the form of crop loans also continues to be problematic.

Approaches and Funding

Estimates of the number of NGOs active in rural development in India range from fewer than 10,000 to several hundred thousand depending on the type of classification used. Some 15,000—20,000 are actively engaged in rural development.

Wide variations in the densities of NGOs exist among states. To some extent these reflect not only differing patterns of poverty, but also historical factors (such as areas of Christian missionary influence or Gandhian activity) and the priorities of foreign donors. Within these states certain districts posses dense networks of NGOs, which overlap and compete for clients, while in other areas there are hardly any NGOs active on the ground.

The most common type of NGO in India is the small agency working in a cluster of villages in a particular locality with a handful of staff; as one moves up the scale there are comparatively few organizations which possess the staff of financial resources to work intensively at the state and national levels, although it is these organizations which are the most well-known in government and donor circles.

Annual NGO revenue from abroad is in the region of Rs. 9 billion (US$ 520 million), up from Rs. 5 billion in the mid-1980s and equivalent to approximately 25 per cent of official aid flows. A further Rs. 500 million—700 million is provided annually by government. When individual and corporate donations are added in, annual NGO income amounts to around Rs. 10 billion. This figure is equivalent to 10 per cent of government's annual poverty alleviation expenditure provision.

NGOs and government share many of the same poverty alleviation objectives. Major points of difference lie in the smaller scale but more focused nature of NGO interventions, a greater commitment to social uplift, and an explicit concern with participation. Some NGOs have chosen to tackle the symptoms of poverty — low educational standards, ill-health, poor sanitation and inferior housing — by means of targeted programmes of assistance. Others have concentrated on enhancing the asset position and income-earning potential of the poor through land improvement schemes, credit and skills training. Both of these centre on a consensual approach to development in which the existing social and economic structure, although inherently important, is not directly challenged. An alternative 'social action' approach for some NGOs, particularly since the late 1970s, has been to politicize poor people, thereby challenging directly many of the social and economic structures established by the state.

NGO approaches have evolved from early relief efforts sponsored largely by Christian organizations, through the 'village uplift' of the Gandhian movement, to a professional development approach stressing sound management planning and co-ordination. A particular feature of the 1980s has been the emergence of NGOs providing support services to other NGOs in the form of training, evaluation and documentation. These agencies are usually financed by core grants from foreign donors and from payments for staff training from individual NGOs. Intermediary agencies responsible for channelling funds from foreign donors to small national NGOs in some cases provide qualified staff for undertaking evaluations.

Since the early 1980s there has been an element of convergence between these various approaches, in which NGOs seek to combine project-specific development work with active organization of the poor. In a reflection of this greater uniformity of approach, community organization is now treated, for the most part, as an essential prerequisite of participatory problem diagnosis and of institutional sustainability. An important corollary now widely recognized among NGOs is that organizational work cannot be sustained unless programme activities generate material improvements and this, importantly in the present context, requires that such programmes be supported by technical skills, appropriate technologies and, in many cases institutions and channels geared to input supply and marketing.

Most NGOs work through groups, although there is considerable variation in both their purpose and in the approach of individual NGOs to group formation. Some, notably the Gandhian agencies, chose to work through existing village institutions but these are invariably dominated by the rural elites. Most NGOs therefore prefer to form new groups which can be organized along class, caste and occupational lines.

Despite problems of competition for clients or for scarce government resources some networks have been established at the state level, which seek to present a common front in negotiations with the government over legislation and policy formulation. Other networks have been formed by foreign donors, although these can also have the effect of creating or widening divisions between groups of NGOs. More recently, there has been an initiative to establish an NGO network at the national level. A number of NGOs, especially the larger and more established organizations, formed the Voluntary Action Network India (VANI) in April 1988 as a common platform for NGOs. VANI provides resource materials, and organizes conferences on strategic issues of broader concern to NGOs. Despite this initiative, co-ordination between NGOs remains relatively weak, which results in a duplication of effort and habits their potential impact on a larger scale.

The Seventh Five-Year Plan (1985-90) provided for an active involvement on the part of NGOs in the planning process together with a massive increase in the volume of government funds (i.e. to Rs. 1,500 million per year, or US $170 million) assigned for use by them in rural development programmes. The work of voluntary agencies was considered supplementary to that of government in offering the rural poor a range of choices and alternatives, at low cost and with greater participation. Most of this allocation was for NGOs to work in government programmes of the type outlined above, in the areas of social forestry, ecological development, primary health-care, the provision of safe drinking water, education, rural housing, land ceilings implementation, enforcement of minimum wages legislation and bonded labour rehabilitation.

Two further types of relationships between NGOs and government deserve mention:

- There are numerous examples of government 'scaling up' of the ideas generated by NGOs, mainly in the health and education sectors.
- Many attempts have been made by government departments to involve NGOs in project or programme implementation in the expectation of reaching beneficiaries more cost-effectively.

General Constraints

Institutional mandates now seriously overlap. Duplication generated by the institutionalization of certain AICRPs and by the spawning of regional sub-stations (166 by 1988) has been particularly severe. Senior staff in ICAR remain largely uninformed of the degree of overlap among institutes and programmes, and of performance in relation to the inputs provided. They are also overwhelmed with detailed management responsibilities to the detriment of strategic planning and professional leadership. Weak mechanisms for monitoring and evaluation mean, in effect, that most research institutes and programmes receive financial allocations, often for multi-year periods, the results of which are rarely subjected to close scrutiny. ICAR is discussing with major donors the possibility of instituting a computerized management information system to address some of these shortcomings, and to strengthen the monitoring and evaluation aspects of the research project cycle.

A high proportion of research budgets is allocated to staff emoluments which leaves little flexibility by materials and equipment to meet new needs as they arise. For every member of scientific staff there are 4.5 support staff, indicating substantial over-staffing in the lower grades.

Buildings are often inappropriate to the research being undertaken, much equipment is obsolete or malfunctioning, and repair and maintenance facilities tend to be inadequate, prompting donor agency suggestions that capital investment needs over the next few years will be at least US $100 million.

Much of the Indian agricultural research establishment sees itself in the role of 'advancing the frontiers of science'. The divorce between research (*de facto,* largely a central government responsibility) and extension (a responsibility of the individual states) is not merely attributable to the divide between the institutions involved, but also arises from a deep-seated view among many scientists that they do not need to co-ordinate with extension services. It is up to extension services to make the most of whatever research results are published. ICAR's own mandate to transfer technology directly to farmers has added to confusion. It has allowed an elaborate and much-criticized set of programmes to be set up, including Lab-to-Land programmes and Krishi Vigyan Kendras (farm science centres).

Research is often designed to produce publishable output, which is virtually the sole criterion of performance among scientists, the generation of technologies adoptable by farmers becoming *de facto* a secondary objective. This, together with the high proportion of total emoluments made up by benefits (sickness, housing, retirement) which are not performance related, makes it extremely difficult to make the overall system more productive, and its output more relevant to farmers' needs.

While the research service has had considerable success in developing Green Revolution technologies for the north-western states, it has faced numerous limitations in developing new agricultural technologies for those parts of (predominantly) eastern and southern states which can be grouped under the following headings:

1. *Resource requirement and availabilities.* CDR areas are characterized by diverse farming systems in which inputs to and outputs from crops, trees and animals are intrinsically linked. Such systems contrast starkly with the monoculture (e.g. irrigated rice) widely evident in more homogeneous areas. To raise agricultural productivity through research in CDR areas is a more complex and expensive task than to achieve a similar increase in homogeneous areas, simply because of the range of crops, trees and animals involved. Further difficulties are posed by the complexities of interactions among them, by the importance of off-farm resources (trees; grazing land) and by the socio-institutional complexities governing, e.g. access to common land and reciprocal labour obligations.

   To achieve a certain percentage increase in agricultural productivity in CDR areas therefore requires more resources per unit of land area than would a similar increase in more homogeneous areas. However, in reality, far fewer resources are allocated to CDR areas.
2. *Research focus.* Much of the reputation of public sector research institutes in India has been built on research into high-yielding varieties of cereals and oilseeds with their concomitant high levels of agro-chemical inputs. This more easily and more reliably generates publishable work than the sustainable low-input technologies more relevant to CDR areas.
3. *Research methods.* Conditions in homogeneous areas are easy to replicate on research stations. On-station experiments under controlled conditions therefore have good prospects of producing technologies adoptable by farmers operating in these areas. By contrast, in CDR areas

much more time and effort needs to be invested in understanding farmers' objectives constraints and practices in the context of the agro-ecological and socio-economic complexities in which they operate. Researchers' relations with farmers need to be participatory and collegiate. These approaches and techniques, however, are still in their infancy in many public sector research institutes, including those in India.

4. *Research-extension linkages.* Major empirical studies drawing on experience from numerous countries have demonstrated that research-extension linkages are weak (e.g. Kaimowitz 1990). Feedback from extension to research on the performance of technologies disseminated has been particularly weak. India is no exception to these general findings: while the introduction of the training and visit extension system has improved management procedures, it does not have sufficient flexibility to tailor the type or timing of messages to areas characterized by unreliable rainfall, for example. Nor does it necessarily improve feedback (Howell 1988). A powerful lesson from reviews is that research-extension linkages require consistent effort from researchers to identify not only ways in which their technologies can be better disseminated, but also how far the technologies have met farmers' requirements and in what ways they can be improved. It appears that only a few individuals within Indian public sector research institutes have begun to take steps in this direction for CDR areas.
5. *Linkages across disciplines and institutions.* The methods and approaches outlined in are necessarily inter-disciplinary, often requiring strong input from social as well as natural sciences. Several reviews (Coulter and Farrington 1988; World Bank 1989b) have drawn attention to the small numbers of social scientists employed in ICAR institutes An alternative approach, relying on inter-institutional collaboration, has so far been little explored in the Indian context. Two ramifications of limited inter-institutional collaboration go far beyond the restrictions they impose on inter-disciplinarity:

   First, contacts between research and implementing institutions (such as special agricultural projects, integrated rural development projects and the plethora of agencies charged with watershed management) have been limited, thereby restricting researchers' knowledge of the implementation constraints faced in the use of existing or new technology.

Second, with the exception of the case studies reported at a recent workshop, links between public sector research institutes and those (non-profit) institutes operating outside the public sector have been very limited.

Given the potential complementarities between the different types of institutes — i.e. the availability of specialist skills and 'lumpy' facilities such as libraries and laboratories in the public sector which NGOs generally do not have, and NGOs' skills in identifying farmers' needs, opportunities and constraints, in participatory approaches and in community organisation—some loss in overall efficiency seems to have been incurred through failure to exploit this potential more widely.

Improving NGO Effectiveness

The level of resources provided to beneficiaries and the commitment of the beneficiaries to particular NGO interventions are essential components of the effectiveness of NGO projects aimed at alleviating poverty. But these factors need to be placed within an array of differing circumstances which will continually affect performance, the exact composition and importance of which will change from intervention to intervention.

This suggests that for NGO projects achieving success is more an art than a science: it lies in having the sensitivity and skill to balance the provision of resources with the sustaining of commitment. The trouble is that no NGO has the time (or the money) to practice the art with precision: money is needed both to provide physical resources and to nurture group commitment. The world in which NGOs live and have to execute their projects is far from ideal. Corners often have to be cut, which inevitably results in a less than ideal project performance. None the less, NGOs, both northern and southern, face the problem of how to improve the effectiveness of their present range of project interventions.

A basic requirement is for more information and analysis in

order to guide the choice of the type of intervention which should be attempted, its form, its size, its progress, its duration, and its continuation once external support has been withdrawn. For the generalist NGO, deciding on the form of intervention is at once both the most critical and the most difficult part of project selection. It requires some understanding of both the poverty of the target group to be assisted and the nature of the society in which this group of poor people is located, including the potential for resolving gender-related questions of poverty. It also requires an understanding of the development work being undertaken and planned by the government, at least at the local level, and ideally of the nature of the role which the government expects NGOs to play in poverty alleviation. Increasingly, too, such an assessment is likely to require knowledge of the activities of other agencies working in the proposed project area, as well as the overall effect that NGO work is likely to have on government efforts in the medium and longer term.

All this suggests that NGOs need to have some sort of local, if not national, assessment of poverty and poverty alleviation into which particular interventions can be placed. Undertaking and utilizing such an assessment has the added advantage of reducing the likelihood of discrete projects being divorced from the more basic processes of development under way in the wider economy. In particular, NGOs have much to learn from different types of projects carried out in the same locality, as well as from similar interventions in different localities. A major problem is that NGOs still prefer to work on their own and to draw on project experience largely from within their own organizations. There is a wealth of untapped experience from other NGOs, and often also from government agencies, either working in similar localities or utilizing similar types of intervention. Such information therefore needs to be shared within and between NGOs in a far more systematic way than occurs at present.

Broader assessment is also important as there would appear to be considerable ignorance within individual NGOs, and even more between different NGOs, concerning methods of effective poverty alleviation and the relative costs of different interventions. Current weaknesses suggest that particular attention needs to be focused on the extent to which the resources (financial and human) committed to a project are adequate to achieve the objectives set, not least if the project contains (as it usually does) a growth component.

While NGOs should not simply adopt projects with low costs per beneficiary, or which are expected to produce the greatest unit quantity of benefit for the costs incurred, they should be aware of the relative anticipated costs and benefits of different forms of interventions, as well as being able to link these to the risk element and the record of project performance. For instance, there are likely to be trade-offs between keeping costs down and a reduced ability to reach the very poorest by means of finely targeted interventions, which by their nature require closer supervision and a greater investment of resources, both human and financial.

The ODI evaluation also indicate that greater care and time need to be taken in both project selection and identification. Establishing discrete projects which have the potential of benefiting the poorest requires, at the outset, that the objectives be clearly stated, even if these change over time. But it also requires greater transparency in relation to the means to achieve these objectives.

At this stage, thought also needs to be given to NGO withdrawal: in the intitial preparation of the project, the issue of self-reliance and how this is going to be achieved needs to be addressed. Pre-project work ought also to address explicitly questions about the size of the beneficiary group; is it adequate (too large or too small) to nurture the community aspects of the project; is the project likely to lead to élitism among project beneficiaries or to a rippling outwards of the anticipated benefits? What all this suggests is that, in drawing up a project, the likely problems to be encountered ought to be addressed explicitly: what sorts of risks are likely to arise, and when, and what methods should be adopted to reduce them?

Greater attention also needs to be focused on the practice and mechanisms of undertaking continuous assessments of achievements and problems, and to have these fed back into the planning process. However, the processes of continuous assessment and monitoring need to be matched both to the nature of the project and to the abilities of the staff involved: there is no point in devising a sophisticated method of appraisal if none of the staff are able to undertake such assessments. Equally, there is little point in outlining detailed targets, for instance annual increases in income, if the staff are incapable of knowing whether these targets are being met.

There is no doubt that monitoring and evaluation procedures

are weak in most NGOs, both northern and southern, and that few, if any, northern NGOs have worked out proper procedures for integrating the information and insights obtained from the few evaluations which are undertaken into the project cycle. However, little practical purpose is likely to be served by recommending that the monitoring of projects should become more formalized, and in particular that a greater number of evaluations should be undertaken by different NGOs, unless mechanisms for incorporating this information into the project cycle are carefully worked out. A major current constraint in utilizing whatever information is, or ought to be, available, is simply lack of time: NGO personnel do not have the leisure to read, reflect, and act upon the data which are currently available within their organizations, let alone devote time to generating, reading, and constructively acting on yet more information. The prior need, therefore, is to examine ways in which the information which does exist within NGOs can be channelled into the work of project officers; only then will it be worthwhile to expand the scope and number of evaluations.

That this need is urgent became increasingly apparent during the present study. The evaluations suggest a certain amount of complacency on the part of some NGOs. Beneficiaries were far from reluctant to voice their criticisms about the running of the projects—not that this is surprising, for criticism is often part of the evaluation process, even one which aims to be constructive. However, the ODI evaluations tended to be far more critical than were the local NGOs of the projects they were running. One reason for this is a high level of ignorance about evaluation and monitoring methods, and of the rich sources of information on project performance and impact that can be tapped without major effort or expense.

The Scale of NGO Interventions

For the foreseeable future, the NGO movement will be subject to continued external pressures for further growth, with the scene set for a period of continued expansion similar to that experienced in the 1980s. These pressures originate in part in the still widely shared view that NGOs make an important, and probably significant, contribution to poverty alleviation in developing countries. They will continue to be boosted by the influential paradigm in which privatization, democracy, and pushing back the role of the state are judged to provide three key pre-conditions for development to occur. In part, too, NGO growth will be fostered by the sheer scale and perpetuation of the problems of poverty, especially in regions like Africa, where governments will continue to have insufficient resources of their own to provide an adequate or even minimum quantity of human and physical resources to promote development. Equally, these pressures are likely to be furthered by the wider fall-out from economic recession and structural adjustment programmes, with NGOs continuing to play a growing role in attempting to address some of the social costs of adjustment.

In turn, all these factors are likely to increase the amount of external funding for NGO interventions in the developing world, both from official aid agencies, and from individuals and private-sector organizations and institutions, resulting in a steady increase in NGO poverty-alleviating projects and programmes. For its part, the World Bank's newly formulated *Operational Directive* on poverty reduction explicitly envisages an expanded role for NGOs in poverty alleviation in the 1990s. It comments thus (1992: 12):

> NGOs have shown that their programmes can reach the poor often more effectively than programmes managed by the public sector, especially when NGOs are brought into the early stages of project preparation. Subject to government sensitivities, Bank policy encourages task managers to involve NGOs as appropriate—particularly grassroots and self-help groups among the poor—in project identification, design, financing, implementation, and monitoring and evaluation.

For individual NGOs, the critical question this raises is the manner in which this continued growth should be directed. For the movement as a whole, what needs to be asked is the extent to which NGOs are capable of making, and have the means to make, a significant dent in the still substantial problems of poverty in the developing world. These questions were addressed at an international workshop held in early 1992 and entitled: Scaling-up NGO Impacts: Learning from Experience (Edwards and Hulme, 1992).

A series of factors lead us to be pessimistic that an expansion in the range and number of NGO projects will have a major impact upon world poverty and hunger. These relate to both the nature of NGO intervention and the broader institutional and political environment in which NGOs operate. As highlighted in the previous chapter, many of the weaknesses of NGO projects revolve around the problems of inadequate and insufficient resources, especially financial resources. With more money, greater care could be taken in project and beneficiary selection; NGOs would have more time to obtain a greater understanding of the dynamics of the poor in relation to other local, regional, and even national groups; more, better, or more appropriate physical resources could be provided; there would be more time for staff to evaluate and monitor projects, to design an appropriate means of withdrawal, and to decide upon the best time for such withdrawal. But the financial constraints on NGOs are usually more deep-seated and complex than even this suggests. Given the massive problems of poverty to be addressed, there is a constant tension between, on the one hand, committing more resources to fewer, better prepared, organized, and structured projects, and, on the other, extending resources more widely to reach, and hopefully make at least some impact upon, a greater number of poor people.

Pressures to spread rather than deepen are increased by two additional factors, financial and human. The first is the wish to keep the costs of helping the poor as low as possible—which is almost bound to have some adverse effect on efficient delivery. The second is the pressure to try to complete projects as quickly as possible so that scarce resources can be transferred to other areas of need. And overriding all this is the tension, within the larger NGOs in particular, of allocating resources to medium to long-term development projects as against the channelling of funds to short-term emergencies. The desire within these organizations is clearly to devote more resources to development projects; but this is tempered by the fact that new emergencies continually occur (and old ones often recur), and also that significant increases in income (from donations tend to arise largely from media coverage of these emergencies, pressurizing the NGOs to spend less income on development.

There are two possible routes of expansion. One is for the number of interventions undertaken to increase, be they particular projects with different communities or an intensification of the processes of intervention with particular groups of beneficiaries. This is the path of replication. Replication could arise from more new NGOs being established, or it could result from existing NGOs executing a greater number of projects. The other route is for the scale of intervention to become larger, so that each includes a greater number of beneficiaries. This is the path of scaling-up (Edwards and Hulme, 1992).

Scaling-up is more likely to occur if existing NGO interventions become bigger. However, the overall impact of scaling-up is likely to be limited for four major reasons:

First, scaling-up requires better performance in a number of areas of NGO intervention which have have been pinpointed as key weaknesses. These include problems of project management, shortages of staff skills, and limited financial resources, all of which inhibit greater impact with current numbers of beneficiaries.

Secondly, scaling-up is likely to reduce the NGOs' political room for manoeuvre, narrowing the range of interventions which conflict with prevailing élites and centres of power, and raising the profile of the groups being assisted.

Thirdly, the scaling-up route is increasingly likely to lead to conflict with the characteristics identified as particularly helpful to achieving success in current NGO interventions. These include smallness, community participation, and high staff to beneficiary ratios.

Fourthly, the bigger and comparatively wealthier northern NGOs, with some important exceptions, have tended in recent years to move away from managing, operating, and running projects themselves, replacing this mode of expansion with the funding of smaller and more indigenously based grass-roots NGOs. In this sense, the movement towards scaling-up has often led, in practice and ironically, to a certain scaling-down. There is little to suggest that this pattern of expansion will be altered for the rest of the 1990s.

All these factors suggest that pressures for expanding and enhancing the impact of NGOs are likely to be met with the replication of the small-scale approach type of initiative. However, this route also presents problems. In particular, there are four precise and more immediate factors which are likely to constrain the continued and rapid replication of such NGO intervention, or to adversely influence its effectiveness. These relate to human-resource capability and finance, the increasingly narrow choice of projects, weakness in NGO co-ordination, and increases in the number of NGOs.

NGO-Government Relations

In addition to human resource and financial considerations, there are a range of structural and institutional constraints which are also likely not merely to limit the impact of individual interventions, but which may well lead to more substantive and deep-seated difficulties for resolving the problems of poverty. Many of these revolve around NGO-government relationships. It is within this context that a number of specific factors which tend to characterize most NGO interventions need to be considered: working with groups, smallness, face-to-face contact, and awareness-building.

In certain instances, the differences between NGO and government projects appear, at least on the surface, to be small or non-existent. Thus, a range of more technically focused NGO projects—building wells, boreholes, dams, houses, etc.—are in large measure the same types of projects which, if it had the resources, would be carried out by the government. However, even in these gap-filling interventions, the NGO almost always brings to the project a greater sense of community involvement, and a higher degree of sensitivity to local needs.

Of most importance in this context is the strong commitment to participation which usually characterizes NGO types of intervention. But this, too, needs to be viewed within a broader perspective. Even where a developing country government embraces the philosophy and approach of participation, it is at a disadvantage *vis-a-vis* the small voluntary organization in making it work in practice. There are various factors at work here. In the first place, NGOs are not normally burdened by the bureaucratic restraints which necessarily characterize state initiatives. Where services are provided and channelled to local communities by central government, they usually need to be provided on a universal basis and are commonly organized within the context of national targets and policies. Even where a particular line ministry wants to respond to a local need, it needs to cover itself from accusations of favouritism, tribalism, or regionalism and to persuade its critics, or its potential critics, that it is providing its services in a balanced way. In marked contrast, NGOs commonly have the freedom to operate in a manner they choose, and often in an area they themselves select.

But there are potential dangers in the NGO approach to which NGOs need to be alert. Thus one of the reasons why NGOs are favoured by local communities is precisely because they bring benefits disproportionately to one area or region over others. What is more, the greater and more extensive the poverty of a region, the less adequate are also likely to be the bureaucratic structures and the services that government provides. This means that NGO projects are likely to be relatively more high-cost and gains relatively less easy to achieve than those to be expected in a more hospitable environment. What this suggests is not only that NGO performance is likely to be limited to areas which government or other agencies are less able to reach, but, perversely, that NGO assistance is likely to be least effective where it is needed most.

Furthermore, it has to be recognized that NGO project expansion is far from a costless exercise for the economies and societies in which it takes place. While some resources (human and physical) for NGO projects are brought into a country, and are therefore provided as free goods, others are clearly not. Northern NGOs in particular, sensitive to criticisms of neo-colonialism, will continue to want to employ (and where necessary train) as many indigenous staff as they can, and engage local contractors, even if short-term efficiency thereby takes a dip. Where possible, they will also try to utilize domestically manufactured or processed consumer and intermediate goods: from desks and tables to cement and bricks. Thus any expansion of NGO projects will necessarily entail an increase in domestic resources—human and capital—utilized by these projects. Clearly in poor countries where resources are scarce, the time will eventually be reached (and sometimes quite quickly) when the NGO use of resources will mean that fewer resources are available to be channelled to other uses. In this process, it could well happen that poor and more marginalized people could suffer disproportionately.

On the human resources front, and in African countries in particular, the expansion of NGOs which is currently under way has already resulted in a significant loss of skilled personnel from the government and increased inefficiencies within the civil service either as NGOs—like official aid agencies—have poached key staff from the civil service, or as their supplementing, or topping-up, of government salaries has led those continuing in government service to devote a disproportionate amount of their time to facilitating donor projects.

One of the main reasons for this is that the larger and northern-based, or northern-founded, NGOs in particular are able to pay significantly higher salaries than can the government. To the extent that NGO expansion continues, the wage and salary distortions which NGOs (and official aid agencies) cause and contribute to, will be perpetuated and become more pervasive, creating widespread problems if and when aid agencies withdraw. In addition, as NGO involvement in development projects expands, there is bound to be an increased risk of duplication of effort between NGOs and other agencies, most notably the government, in rural development interventions unless a rational deployment of human resources and technical staff emerges. For instance, in Zimbabwe NGOs employ an additional 25 per cent agricultural extension or related personnel to those deployed throughout the country by the government, yet there is little or no co-ordination of the work of the government and NGO extension staff.

But the adverse consequences are more profound than simply affecting salary differentials or leading to an inefficient deployment of skills. However distinct, separate from government, and geographically isolated individual NGO projects are, NGOs operate within the overall administrative system and so are affected by government and government institutions. Like the private sector, NGOs and other donors need a well-ordered administrative system in order to operate efficiently. As numbers of NGO projects expand, the efficiency of the public administration system in general and of line ministries of particular is bound to be affected by increased defections of personnel to the aid sector, adding to the problems caused by direct defections to the private sector, while the increased number of NGO projects will demand an even greater degree of public service efficiency to administer. In time—and already that time has arrived in a number of poorer African countries—the level of defections will be so great as to frustrate not only the development efforts of the government but even the development efforts of the NGOs themselves. The consequence of this trend continuing is that NGOs will increasingly need to consider the impact that their interventions are having on the ability of the host government to operate in the development field. Hanlon (1991 : 107) has documented an extreme case, in Mozambique, where, in his view, the effect of NGOs has been not only to create parallel institutions to those of the state but to undermine state structures and severely reduce the government's ability to assist the people: 'donors have used aid to weaken and break the Mozambican government.'

There is also the problem of lack of co-ordination. Like their official counterparts, a feature of NGO operations has been and continues to be their lack of co-operation, consultation, and sharing of information about their areas of operation, their successes and failures, and reasons for varied project performance. This has been exacerbated by the explosion in the number of NGOs in many countries, encouraged in large measure by the increased availability of funds from government and official aid donors. In many of the larger NGOs, too, there is often a recognized and acknowledged lack of intra-organization sharing of information and data. As individual NGO interventions increase in number, poor co-ordination is bound increasingly to limit effectiveness unless and until the problem is addressed in a comprehensive fashion.

Southern NGOs, in particular, tend to spend far more time and devote far more resources to promoting individual and discrete interventions than in analysing the broader policy issues which have a bearing on their mostly micro-level poverty-alleviating interventions, and in seeking to influence government policies which have a direct bearing on the lives and incomes of poor people. There is thus often substantial scope for NGOs in the south to lobby governments to influence policies and the legal framework to make it operate more in favour of the poor and marginalized over against the richer and more affluent beneficiaries of the prevailing social, political, and economic system (Bratton, 1990; Edwards and Hulme, 1992).

The precise way in which change could occur will depend, of course, on an array of issues not least of which is the nature of the southern government. However, this broader role has become increasingly important as governments have adopted structural adjustment programmes, many of which are adversely affecting different groups of the urban and rural poor. Although NGOs are often in a comparatively advantageous position to engage in such lobbying, in Africa in particular, they appear to have been reluctant to take on such an advocacy role. In Asia the influence and importance of this type of action by NGOs is of far greater importance, even if in the last few years the contribution of NGOs to the current process of democratization in Africa is becoming the subject of growing interest and debate (Fowler, 1991).

To enhance their capability to undertake these types of activities, southern NGOs need funds both to analyse where the gaps are and the potential exists to pursue more widespread lobbying exercises for the poor, and to provide a local capability to undertake such activities. There is clearly scope for northern NGOs to fund such initiatives, and to share their expertise in campaigning with their southern partners (Clark, 1991; Vasant, 1989). In certain circumstances even more could be done in this area: in particular because they are external bodies, northern agencies often have a greater ability to raise certain issues, especially those related to human and land rights, and democracy, than do southern NGOs whose staff tend to be more vulnerable to intimidation—or worse.

But even beyond these more sensitive issues which ripple over into politics and challenge the entrenched positions of various national and regional interest-groups, relationships between NGOs and governments in the south are likely to face increasing pressure for change in the 1990s. In particular, growth in the numbers of NGOs present in a country, and in the number of projects they undertake, has led increasing numbers of southern governments to discuss the need for, and often to introduce, a more formal system of monitoring and co-ordinating the activities of NGOs. Few, however, have yet gone as far as the Indian Government, which has incorporated NGOs into its recent development plans and substantially funds some of their activities.

Most governments now require foreign (and local) NGOs to register their presence in a country, and to specify their area of development activity; many require NGOs to seek agreement from the local authorities to operate in a particular locality. To the extent that NGOs become an increasingly significant influence in a country, their potential for policy influence up to the national level is bound to increase. As this happens, it is understandable that a government will want not only to co-ordinate their development efforts but also to increase its ability to monitor, control, and put boundaries around their operations.

At the same time, and often at the instigation of official donors, governments are viewing NGOs as sub-contractors who can take on the responsibility for delivering services and implementing large-scale development projects (Robinson, 1995). What remains uncertain is the extent to which, as NGOs grow in influence and importance in the development sphere, issues of control will become the dominant motive in government action. In deciding how to draw the boundaries, governments run the risk of restricting and limiting NGOs to the extent that their independent and flexible style of operating is stifled. If they are so restricted, the NGO movement is likely to remain relatively stagment and marginal, or even to wither. This would clearly have serious effects not only on actual and potential NGO interventions, but also upon far wider attempts to foster self-reliance and nurture community-based activities. Most NGOs would argue that if these are stifled, the potential for development for the poor dies as well.

There will therefore be an increasing need to find a compromise between competing pressures. Governments need to create a mechanism in which the insights and experience of NGOs are utilized and disseminated, while NGOs need to be sufficiently confident in the government to want to share their experiences. Clearly this is an ideal and, in practice, will continue to be far removed from reality. However, if governments believe that NGOs do have a role to play in development, they will wish to establish a mechanism which will both provide feedback from individual NGO experience to government agencies and to other NGOs, and enable NGOs to tap the experience and knowledge of the government and its various institutions.

The initial reaction of most NGOs to government interest is to try to defend their territory, fearing that to the extent that they conform and submit to the rising demands put on them by the government, their uniqueness will be threatened. To the extent that they refuse to conform to increasing bureaucratic attempts to put boundaries around their activities, they will be increasingly faced with the options of either running down their activities (and thereby lessening their influence) or—if they are northern-based NGOs—simply of pulling out.

One possible way out of this growing dilemma is for governments to institutionalize their relations with NGOs in different ways at different levels. In some countries a national register of developmental NGOs has been established, divided into local and foreign. However, if governments wish to encourage the (controlled) growth of NGOs, they need to avoid the creation of complex legislation, or the introduction of complex procedures, which inhibit NGO activity or delay the speedy implementation of their projects.

Northern NGOs and Official Aid Donors

In the future there are likely to be even closer relationships developing between northern NGOs and official and agencies, with a continued increase in the level of funding and greater NGO involvement in policy dialogue and project implementation. It is also becoming increasingly common for northern NGOs to fund projects and programmes undertaken by southern NGOs rather than to execute projects themselves, and for northern NGOs to channel funds to partners in the south, who themselves fund projects.

It is therefore of interest to these agencies that the interventions they fund more effectively achieve the objectives set; addressing the range of constraints which limit NGO project success is clerly as relevant to official aid funders as it is to the NGOs themselves. In terms of much current practice, it would appear that greater attention often needs to be given by official aid agencies to the following: the funding of pre-project preparation; assisting overall contextual assessment and analysis; helping assess ways in which current data within NGOs might be utilized more effectively; and assisting with the enhancing of management and technical skills within NGOs.

All this points to an enhanced role for external donors in promoting NGO institutional development with a view to enhancing their overall impact and effectiveness. This may require a greater flexibility in the type of funding that donors are willing to provide, possibly through more core funding for NGOs with a proven reputation for sound development work. A more specific initiative would be to incorporate the costs of ongoing monitoring and evaluation into NGO project funding. At the same time, northern NGOs might profitably consider providing, or increasing the level of, block grants to southern NGOs or consortia to enable them, in turn, to build up their own institutional competence.

To the extent that official aid agencies feel the need to continue to fund NGO interventions on a project-by-project basis, NGOs should be further encouraged to devote more time and resources at the outset to describing how the precise objectives of their projects are to be met, how they will be sustained after their withdrawal, pinpointing the risks involved, and discussing, however crudely, how risks could be reduced. NGOs will also need to do more to specify the management and staff requirements of projects and how these are to be met and to provide a breakdown of total costs and cost per beneficiary, perhaps also comparing these with their other interventions.

Although northern NGOs have been reticent in addressing their own shortcomings, they have been sensitive in trying to address management weaknesses and inadequate human-resource skills in the south. A widespread practice has evolved whereby individual northern NGOs pay for southern NGO staff to travel abroad on exposure-cum-training and study trips or to develop international networking contacts. However, what is often missing is provision for the enhancement of local skills for a wider group and larger numbers of NGO personnel, as well as for project managers. Just as the World Bank has highlighted the need for capacity building at the national level, so too there is a pressing need to build skills capacities within and between southern NGOs. The problem is accentuated because there is usually little liaison between the NGOs capable of funding national or regional facilities which could provide this function; it would usually be prohibitively expensive for just one NGO to fund such centres.

An alternative way of addressing the same set of problems is through more targeted training. Official aid agencies have been accused of placing too much emphasis on project execution and too little time on training local people. If NGOs are serious about self-reliance in the communities with which they work, then they need to consider building in—and funding, or requesting funding from official aid agencies for—a training component in all their projects, even though the total project costs are bound to increase as a result, and the more immediate and tangible benefits arising from particular project interventions are likely to be slower in coming.

An important theme woven through the pages of this book has been the difficulty of making firm generalizations about the role and impact of NGOs in poverty alleviation. There is still insufficient evidence of what they have achieved in the past, as there is of the differing influence of the range of internal and external factors which influence performance, to be able to draw uncontestable conclusions about the impact of NGOs in poverty alleviation.

NGO know and recognize the constraints under which they work, and the limitations of their interventions. Yet many appear reluctant to expose their own supporters and the general public to these shortcomings and, more broadly, to acknowledge that, in isolation, even a wide array of different poverty-alleviating projects is unlikely to make a major dent in the problem of world poverty.

Even when NGOs have tried to move away from a concentration on isolated projects to try to tackle more of the deeper structural problems of development, the results have frequently been limited, not least because voluntary agencies will always be vulnerable to powerful social and political forces, especially when they choose to play a more visible role in trying to resolve conflictual national issues.

Part of the reason that northern NGOs tend to exaggerate the potential impact they can make is that, historically, most have built their domestic support more on the basis of eliciting a response to the unacceptability of the extent and depth of developing-country poverty (as well as to the immediate dangers to life which emergencies bring), and less on the manner in which the projects and programmes undertaken contribute to the fundamental resolution of these problems. To the extent that the moral appeal to do something for the poor and vulnerable is used to legitimize the action undertaken, any assessment of impact tends to be set aside, or relegated to a subsidiary and secondary level.

There are practical (as well, perhaps, as moral) dangers in continuing to maintain such an approach. In the first place, it discourages NGOs from critically assessing their work, and from informing the public of the impact of their projects and programmes. And as we have seen, weaknesses in absorbing the lessons of experience tend adversely to affect future impact. One result is that this places those critical of NGOs and the whole NGO approach to development in a stronger position to be able to make use of the evidence of poor individual project performance in order to try to influence the public not merely to hold the view that NGO projects do not solve the problems of local poverty, but to question the very basis for continuing to support NGOs and to respond to the moral imperative upon which this funding is largely based. If the belief becomes widespread that the money provided makes hardly any difference at all to the lives of the poor, there would be little point in continuing to contribute to and support the activities of NGOs.

THE INDIAN CASE

There is widespread agreement among development practitioners, government officials, and foreign donors that NGOs play an important role in helping to alleviate rural poverty in India, complementary to that of government, both in terms of providing additional resources and in making government programmes more effective. This view has formed the basis for a sustained increase in the level of funding from government sources and official aid donors. It is also a view shared by many NGOs, although some see their role in terms of empowering the poor rather than in implementing development programmes.

In a country the size of India, with major differences between individual states and regions, NGOs are characterized by a rich diversity of approaches, traditions, and activities, rendering the task of generalization problematic, if not impossible. They cover most areas of the country and their activities affect a significant proportion of the population living in poverty. A number of studies have identified a particular set of attributes with which they are associated, but there is relatively little information on their aggregate impact in alleviating poverty.

Estimates of the number of NGOs active in rural development in India range from less than 10,000 to several hundred thousand depending on the type of classification that is used. Nearly 20,000 organizations are registered with the Ministry of Home Affairs for foreign funding, although the list does not distinguish between religious organizations (such as mosques and temple management committees), commercial bodies, and voluntary agencies; only half of these fall into the NGO category. In addition, there are many others which derive their financial support from internal sources, such as businesses and private donations. A realistic estimate of the number of NGOs actively engaged in rural development in India would be in the 15-20,000 range, including local and regional branches of national organizations which operate as NGOs in their own right.

Aggregate numbers reveal only part of the picture as there are significant variations in the number of voluntary agencies in different states, with a marked concentration in the south of the country. For example, a directory produced by the Council for Advancement of People's Action and Rural Technology (CAPART) in 1990, listed 470 NGOs in West Bengal and 373 in Tamilnadu as compared to 77 in Madhya Pradesh and 11 in Jammu and Kashmir. To some extent these reflect differing patterns of poverty, but also historical factors (such as areas of Christian missionary influence or Gandhian activity) and the priorities of foreign donors. Some districts possess dense networks of NGOs, which overlap and compete for clients, while in others there are hardly any NGOs active on the ground.

NGOs in India can be grouped into six categories according to their scale of operations and the location of their head office:

- large indigenous NGOs working in several states in different parts of the country;
- large indigenous NGOs working in most districts of one state;
- medium-sized indigenous NGOs working in a large number of villages in one or two districts of one state;
- small indigenous NGOs working in a group of villages in one locality (the most common type);
- large international NGOs with in-country representation providing funding and support to indigenous NGOs;
- small international NGOs working directly in one or two localities.

Comparatively few possess the staff of financial resources to work intensively at the state and national levels, although it is these organizations which are best-known in government and donor circles. A number of the larger NGOs perform an intermediary role in channelling resources from donor agencies to small local NGOs, and are not generally involved in project implementation. Most international NGOs have no direct representation in the country and prefer to work through intermediaries, although several have regional offices.

NGOs are generally reluctant to divulge detailed accounts, but some of the larger national ones have budgets amounting to tens of millions of rupees. One survey reported fifty-four NGOs with annual turnovers in excess of Rs. 1m., although this is probably an understimate. The same survey found that nearly half the respondents had budgets below Rs. 2,50,000, which provides some support for the view that the majority of Indian NGOs are small-scale and localized (Nath, 1989).

Recent estimates suggest that the amount of foreign funds coming into the country for use by NGOs each year is in the region of Rs. 9bn. (US$ 520m.), up from Rs. 5bn. in the mid-1980s. In quantitative terms, this is equivalent to approximately 20 per cent of official aid flows, which stood at $2.4bn. in 1991. A further Rs. 500-700m. is provided by the government. When individual and corporate donations are added in, an annual income figure of Rs.

10bn. would seem a reasonable estimate of the total available resources, although this does not take into account unofficial payments or contributions in kind by project beneficiaries. This figure is double the government's annual expenditure on IRDP, and 10 per cent of its overall budget for poverty alleviation and service provision, which indicates that the resources mobilized by NGOs are important but essentially supplement those provided by the government.

Evolution and Approach

The fundamental objectives of NGO activity in rural India are poverty alleviation and the empowerment of the poor, primarily through small-scale development projects. Some NGOs have chosen to tackle the symptoms of poverty manifested in low educational standards, ill-health, poor sanitation, and inferior housing by means of social welfare programmes. Others, among them the four NGOs examined in the present study, have concentrated on enhancing the asset position and income-earning potential of the poor through land-improvement schemes, credit, and skills training. An alternative approach has been for NGOs to empower poor people to demand resources from the state or to challenge injustice and exploitation.

The foundations for the contemporary voluntary agency movement were created in the pre-Independence period, some of them associated with the social reform movements of the late nineteenth century, largely concerned with educational and cultural matters and only tangentially with the question of poverty. Christian missionary groups established a network of hospitals, schools, and welfare services for the poor in the first half of the twentieth century. A third tradition was the Gandhian approach, which combined social reform with village development activities (Alliband, 1983).

The Christian and Gandhian approaches continued to predominate after Independence. In the early post-Independence period, disaster relief and food-for-work programmes came to be associated with Christian organizations in particular. Social welfare provided critical back-up for public service provision in the 1950s and early 1960s, and agencies steeped in Gandhian values emphasized village self-reliance and provided the foundation for development activities centred on small-scale agriculture and cottage industry. The integrated development approach became popular in the late 1960s and early 1970s, with NGOs combining health and education with economic programmes in pursuit of poverty alleviation. It was also at this time that funding from international NGOs began to make its mark.

During the latter half of the 1970s, a more radical trend emerged, with social action groups taking the view that poverty was a structural phenomenon which had to be tackled head-on through the active mobilization of the rural poor. They abjured violence but the thrust of their activities was confrontational, initiating struggles over issues such as land reform, wages, and bonded labour, while another dimension of their work rested on empowering the poor to demand efficient delivery of services from the state and pressing for the implementation of progressive components of government legislation. With liberal foreign funding, social action groups proliferated throughout the late 1970s and early 1980s, and established themselves as the dominant type of NGO in some states, notably Tamilnadu and Bihar, in sharp contrast to the programme-focused approaches which had found favour from the 1960s (Unia, 1991). By the mid-1980s, however, their relatively limited economic achievements led to a questioning of the basic tenets of this approach. At the same time, there was growing criticism of the lack of participation by the poor in the design and implementation of NGO integrated development programmes.

From the mid-1980s, a further trend emerged within the NGO movement, emphasizing the importance of a professional approach based on sound management, planning, and co-ordination. A parallel development was the creation of resource agencies which work directly with the poor but also provide support services to other NGOs in the form of training, evaluation, and documentation. These agencies are usually financed by core grants from foreign donors and payments for staff training from individual NGOs. Intermediary agencies responsible for channelling funds from foreign donors to small national NGOs in some cases also provide these types of services, for example, in assisting with evaluations.

In recent years there has been an element of convergence between these various approaches, with NGOs seeking to combine project-specific development work with active organization of the poor. Reflecting this greater uniformity, community organization is now treated, for the most part, as an essential prerequisite of the successful introduction and implementation of specific programmes. Similarly, most NGOs now recognize that organizational work among the poor cannot be sustained without material improvements derived from programme-specific activities.

Most NGOs work through groups, though with considerable variation in purpose and approach. Some, notably the Gandhian agencies, chose to work through existing village institutions (*panchayats or gram sabhas*). But these are invariably dominated by the rural elite, and most NGOs therefore prefer to form groups which exclude the wealthier members of the village community. In some cases, caste or tribal affiliations constitute the basis for group formation, while others, particularly the social action groups, restrict their membership to the landless or marginal farmers. Another approach is to include all the poor, irrespective of caste or class. In some cases membership is defined by a common occupation, such as farming or fishing.

This diversity of approach has tended to make co-ordination difficult to achieve, since there are often sharp differences of perspective and orientation. At the local level, these differences are sharpened by competition over areas of operational activity, especially where there are dense networks of NGOs, and by personality conflict. Another difficulty is the preoccupation of many local NGOs with projects in the villages where they are already working, and their failure to perceive the need for or the potential benefits of sharing insights or resources with other organizations. Rivalry over scrace government resources and official patronage also hinders co-ordination at the local level.

Nevertheless, some networks have been established at the state level to present a common front in negotiations with the government over legislation and policy formulation. Some NGOs have sought to form networks with specific advocacy objectives such as trying to encourage the government to introduce a guaranteed employment programme nationally. Other networks have been formed by foreign donors, although these can also have the effect of creating or widening divisions between groups of NGOs. More recently, there has been an initiative to establish an NGO network at the national level. A number of the larger and more established NGOs formed the Voluntary Action Network India (VANI) in 1988 as a common platform, initially to exert pressure on the government to amend or revoke contentious items of legislation, but now with an expanded remit to provide resource materials and organize conferences on foreign funding and strategic issues of broader NGO concern. Co-ordination between NGOs remains relatively weak, however, and this results in a duplication of effort and limits their potential impact on a larger scale.

Relations with the Government

As NGOs have grown in size and influence, their activities have brought them into closer contact with government, the implications of which have been the subject of extensive debate. A dominant consideration here is the increasing volume of programme funding from government sources.

The government has long recognized the positive NGO contribution in the field of social welfare, and provided limited funds to support these activities, but it has only been in the latter half of the 1980s that the NGO role in rural development has received explicit recognition. The Seventh Five Year Plan (1986-90) marked a watershed. The work of voluntary agencies was considered as complementary to that of government in offering the rural poor a range of choices and alternatives, at low cost and with greater participation. The plan document provided for an active NGO involvement in the planning process and Rs. 1.5bn. were allocated from government funds for a wide range of anti-poverty and minimum needs programmes. A semi-autonomous body called the Council for the Advancement of People's Action and Rural Technology (CAPART) was created to administer these funds, which include a small proportion of bilateral aid. To be eligible for CAPART funding, agencies have to be registered with the government for at least one year and working in rural areas.

Many NGOs seek government funding in preference to foreign aid principally because it obviates the need for registration under the Foreign Contributions Regulation Act. A strong nationalist tradition has in any case always existed among Indian NGOs, which abjures foreign funding on the grounds that it undermines their independence and limits their freedom to determine programme priorities. At the same time, the legitimacy derived from government funding can provide them with a degree of protection from harassment from vested interests.

Against this, dependence on official funds leaves NGOs susceptible to changes in government policy, and can result in programme modification to accommodate official priorities. It can also lead to co-option, whereby voluntary agencies tone down their social and political objectives in order to secure financial support. In practice, however, there is not such a sharp dichotomy between organizations in receipt of government funds as opposed to foreign funds, since most seek a blend of funding from both sources.

Another dimension of the relationship with government is in the realm of programme replication. The government has frequently sought to replicate voluntary initiatives on a larger scale, especially in the case of technological innovation, health care, and education. Related to this, there is a growing tendency for government bodies, particularly at the district or sub-district levels, to ask NGOs to implement specific programmes or schemes. Government officials believe that if NGOs are made responsible for project implementation, the administrative costs will be lower, and the scheme will be executed with greater efficiency and with active participation of the intended beneficiaries.

Local co-operation leads to NGO representation on consultative committees, for example, those responsible for determining government funding priorities or for preventing atrocities against tribals and scheduled castes. Contacts with local government officers and bank officials provide them with information on funding and can help safeguard their projects. However, relations with local government are not always cordial, and there are numerous instances of obstacles being placed in the way of voluntary agencies, either out of official jealousy or to contain efforts at mobilizing the poor.

While the government has been increasing the level of funding that it provides to NGOs, it has also sought to regulate their activities more closely. Over the years, an elaborate legal framework has been devised. All voluntary agencies with seven or more members are compelled by law to register with state or central governments under the Societies Registration Act, 1860 (or the corresponding state act), as a trust under the Indian Trusts Act, 1982 or, in the case of religious organizations, the Charitable and Religious Act, 1920. This is a formality which rarely poses a problem, but registration is essential for NGOs wishing to apply for grants through CAPART or to receive foreign funding.

The government has also attempted to establish a regular forum where NGOs and officials can interact and exchange views. In 1985 it backed a proposal from a group of voluntary agencies for the formation of a National Council of Rural Voluntary Agencies, with corresponding state councils, whose main purpose would be to investigate complaints in regard to official obstruction and harassment and look into allegations of NGO mismanagement and misuse of funds. The proposals met with widespread opposition (much of it co-ordinated by VANI) on the grounds that they would constrain the autonomy of voluntary agencies, and the government decided not to put forward legislation.

Clearly, closer co-operation with government has had its costs. While the government has provided an increasing level of financial support to voluntary agencies and has encouraged their participation in policy formulation, it has also placed a number of restrictions on their freedom to function independently. It is less clear, however, whether increased co-operation has resulted in greater development effectiveness; several of the case-studies attempt to throw light on this question.

Rural Development Trust

The Rural Development Trust has been promoting development activities in the Anantapur district of Andhra Pradesh since 1969. Its Community Organisation Programme forms a key component of an integrated rural development project which includes health, education, skills training and, more recently, ecological development, covering some 280 villages in the district. Credit is provided to small and marginal farmers through village associations (*sangams*) for investment in agricultural inputs, enabling them to cultivate their land more intensively without having to rely on high-interest loans from money-lenders. The case-study examines the impact of the credit programme on the economic and social status of poor households in six *mandals* (administrative divisions) in Anantapur district where ActionAid UK was the main funding agency.

Anantapur district is located in the drought-prone region of Rayalseema. The harshness of the local environment cannot be overstated: vegetation cover is sparse, consisting mainly of scrub and thorny undergrowth, and rainfall is low and intermittent, with an average of one in every four years declared a drought year. The main cash-crop, groundnut, has undergone a substantial increase in acreage over the past twenty years. Millet is the major food crop, although there has been a marked decline in production in recent years. Paddy is also grown during the winter season. Most people living in the area are engaged in farming, with 80 per cent of the workforce classified as cultivators or agricultural labourers. Land ownership is highly skewed: farmers owning less than 5 acres account for the majority of cultivators, but a relatively small share of the total cropped area. Agricultural labourers constitute one-third of the rural labour-force, but most own some land. Agricultural work is mainly restricted to planting, weeding, and harvesting during the June to December groundnut season, which typically generates two to three months of employment.

The main impediments to removing poverty are the environmental constraints, the uneven pattern of land distribution, and the limited availability of off-farm employment. Farmers with less than 5 acres of dry land cannot meet their basic consumption needs without undertaking casual wage labour. The majority of small and marginal farmers are below the poverty-line. Even in a good year, they can only just make ends meet from groundnut cultivation: when the rains fail, yields are barely sufficient to cover the costs of inputs. Sharecroppers secure only marginal returns from leasing arrangements with the added benefit of fodder. Only the minority of farmers, with access to irrigation, can be assured of higher incomes from paddy cultivation.

The RDT was formed in 1969 by a former Jesuit priest, with the initial aim of improving irrigation facilities for poor farmers; community wells were constructed during the 1970s through an extensive food-for-work programme. The programme was discontinued in 1978 with a reorientation and expansion of the project in favour of an integrated development approach. This also marked the launch of an extensive child-sponsorship programme funded by ActionAid UK. Health, education, and community organizations were established as the key sectors of the project, with a separate women's programme from 1982, and skills training from the late 1980s. A massive ecological programme started in 1988, which combines water harvesting measures and social forestry with employment generation, is now the largest component of the project in terms of funding and human resources.

The Community Organisation Programme (COP) was born out of the realization that many poor farmers failed to benefit from the irrigation programmes of the early 1970s. It was founded on the assumption that poor people had to be more explicitly targeted for development assistance. The target population included small and marginal farmers with less than 5 acres of land, and the landless. Its objectives were as follows:

- to create an awareness among the rural poor of their common social and economic problems and to provide them with the means to overcome these through the formation of village associations (*sangams*);
- to improve the income levels of poor farmers through the provision of credit and extension in appropriate agricultural practices;
- to promote increased self-reliance by enabling poor people to manage programmes themselves on a sustainable basis.

For ease of administration, *sangams* were formed on caste lines, and became the focal unit for all the sectoral programmes, especially health and eduction, and later credit. All those below the poverty-line (roughly 60 per cent of the population) or with a child in receipt of sponsorship, were eligible for membership.

RDT regards development as a long-term process, in which economic and social changes are equally important. Poverty is thus seen both as a structural phenomenon arising from inequalities in the distribution of wealth and assets and as a social phenomenon characterized by poor education and a limited awareness of individual potential. Long-term poverty alleviation is intended to address basic needs at the local level, namely for food, clothing, shelter, knowledge, and services, as well as social and political rights. In this context, the *sangam* is intended to act both as the starting-point for village development activities and as a forum for uniting poor people. In short, the *sangams* were conceived as enabling people to achieve an awareness of common problems for collective action, and thus as the pivotal unit around which other programmes would function. The administration of credit at the local level is considered to be the joint responsibility of the *sangam* and village-level field staff.

A central Community Credit Fund (CCF) was established soon after the formation of the *Sangams* in 1980. For the first three years, it was built up by annual contributions from RDT (in effect from ActionAid) of Rs. 60 per family of which individuals could draw to meet petty expenses, provided they had no record of default. After 1986, the CCF evolved into a fully fledged crop loans scheme and RDT's contribution gradually increased each year in line with a matching amount from the farmers, with loans carrying an interest rate of 11 per cent, on par with that charged by the commercial banks. Farmers were entitled to borrow on a regular annual basis at the time of sowing in June, rather than intermittently according to specific needs. The credit was used primarily for the purchase of inputs such as fertilizer, pesticide, seeds, and bullock hire for ploughing and labour expenses, with the aim of enhancing production. Individual contributions steadily increased, in some cases to Rs. 200, with RDT continuing to provide a matching amount. This allowed the CCF to grow quickly, enabling individual farmers to borrow up to Rs. 1,500 provided they repaid regularly and in full. The CCF was designed to become self-sufficient once the amount available for loans reached an optional level in relation to farmers' needs, which was estimated at Rs. 2,000 for a 5-acre plot. The programme also aimed to make the *sangams* increasingly self-reliant so that over time they would be able to assume greater responsibility for credit management.

In the 135 villages covered by ActionAid the target-group population numbered to 13,800 households (70,000 people), out of a total of 24,800 households. Assuming that some 60 per cent of the population can be classed as poor, the number of families reached by RDT was equivalent to 6 per cent of the rural poor in Anantapur district (population 2 million). Sixty-four staff were employed in administering the COP, divided between three field officers; eight community organizers were responsible for supervising the work of forty-nine field-workers who interacted with the *sangams* on a regular basis, in administering the Community Credit Fund.

The main cost incurred (Rs. 1.4m. in 1989) was for administration and staffing. With 5,765 borrowers, the average cost per beneficiary worked out at just over Rs. 200 per head in 1989, although this included provision for non-credit activities. Further costs were incurred by borrowers in terms of the opportunity cost of attending regular *sangam* meetings and making repayments, but these were offset by lower interest rates compared to those charged by money-lenders and the accessibility of the credit. Nevertheless, they suggest that the credit scheme was expensive to administer relative to loan size, even if the credit disbursed ultimately had a positive impact.

Changes in cropping patterns and improved economic status. From 1986 CCF credit encouraged a rapid shift towards groundnut production on the part of small and marginal farmers. Alongside the supply of credit, a land reclamation scheme initiated by RDT in the wake of the 1985/86 drought also enabled many farmers to extend the area under their cultivation. Factors external to the project also had a bearing on the trend towards groundnut cultivation. One such was the demonstration effect exerted by larger farmers with access to institutional credit who had been steadily increasing the acerage of land under groundnut in response to the favourable market price arising from increased demand for edible oils.

The most visible effect of this shift in cropping patterns has been increased incomes for the majority of farming households. The returns on groundnut cultivation were found to be three to four times higher than for traditional foodgrains. The cumulative effect of three successive good crops of groundnut after 1986 undoubtedly raised the incomes of target-group farmers substantially, enabling many households to cross the official poverty threshold (Rs. 6,400). It is questionable whether such changes are sustainable in the longer term however, given the continued vulnerability of farmers to drought and crop failure and their limited capacity to save. While groundnut production is more profitable than foodgrains, yields varied considerably according to rainfall, soil type, seed quality, extension advice, and the aptitude of individual farmers. Farmers also benefited to varying degrees depending on the size of their landholding, their possession of assets, and the nature of leasing arrangements.

Evidence of improvements in the economic status of beneficiaries was seen in the form of improved food consumption, more regular purchase of clothing, and the acquisition of basic household utensils. Farmers were also able to purchase bullocks and small plots of land, and clear off outstanding debts to money-lenders. The sale of groundnut provided farmers with cash to purchase rice which became the main food staple, and although nutritionally inferior to the traditional millets, was perceived to be a higher status food. A further factor was the availability of subsidized rice from the government, at prices below the cost of traditional food staples. Families tended to eat more varied and regular meals and having to go without food at night during the lean season became a thing of the past for most people.

Increased income from agricultural production to some extent enhanced farmers' ability to cope with calamities, such as drought and sickness. Seed saved from the previous year's harvest provided security in times of need; small quantity could be sold if the need arose. Moreover, many of the poorest families no longer migrated out of the area in search of temporary employment during the lean season, as returns from groundnut cultivation were sufficient to meet household needs if supplemented with additional income from wage labour.

Distribution of benefits. Small farmers owning between 2 and 5 acres of dry land (the principal target-group) were the main beneficiaries. Those with a pair of bullocks or access to irrigation gained relatively more than those without such assets, since the costs of ploughing were also incurred by those without bullocks. Marginal farmers owning less than 2 acres, sharecroppers, and tenants gained less: their capacity to generate a sufficiently high yield to repay the loans is lower than that of farmers owning more land, even in relative terms. They also depend to a higher degree on income from agricultural labour for their family needs. Nevertheless, the extra income generated from groundnut cultivation was considered to be important.

Returns for sharecroppers are generally too low to generate a significant level of income. Many marginal farmers using crop loans for sharecropping were primarily interested in the fodder value of the crop. Landless agricultural labourers, who constitute around 11 per cent of the target population, benefited least of all. Such people cannot invest in land; borrowing for sharecropping is unremunerative as the returns are low; a number are simply too poor to borrow with their limited capacity to repay. Nevertheless, those landless beneficiaries with non-agricultural sources of income—such as basket-making, mat weaving, leatherwork, and the sale of hides—were able to purchase raw materials in bulk at lower prices using CCF credit. A significant number used their loans for consumption purposes, to benefit from the marginal saving on bulk purchases of foodstuff. And a number of former bonded labourers managed to pay off their debts and take up cultivation.

Other factors have had an influence on local employment opportunities. A gradual expansion in the area under irrigation has led to an increase in the demand for labour. In particular, the availability of employment on irrigated paddy and groundnut land owned by richer farmers has helped to reduce out-migration. At the same time, the tendency for small and marginal farmers to take up groundnut cultivation on their own plots reduced the availability of labour during the June-December groundnut season, and may have contributed indirectly to an increase in wages.

Widows of small farmers who joined the *sangam* following the death of their husbands used the credit to purchase assets for other members of the household to cultivate the land or leased it out on a sharecropping basis. Since they rarely have any independent means of support once their husbands die, the income derived from cultivation of the family plot with credit from the CCF played a critical role.

A small proportion of borrowers became relatively better-off through being able to double-crop as a result of acquiring land or access to irrigation facilities. Others had access to non-agricultural income such as remittances, but few could be considered wealthy. For farmers owning 5 acres and above the loans available through the CCF were relatively incidental to their overall investment needs. Most in this category, especially those with land under irrigation, borrow from institutional sources, notably co-operative societies and the nationalized banks in the range of Rs. 2-4,000, as compared with the Rs. 700-1,200 available through the CCF. For them loans under the CCF were useful in so far as there was a matching contribution from the RDT together with other advantages related to timeliness and low interest.

Social development. The purpose of the *sangams* is threefold:

(i) to facilitate discussion and action on issues and activities for the benefit of the community,
(ii) to practise democratic processes in decision-making, and
(iii) to develop local leadership qualities.

However, the field investigations suggest that most of the *sangams* fell well short of these objectives. They primarily functioned as credit groups, bringing farmers together to discuss issues such as size of contributions and repayment problems, facilitating loan distribution, and providing an organizational structure for repayment. Some provided a forum for the exchange of information on agricultural practices such as cropping patterns, use of fertilizer, and seed varieties. There was little sense of ownership attached to the crop loans scheme, although the *sangams* varied considerably in terms of the beneficiaries' involvement in the administration of credit. Many continued to depend on RDT social workers to disburse credit and to collect repayments, which had important implications for the sustainability of the scheme.

Sangams varied considerably in their capacity for independent action and decision-making. In a few instances they fulfilled a broader role in providing a forum for collective action. In one case, the *sangam* enabled its members to seek redress of outstanding grievances related to the distribution of surplus land by the government. In another, members petitioned the government for permission to cultivate a substantial tract of land owned by temple authorities. However, these were the exception rather than the rule.

Although in most cases members were unable to explain the broader purpose of their *sangam*, there have clearly been some important qualitative benefits from *sangam* membership, especially for the scheduled castes. Many reported that the practice of untouchability had diminished, and better education of their children assisted in this process. Comming together as a group has given members greater confidence to approach local government and bank officials. Such changes are indicative of enhanced social status for scheduled caste villagers in the wider community, although not all of these can be attributed to the existence of the *sangam*.

Sangams clearly perform an important role in bringing poor villagers together in a common forum where they are able to articulate and discuss shared problems, which is not the case with *panchayat* councils, where the poor are usually denied effective representation. Nevertheless, it is not evident that all members participate equally in *sangam* meetings. The landless members in particular do not play an active role, as discussions often relate to the interests of farmers owning land, who have been the principal beneficiaries of the programme. Moreover, *sangam* leaders exercise a fairly dominant role in meetings and have a tendency to speak on bahalf of others. This has a positive side in so far as leadership among the poor is developing, but also a negative dimension as regards limits on participation.

Advantages of the crop loans scheme. Aside from its direct benefits, there were a number of benefits related to the CCF as an alternative source of credit. The most important one cited by farmers was reduced dependence on money-lenders. The majority of small and marginal farmers (and to a lesser extent middle-income farmers) have traditionally depended on private money-lenders (usually big landlords) for the bulk of their credit needs, mainly for consumption purposes (especially following crop failure) and for marriages and festivals. Many marginal farmers and agricultural labourers were tied into bonded labour contracts as a result of incurring debts which carried high rates of interest (typically 24 per cent).

With the spread of groundnut cultivation, farmers began to borrow for seed, fertilizer, bullock hire for ploughing, and labour costs. To secure a loan they had to make frequent visits to the money-lender, in the process wasting time that could have been spent tending crops, and where the money-lender lived outside the village incurring additional travel costs. The need to petition for loans was also a demeaning process which reinforced traditional caste and patron-client relations. The provision of a loan was commonly made conditional on farmers having to work on the landlord's plot before working on their own land, this incurring delays in sowing and harvesting. Even when the money-lender finally agreed to a loan, it often came too late to enable a farmer to purchase seed and other inputs at the optimal time, i.e. at the onset of the rains. Output was reduced as a result.

In addition to reduced dependence on money-lenders, loans from the CCF were timely, as they came just before sowing in June, and they carried a lower rate of interest. The matching contribution from the RDT was clearly regarded as an important benefit, especially since higher contributions by farmers were matched by the RDT, enabling them to increase the amount they could borrow over time fairly quickly. In some cases, access to CCF credit had encouraged farmers to approach banking institutions for additional loans for agricultural purposes. There were, in addition, several cases where families had two, and in some cases three, members taking loans from the CCF for the same piece of land which was farmed jointly, giving them access to quite substantial sums.

However, for a significant proportion of farmers interviewed in the study, the volume of credit available through the CCF failed to meet their full requirements, and many continued to borrow from money-lenders and banks to supplement the CCF loans. This was especially true of middle-income farmers who had ready access to institutional credit. Other farmers borrowed from the CCF for their agricultural needs and resorted to money-lenders for loans to cover marriage expenses and dowries, although there was an element of fungibility between these two sources of credit, and their end use was not always clearly demarcated.

Some costs were incurred in moving away from money-lenders to the CCF. The patron-client system contained an element of reciprocity and was not purely confined to rent extraction by rapacious money-lenders, especially where the money-lender was also the local landlord. Some farmers complained that the CCF was more inflexible in demanding repayments within a fixed time-schedule irrespective of crop performance. In times of drought some money-lenders would waive interest payments or stagger repayments, in return for labour commitments or other favours. The reciprocal dimension of the patron-client relationship therefore helped to explain the propensity of some poor farmers to continue taking loans from the money-lenders, particularly where the latter rely on a regular supply of casual labour during the harvesting season.

Sustainability. A major impediment to achieving a self-sufficient revolving credit scheme was the vulnerability of small and marginal farmers to crop failure as a result of drought, which is a recurrent feature in the area. Even if the CCF had been built up to an optimal level, a severe drought would have led to widespread default and depleted resources within the fund. If the RDT contributions had been discontinued, the scheme would have been in danger of collapse. By 1988 the cumulative amount of outstanding dues had reached Rs. 1.06m., shared among 2,272 borrowers, giving an average of Rs. 466 per borrower.

Three relatively good years from 1986/87 were followed by poor and uneven rainfall in 1989/90. Marginal farmers in particular repaid their CCF loans only by the sale of seed, leaving none available for the next sowing season. There was evidence that many such farmers were preparing to borrow from private money-lenders to fulfil their CCF obligations, since failure to repay would have debarred them from future loans.

A related issue was their dependence on income from cash-crop production. There are two aspects to this. Good returns are related not only to favourable climatic conditions, but also to the prevailing market price for groundnut, which is subject to fluctuations resulting from local variations in output as well as to longer-term trends in national demand for groundnut oil in the domestic market. Should a cheaper substitute become available, groundnut prices, and hence farmers' incomes, could be adversely affected, although it would be theoretically possible for them to switch crops again. Present trends indicate strong demand for groundnut oil, but there is no guarantee that this will hold for the longer term.

One consequence of the transition to groundnut production has been an increase in the amount spent on inputs, especially artificial fertilizers and pesticides purchased with credit from the CCF. This spending may raise production in the short term, but there are also some disadvantages. There is clearly a greater risk involved when the costs of investment are higher: In drought years production may be insufficient to cover input costs, and lack of rainfall can actually cause the fertilizer to damage the crop. A shift from food to cash-crop production also has implications for household expenditure patterns, rendering them susceptible to price inflation. Such considerations are important when considering potential sustainability in the longer term.

In theory, *sangams* were responsible for the administration of loans from the CCF. Most were capable of disbursement, but their involvement in loan recovery varied enormously. NGO staff did the hard work of physically collecting repayments. A number of borrowers interviewed did not know how much they had borrowed or the rate of interest on the loans, but nevertheless acknowledged the benefits of the scheme. For these reasons it was judged that the withdrawal of the direct support of field staff would in many cases result in the collapse of the scheme and perhaps the *sangam* itself.

A number of other problems with the mechanics of the scheme raised important questions about its longer-term existence. Farmers were still under the impression that their own contribution to the fund would continue to be matched by the RDT. In some cases they had been pushing for higher levels of individual contributions, underlining the importance of the incentive effect of the RDT matching contribution, which amounted to a subsidy as there was no mechanism for retrieving the organization's inputs. Since farmers had come to expect continuing contributions from the RDT, it was evident that they would lack the incentive to persist with the scheme if these were discontinued. This was borne out in practice in late 1991: when RDT decided to end its contributions, the majority of the *sangams* voted to terminate the scheme.

Strengths, Weaknesses, and Lessons

Two factors that may have played a vital role in the success of the crop-loans scheme up to 1991 were the community organizations and the quality of programme staff. As noted above, village *sangams* played a functional role in bringing poor farmers together to discuss their credit needs and to facilitate the administration of the scheme. Yet field staff exhibited varying degrees of commitment to the programme. Although they proved capable of administering credit and ensuring a certain level of repayment, this did not prove central to the success of the programme. Rather, success was primarily attributable to the fact that loans from the CCF provided a viable alternative to high-interest credit from money-lenders.

One of the limitations of the programme was that the benefits accruing to landless labourers were relatively marginal. While some opportunities for wage employment were created by the ecological development programme during the lean season, the needs of the landless were not specifically addressed. Although a number of *sangam* members acquired assets under the government's Integrated Rural Development Programme (IRDP), there was not a systematic effort to secure subsidized loans for non-agricultural income generation for the landless.

The major limitation of the programme lay in its lack of sustainability, which was directly related to the harsh environment in which credit was being introduced, although it was hoped that the ecological development programme would provide a longer-term solution to these problems. Another weakness relates to the role of the *sangams*. Most were not directly concerned with social issues and few displayed the potential to become self-reliant. A further limitation was the reliance of the programme on refinancing from external sources, and the fact that the CCF did not fully meet current credit requirements. Little attempt was made to encourage farmers to take out loans from banks or to make more use of government resources, which reinforced their reliance on the CCF and, by implication, on funding from foreign donors.

In many ways the Community Organization Programme was unique in terms of its scope and approach. Few other NGOs were likely to have been able to mobilize resources on a comparable scale. However, the very success of the CCF in raising the productivity and incomes of small farmers underlines the importance of alternative sources of credit, while the limitation of the programme in terms of sustainability in a drought-prone environment points to the need for NGOs considering credit provision to incorporate compensatory machanisms as an insurance against crop failure under such circumstances.

3

NGOs and Health Care in Third World

Health care in India has a long tradition of voluntarism. For centuries, traditional healers have taken care of the health needs of their own community, as a part of their social responsibility. they have used the knowledge that has passed down the generations, regarding the medicinal value of locally available herbs and plants. This tradition still continues, particularly in the tribal pockets of the country.

Unfortunately, the institutionalised voluntarism that evolved during the colonial era was completely dominated by the thinking of the colonisers. They completely ignored the rich traditional systems of health care in India. This was partly due to the fact that much of this effort grew out of the activities of Christian missionaries, most of whom came from the West. The Indian elite, who had been partially involved in the voluntary effort during that phase, also firmly believed in the supremacy of everything Western. Consequently, there was little possibility of evolving a health system which assimilated the best of both schools. Perhaps, the major exception was Mahatma Gandhi's continuous effort to popularise naturopathy, yoga and vegetarianism through the ashrams that he had set up in various parts of the country.

After Independence, till the mid-sixties, voluntary effort in health care was again limited to hospital-based health care by rich family charities or religious institutions. In the mid-sixties, the effectiveness of the Western curative model of health care in the less developed countries came under serious attack by development planners. The Chinese experience of decentralised health care through effective use of motivated health cadres at the grassroots level, also received widespread attention. Out of this rethinking, grew various models of community health programmes which emphasised decentralised curative services. In these, trained village level workers played a key role. Much more importance was given to preventive aspects, where the community plays a more effective part in their 'own' health care.

Unfortunately, this refreshing trend too ignored the important role of traditional healers and dais in health care, and very little attention was paid to the Indian systems of medicine.

The voluntary health effort as it exists today, can be broadly classified as follows:

- *Specialised Community Health Programmes:* Many of them go a little beyond health, by running income-generation schemes for the poorer communities, so that they can meet their basic nutritional needs.
- *Integrated Development Programmes:* In these programmes, health is a part of integrated development activities. Consequently, their emphasis on health care may not be as systematic or as effective as that of the previous group. However, the long-term impact of their work on health and the development of the community is significant.
- *Health Care for Special Groups of People:* This includes education, rehabilitation and care of the handicapped. These specialised agencies are playing an important role, keeping in view the fact that hardly any government infrastructure exists in this sector of health care.
- *Government Voluntary Organisations:* These are voluntary organisations which play the role of implementing government programmes like Family Planning and Integrated Child Development Services. These bodies are marginally more efficient than the government system but their overall approach is the same.
- *Health Work Sponsored by Rotary Clubs, Lions Clubs and Chambers of Commerce:* They usually concentrate on eye camps—conducting cataract operations in the rural areas on a large scale with the help of various specialists, etc.
- *Health Researchers and Activists:* The efforts of these groups

are usually directed towards writing occasional papers, organising meetings on conceptual aspects of health care and critiquing government policy through their journals *(which usually have limited circulation).*

- *Campaign Groups:* These groups are working on specific health issues, such as a rational drug policy and amniocentesis, among others.

According to a rough estimate, more than 7,000 voluntary organisations are working in the above areas of health care throughout the country. Voluntary agencies have played a significant role in developing alternative 'models', as well as providing low-cost and effective health services in many parts of the country. They have been able to develop village-based health cadres, educational materials and appropriate technology. They also help in filling the critical gaps that exist in government health services.

However, these 'models' are far from perfect; they do not possess the conditions of replicability, as does the government sector. On the other hand, the vastness and regional diversities that characterise India also make it extremely problematic to think of replication or standardisation of 'models'. In fact, it is being increasingly acknowledged that the term 'model' itself when applied to people's health care systems, is suspect. There can be no prototype. An appropriate system should evolve from the people themselves. Just as health conditions emerge from the community's interaction with its surroundings, it is the people's struggle through time that determines the nature of the services that they receive.

It is also recognised that the task of formulating a 'model' or an appropriate system of health care becomes a highly challenging managerial, sociological, technological, epidemiological and political task which, if simplified to the current level of health planning, will produce imperfect results.

The concept of 'participation', currently in vogue, is another problem. In the case of the establishment, for whom anything referring to empowerment of the people is hard to accept, the term has come to mean compliance, contribution or collaboration. In its true sense, 'participation leading to empowerment' stands as a challenge to the interests of the establishment.

The effect of community health experiments in shaping

government policy with regard to health care has been limited, although a few of the concepts have been incorporated in government programmes. Some representatives of voluntary agencies have been absorbed in the government's policy-making bodies. This is a critical area, totally neglected by voluntary agencies.

All voluntary initiatives are not necessarily in the area of extreme needs. One finds very limited voluntary initiatives in the BIMARU states (*Bihar, Madhya Pradesh, Rajasthan and Uttar Pradesh)*, as compared to the better-off states like Kerala or Maharashtra. Even in Kerala, they are not necessarily in the least developed parts of the Malabar coast or the highlands.

Hardly any effort has been made to form public opinion or mass organisations like trade unions, people's movements or political bodies, to generate a demand for more appropriate and effective health services. Inspite of these limitations, however, the contributions of voluntary health organisations in providing appropriate health services in needy areas is highly appreciable.

The Kerala Sastra Sahithya Parishad (KSSP) is one of the few voluntary organisations which has attempted to demystify medicine. Special campaigns on the drug policy, anti-smoking and amniocentesis have had some limited impact, both at the policy level as well as in educating the consumers. The KSSP emphasises that the greater health problem is poverty, and that the majority of ailments arise from the inadequacy of proper food and an unhealthy living environment. The KSSP has organised numerous health camps, published several documents on people's health, and are in constant touch with various organisations like the Voluntary Health Association of India (VHAI) and Medico Friends Circle. The KSSP believes that health care is a basic right of every citizen, and that an effective health care delivery system should work towards keeping the entire population physically and mentally healthy. It warns people against modern health care systems controlled by multinational drug companies, stressing instead the wealth of knowledge that exists in traditional systems of medicine.

The health groups are also divided on ideological grounds—foreign or locally funded, those following traditional or modern medicine, etc. Most of these groups are dominated by a group of elite, who meet nationally or internationally, to express concern and share information: however, they do not have any mechanism by which to transfer this information to either the common people or social activists, who might be able to use this in their struggle. To this elite, even paramedics and village health workers are mere functionaries and not agents of change.

Given this situation, as well as keeping in view the tremendous potentiality of promoting and strengthening the voluntary sector in meeting the critical needs of health care, we propose that the following mechanism be put in place within the Ministry, to strengthen and encourage voluntary effort in key areas of health care. A National Co-ordination Committee, consisting of the Director General Health Services, Secretary *(Health)*, three representatives from voluntary organisations and one representative from the state government, should work as an active listening post for all the voluntary agencies working in the field of health. This committee should meet periodically to monitor the implementation of the committee's recommendations, and provide inputs on the planning and implementation of health services in the country. Its functions should include:

- Promoting collaboration and co-operation between the government and voluntary organisations in primary health care.
- Identifying people's health needs and bringing them to the notice of planners.
- Assisting in developing comprehensive national health policies and action plans at all levels.
- Working out the modalities of administrative relationships between the government and voluntary organisations for health care delivery to the people.
- Identifying voluntary organisations at the state, district and block level which are capable of taking up, in collaboration with government agencies, health education, primary health care services and operational research.
- Monitoring and providing feedback to the government on various National Health Programmes.
- Providing guidance and support to voluntary organisations in the health field.
- Calling an annual convention of all voluntary organisations in health, to provide healthy interaction between the health functionaries responsible for policy-making and planning at the national level and various representative voluntary organisations.

- Updating the national directory of voluntary organisations, which should be a priced publication *(profits should be used to update the directory every year).*
- Organising periodic quarterly meetings of the National Co-ordination Committee.
- Sanctioning innovative projects in the voluntary sector to conduct research, health service delivery and the production of educational materials. It is proposed that about 100 projects should be sanctioned in the first year and, subsequently, 50 projects every year. Projects should be run for three to five years, and every project should have a reasonable budget. The Ministry of Health and Family Welfare may consider decentralising the power of sanction to the states.
- Screening, monitoring and evaluating, as well as providing support to all the sanctioned projects.

The National Co-ordination Committee should evolve a working mechanism with a state level counterpart or a state level co-ordination committee. Its activities should be aimed at:

- Preparing and updating a state level directory of voluntary organisations in the health sector.
- Convening a people's health assembly annually, comprising of information leaders, religious leaders, trade unions, media representatives, policy-makers, planners and voluntary organisations.
- Identifying voluntary organisations which have the training and resource potential to undertake orientation programmes for the government and other voluntary organisations.
- Responding quickly to epidemics.
- Meeting quarterly for effective co-ordination and co-operation.
- State health secretaries should act as Convenors to the state co-ordination committees.

Voluntary organisations should be involved in various activities at the district and block level, such as innovative health service delivery, training and special programmes for endemic areas. A fine example of voluntary agencies taking up health and development initiatives in remote areas is VHAI's initiative through its KHOJ projects.

Certain criteria should be followed when providing financial support to voluntary organisations. Only those registered as Societies or Trusts should be considered for assistance. Moreover, only those voluntary organisations which have worked for at least three years in primary health care and development, and are currently engaged in such work, should be provided financial assistance. These strategies, if realistically pursued, could go a long way towards improving the provisions of health care in the voluntary sector. The Commission feels that voluntary agencies working in the health sector need to focus on the following issues of concern:

- How they can join together in a broader struggle for social justice with other progressive forces.
- To systematically and effectively take up issues of socio-economic justice, in the areas where they are operating.
- To work systematically towards a viable alternative health strategy.
- To build up general awareness on rational and holistic health among the public at large, so that a conducive atmosphere is created for a shift in policy.
- To build up an atmosphere for greater public accountability of the existing government health infrastructure.
- To build up a consumer movement to ensure quality health care, at a reasonable cost, from the private sector in health care.

The major shift of focus will very often put the voluntary organisations in conflict with the state, medical establishment and medical industries. But to make an overall impact on health of the nation, the above concerns need to be addressed on a priority basis by voluntary agencies working in the health sector.

HEALTH STATUS IN INDIA

The health of a nation can best be judged by the health status of its people. So far, experts have considered general mortality, infant mortality and expectation of life at birth to be the primary determinants of improved health status. However, studies on fertility, morbidity, the impact of health programmes and the use of health services, have recently been introduced to assess the health status of a population. Mortality data, nevertheless, still remain an integral part of health situation analysis.

Historically speaking, at the time when India won its Independence, the health situation in the country was extremely dismal. However, considerable progress has been made over the last five decades; this is reflected in the improvement in some health indicators *(like the crude death rate, infant mortality rate and life expectancy)*. Overall, mortality *(in particular, infant mortality)* has declined dramatically and life expectancy at birth has increased to 62 years.

In India, life expectancy *(average number of years a new born child is expected to live under current mortality conditions)* has almost doubled, from 32 years at the time of Independence to 62 years in 1995. Neighbouring countries like China, which had a similar health scenario 50 years ago, have done comparatively better *(for instance, life expectancy in China is now 69 years)*. While 62 years is a fairly acceptable figure for life expectancy for India as a whole, when we look at state-wise figures, we find vast variations. For instance, in 1990, Kerala had the highest life expectancy (69.6 years) whereas Uttar Pradesh and Madhya Pradesh had the lowest figure (53.4 years). While the percentage change in life expectancy for India was 7.52 per cent over the decade 1980-90, statewise, Bihar had the least increase (4.40%) and Uttar Pradesh had the largest increase (14.10%). Seven major states have a life expectancy lower than the national figure.

The increase in life expectancy is the direct result of a decline in the death rate *(annual number of deaths per 1,000 population)* from 27.4 deaths per 1,000 population at the time of Independence to 9 deaths per 1,000 population in 1995. However, that the statewise disparity is large, ranging from 6 deaths per 1,000 in Kerala in 1990 to more than double in Madhya Pradesh and Orissa. The maximum decline in the decade 1980-1990, has occurred in Rajasthan (33.82%). One-third of the major states in India have a death rate higher than the national average.

The infant mortality rate *(annual number of deaths of infants under one year of age per 1,000 live births)* is widely recognised as a sensitive indicator of the general health status of a population. In India, the infant mortality rate has declined dramatically. From 146 infant deaths per 1,000 live births at the time of Independence, it has almost halved to 74 (1995). As with the other indicators, there are vast statewise variations. In 1993, Orissa and Kerala had the highest and lowest infant mortality rates, of 110 and 13 respectively. When the 1983 figures are viewed there is a major gap between the infant mortality rate in Kerala (33) and Uttar Pradesh (155). Over the last decade (1983-93), infant mortality has decreased by 29.52 per cent, on an average, over the country. However, when viewed statewise, the infant mortality rate in Kerala has decreased by 60.61 per cent whereas in Karnataka it has declined by only 5.63 per cent. In five of the major states, the infant mortality rate is still higher than the national average.

The improvement in infant mortality is directly linked to the decline in the birth rate *(annual number of births per 1,000 population)*. In 1947, the all-India birth rate was 39.9 births per 1,000 population; at present it is 28.7 births per 1,000 population. However, within India, there are vast disparities. The figures indicate that statewise, Kerala has the lowest birth rate of 17.4 while the birth rate in Uttar Pradesh is as high as 36.2. In terms of decline in birth rate, between 1983 and 1993, Kerala and Tamilnadu showed the most dramatic decline (more than 30%), while the lowest was in Uttar Pradesh (5.73%). Six of the major states still have a birth rate higher than the national average.

Demographic indicators have also been affected by the improved health status of the country. The total fertility rate *(average number of children that would be born to a woman, if she experiences the current fertility pattern throughout her reproductive span: 15-49 years)* in India has gone down from 5.97 during Independence to 3.6 in 1992. That Kerala has the lowest total fertility rate of 1.7, while Uttar Pradesh has the highest rate of 5.2. The maximum and minimum decline (of 26.09% and 5.45%) are in Kerala and Uttar Pradesh respectively. Five of the major states have a total fertility rate higher than the national average.

Similarly, the general fertility rate *(number of live births per 1,000 women in the 15-49 years age group in a given years)* has also declined from 136.3 in1985 to 118.6 in 1992. Again, Kerala has lowest general fertility rate of 62 and Uttar Pradesh has the highest rate of 161.9. Also, in the last decade, the maximum and minimum decline was in Kerala and Uttar Pradesh respectively. Six of the major states have a general fertility rate which is higher than the national average.

The sex ratio figures *(number of females per 1,000 males)* have been declining considerably since Independence and, therefore, are a cause for serious concern. The all-India sex ratio, which stood at 946 females per 1,000 males in 1947, fell to 935 in 1981 and 927 in 1991. In fact, only in one state *(namely Kerala)* is the sex ratio favourable to females. In Haryana, Uttar Pradesh and Punjab the sex ratio is less than 900 females per 1,000 males. Over the last decade, the sex ratio has gone up marginally in five major states. Only in nine major states is the sex ratio higher than the national average.

The population in these areas—be they tribals, scheduled castes, displaced or migrant populations in search of work, remain underserved, ignored and are forced to meekly accept a lower quality of life. Primary health care services, preventive care and public health measures do not reach them adequately. The mere existence of constitutional safeguards and protection, for example, for scheduled tribes, is not sufficient to ensure the provision of proper preventive and curative services, and adequate and willing health manpower or resources.

In the course of public hearings, the Commission repeatedly noted a degree of helplessness and lack of faith in the system amongst this segment of the population. In addition, in the Indian social context—children, women, migrant labour, in particular, are marginalised. The political system has gravely failed to respond to the special needs of such population groups.

Some major issues bearing on the health of society have also been overlooked. For instance:

- Occupation-related health problems of workers employed in stone quarrying, leather industry, etc.; children employed in the carpet or match industry, etc., have not received appropriate and sustained attention.
- Often, age-related or gender issues, for example, problems of the rural aged with disabilities, widows, etc. do not get noticed at all, as health care is not seen to be the bedrock of social security.
- The extent to which people make use of indigenous systems of medicine is not matched by the attention paid by the government to the development of such systems.
- There is no defined role for, nor regulation of the private sector in medicine, even though a large part of health expenditure, especially among the poor, is spent on private medical care.
- Another overlooked issue is the need to pattern a system of health care that responds to seasonal variations in the availability of work, income, food to rural labour, and the

ways in which they influence preventive and curative care.

In the face of the disparities that still remain between the more advanced areas and the difficult/needy/vulnerable areas in terms of health and development, some crucial policy questions need to be posed. For instance, what should be done in concrete terms, to bring the standards of health care and health outcomes in the vulnerable regions/states to an acceptable minimum? How should the standard of health care in these vulnerable regions and areas be raised, and how should the access of the poor/backward/underprivileged/vulnerable people be increased? These are some of the guiding questions of the Report. Solutions to these questions will need new ways of thinking, technology and management. Above all, it will need political action *(not political will alone)* to place health status and medicare in an appropriate context.

The identification of vulnerable regions should not be left to commonsense, adhoc decisions or political judgement but should be scientific and ruthlessly objective. At the same time, one should not get caught in complex statistical exercises and hair-splitting statistical weights in an attempt to identify such areas.

The health of a nation can be gauged from health and demographic factors like the crude death rate, infant mortality rate and total fertility rate. Environmental factors *(in particular, drinking water and sanitation)* play a crucial role in influencing morbidity and mortality, apart from nutrition and the income level of the people. Considering environmental, health and demographic factors together, and using a few more parameters, the Independent Commission conducted extensive exercises and identified some of the regions/states/districts of the country which could be termed vulnerable regions *(states/districts)* in terms of health and development.

Methodology to Compute the Household Misery Index (HMI)

The 1991 Census of India gives valuable data at the household level *(rural as well as urban)* on housing and basic amenities like availability of safe drinking water, toilet facilities and electricity. Data are also presented for the first time on the type of fuel used for cooking *(cowdung cake, wood, coal, charcoal, kerosene, cooking gas, electricity, etc.*). The housing data classifies houses as pucca, semi-pucca or kutcha (for details, see GOI 1991, 1994a).

On the basis of this data we constructed a Household Misery Index (HMI), which reflects the extent of deprivation at the household level of basic needs like pucca housing, safe drinking water, toilet facilities and electricity, and also the availability of proper fuel for cooking. The HMI was calculated separately for rural and urban households of each district and state, and a composite weighted index worked out *(weighted by the proportion of rural and urban households)*. The five indicators of misery chosen were:

- M1: Households without pucca housing.
- M2: Households without safe drinking water
- M3: Households without toilet facilities
- M4: Households without electricity
- M5: Households using cowdung cake and wood as cooking fuel.

To simplify matters, M1 to M5 were given equal weights, though in a sophisticated index, one can assign different weights to these indicators. To compute the index, the scale used was 0-5 for rural areas and urban areas, and 0-10 for the combined figure *(unweighted)*. The composite weighted index had a scale of 0-5 for each district/state. For the sake of simplicity, in the final tables, the scale was 0-100. All the states/districts were arranged in descending order, which determined their HMI rank.

However, it must be kept in mind that these figures are indicative rather than definitive. The ranking of districts is according to the extent of misery, rather than in terms of absolute values. Because of the limitations of Census data, one must interpret these figures with caution. A close examination of the data reveals that there may have been considerable subjectivity in classifying houses as pucca or semi-pucca. In some districts, the figure for semi-pucca houses are very high while that for pucca houses is low. Curiously, in some districts which are supposed to be more advanced, the proportion of pucca houses is less than in backward districts. The Census instructions may not have been properly followed in Kerala, where the data reveal abnormally low figures for safe drinking water at the household level *(in Kerala, the Census figure for households with safe drinking water is only 18.9%, compared to 46.3% in Andhra Pradesh and 67.0% in Tamilnadu)*.

Despite our serious reservations about the Census figures for Kerala, this exercise, based on Census data, does give an idea of the lack of basic amenities at the district level *(which helps in identifying the most vulnerable districts in each state).* Using this data, districts were classified as vulnerable. It may be noted that even comparatively developed states have vulunerable districts, while most under-developed states have a few districts which are moderately vulnerable.

The HMI values indicate the most vulnerable districts in each state of India. To validate the results, a comparison has also been made with the estimates of fertility, mortality and infant mortality for 1981 for each district, as presented by the Office of the Registrar General of India (GOI 1994b).

The state of Orissa, alongwith other states, namely, Bihar, Madhya Pradesh, Rajasthan and Uttar Pradesh and the entire north-east region, have been identified as vulnerable in terms of health and development. Coincidentally, the regions which have been identified by the Commission as vulnerable are invariably found in the following areas:

- Hilly/mountainous
- Tribal
- Arid/semi-arid (including desert)
- Drought-prone
- Flood-prone
- Water-logged
- Marshy
- Coastal

Thus, ICHI has made a modest attempt in this report to identify the critical areas in the field of health care which call for a thorough restructuring of the health delivery system and, above all, a rethinking on the vital but neglected health sector within the developmental context.

The current view of allocating more funds to create buildings for PHCs and SCs, and expanding a largely ineffective army of health workers, has to change in favour of policies and programmes which genuinely focus on a health care system that ensures equity and concern for the deprived and unreached people.

It is hoped that planners and policy-makers will give the highest priority to the most vulnerable districts in each state.

Health—Family Planning

Not surprisingly, Gujarat is far ahead of Rajasthan in the demographic transition. The crude death rate and the infant mortality rate are slightly lower in Gujarat. The differential between the two states is larger in the case of maternal mortality. The crude birth rate and the fertility rate of Gujarat are well below the corresponding figures for Rajasthan. A much larger portion of the reproductive age group is using contraceptives in Gujarat and on average couples are sterilised there after producing a lower number of children. Trained personnel attend births to a much larger extent, reflecting the better development of health services. Antenatal care in rural areas is received by a higher proportion of mothers in Gujarat, although the figures are low for both states. Per capita health expenditures by government are somewhat higher in Gujarat, although Rajasthan has been catching up. The rate of growth of health outlays in the latter state was much higher.

Rajasthan has the dubious distinction of being one of the four large North Indian states, (Bihar, Madhya Pradesh, Rajasthan and Uttar Pradesh) called BIMARU (literally meaning sick) states, where statistical measures of mortality and fertility remain high despite all efforts made by government and volags.

Health is a state subject and FP was put on the concurrent list in the Indian Constitution in 1976. FP is centrally funded in its entirety. Rajasthan and Gujarat, as well as other states, basically follow the Central health and FP model in terms of policies and programmes.

- There is a marked orientation towards allopathic medicine and a corresponding neglect of indigenous approaches.
- There is a strong emphasis on clinic-based, curative medicine.
- An attempt was made to build a delivery system in rural areas based on primary health centres, sub-centres and community centres. Difficulties in mobilising suitable health personnel to locate in these centres has been a source of frustration, however. The implicit and explicit incentives were all biased in favour of practising medicine in metropolitan cities or migrating abroad.
- A major attempt was made during the seventies to achieve ambitious targets in spreading FP based on male sterilisation. This became coercive during the Emergency

period in the mid-1970s and generated a backlash which still continues to some considerable extent.

The Seventh Plan changed direction, to some extent, as the limitations of the earlier doctrine came to be recognised. There was a move to use traditional practitioners and to educate the people so that they could be self-reliant. Ayurvedic dispensaries were built. Emphasis was placed on a Minimum Needs Programme and the training of multi-purpose health workers. More attention was given to creating demand for FP services than before.

Considerable progress was made. Average life expectancy for India as a whole rose from 32 years in 1947 to 58 years in 1990. The infant mortality rate fell from 129 in 1971 to 80 in 1990. The crude birth rate declined from 37 in 1971 to 29 in 1990. The contraceptive prevalence rate increased to 42 but did not cause a commensurate fall in the birth rate because many couples started using contraceptives only after three or more children. The rate of population growth remains high and the total number of people increases by 17 million every year.

The government recognises the following weaknesses in its approach and in the way it is implemented:

— The backlog in the building of the physical infrastructure for health and family planning is "staggering", according to the Eighth Plan. Although access to these services has increased considerably over time, a substantial part of the rural people are still beyond reach.

— Average vacancy rates for government health personnel in rural areas are very high: doctors 14 per cent, specialists 30 per cent, female health assistant 11 per cent. There is far too rapid a turnover of personnel in key government positions leading to a loss of continuity and accountability.

— The quality of services provided by the public health system remains poor. Access to nominally free services and drugs actually requires substantial payments. Shortages of drugs are frequent. It can take a long time to see a doctor.

— The coverage of ante-natal care is low, partly because of lack of demand. Women have a subservient position in society and lack the awareness and self-confidence to use existing facilities. The programme to deal with anemia that affects many women is ineffective. Findings of recent studies by the Indian Council of Medical Research, the Operations Research Group and the Centre for Operations, Research and Training reveal that women's access to health services is much less than that of men. Khan and Patel (1993) summarise these studies and state:

> The quality of services provided at MCH clinics held at the primary health care centres and sub-centres are poor. Even minimum routine tests and examinations are not carried out. The ANMs (auxilliary nurse midwives) and LHVs (local health volunteers) lack proper knowledge about pregnancy care, safe delivery and the risk approach.

— Targets of the Universal Immunisation Programme for diptheria, whooping cough, tetanus, polio, measles and tuberculosis could not be met on time.

— FP targets are set first of all in Delhi with the aim of getting each state to reach the national goal, that is a contraceptive prevalence rate of 60 per cent. Some states raise these Delhi targets to put pressure on field staff while others lower them to take into account the varying abilities of various districts to achieve them. Some states assign FP targets not only to FP agencies but also to other government development departments. District authorities assign targets to field workers on the basis of population and they are the basis of performance evaluation of field workers. The consequences of not reaching targets vary depending on the political and bureaucratic attitudes prevailing in particular areas and at different times.

— Targets for India as a whole for IUD, oral pills, condoms were fully achieved or exceeded but there was a shortfall of 24 per cent with respect to sterilisation in 1989-90. Sterilisation has been the predominant method for contraception all over India for a long time. It accounts for over 70 per cent of all contraceptive acceptors today. Reliance on sterilisation has diminished greatly in recent years. Currently, it accounts for roughly one-fifth of new family planning acceptors and nine out of ten sterilisations are performed on women. Despite the trend towards reversible methods, the official programme continues to reward excessively the recruitment of sterilisation acceptors and to arbitrarily penalise workers held responsible for the shortfall with respect to sterilisation targets. Not enough attention is given to provision of services for spacing methods and there is little emphasis on continuous use of reversible methods.

— The usefulness of setting method specific targets, backed up by strong incentives and penalties, has been a topic of considerable controversy. A recent study by Visarias and Jain (1992) found that service statistics, such as those quoted above, are considerably inflated owing to the pressure on service providers to meet targets handed down to them from the top. On the basis of a comparison of these data and survey information for four districts in Gujarat, the authors concluded that sterilisations were over-estimated by 6 per cent and reversible methods by 10 per cent.

— The family planning programme remains the concern of the Central Ministry of Health and Family Welfare. Other Central ministries (such as Education, Women and Child Development) whose activities are crucial for achieving progress in family planning do not assign high priority to this task. Family planning is a 100 per cent centrally sponsored scheme and state governments are responsible for implementation. The commitment of the latter to the programme varies a great deal from state to state. Little is done to adapt the design of programmes to the very considerable diversity that is encountered in the field. There is unwillingness to devolve real decision-making authority to the states, to say nothing about district and lower levels of administration.

— Doctors, demographers and bureaucrats have exercised far too much influence in the formulation of policies and programme design in the field of family planning.

— There is insufficient emphasis on training of staff at all levels, leading to insensitive and ineffective implementation.

— Information, education and communication activities are geared to national concerns while the decision to limit family size is a personal decision.

The Government of India (GOI) is the dominant actor in terms of policy and programme in both health and FP. Both the GOI and the FPAI have tried since 1986 to make family planning a "people's movement" but the results so far have not been encouraging. Only 138 volags have taken advantage of these schemes. Many women's organisations are critical of FP and many environmental organisations tend to shy away from the population question, as we have noted already.

GOI schemes aimed at promoting the interest of volags in FP take the following forms:

1. *Six-bedded Sterilisation Ward with Operation Theatre.* Volags can obtain funds to set up such a facility in areas where the CPR is less than 35 per cent and where the government's own delivery system lacks such a facility. This scheme is said by the Ministry to be popular. No independent assessment is available, however.
2. *Scheme for Encouragement of Spacing Methods and Sterilisation.* Volags in areas with a CPR of less than 50 per cent can obtain funds for motivational work, including establishment of Mahila Mandals (women's groups), Yuvak Mandals (youth groups), etc. The volag is expected to register all marriages and to follow up old and new couples. Very little could be found about the response to this scheme, despite enquiries addressed to the ministry concerned.
3. *Mini Family Welfare Scheme.* Volags in areas with a CPR of less than 35 per cent can obtain funds to generate demand for FP and maternal/child health services. All eligible couples have to be covered. Links have to be established with the government's delivery system and with volags working in related fields. The response to this scheme could not be ascertained, despite enquiries made at the ministry.
4. *Promotion of Small Family Norm through Innovative Methods.* Volags in areas with a CPR over 35 can obtain funds for projects that they themselves have designed using traditional systems of medicine and community participation. The ceiling is Rs. 1.5 million. There is not much response to this scheme so far.
5. *Private Voluntary Organisations in Health (PVOH).* This scheme is funded by the USA. In 1992-93 assistance was

given to 40 volags.

6. *Mother Unit Scheme.* Bigger and more experienced volags can get funds from government to enable them to support small volags. Currently, there are five mother units; FPAI in Bombay, Gandhigram in Tamilnadu, Centre for Labour and Educational Research in Madhya Pradesh, Child-in Need Institute in West Bengal and Centre for Research, Planning and Action in New Delhi.

Although some of these efforts have had a measure of success, altogether the net impact has not amounted to a "people's movement" aimed at FP. We are not quite sure we understand all the factors, or their relative importance, that make FP relatively unattractive to volags but the following list may shed some light on the current situation:

— Volags may admit that population growth needs to be curbed but insist that the right way to go about it is to raise literacy, reduce infant mortality, eliminate gender inequality and eradicate poverty. Many women's groups espouse this view. Gandhian volags may believe that supplying modern contraceptives is not the moral answer and that emphasis should be put on sexual abstinence instead.

— The GOI is the major player in FP and its approach has tended to be pre-emptory rather than participative. It is not respectful of governments at state or lower levels and it expects volags to implement GOI's detailed and rather rigid design, irrespective of very different field situations. Volags have little room for manoeuvre in adapting the design to diverse needs of the communities they are serving.

— The GOI's programme design for FP (which is copied by most state governments), administered by the Ministry of Health and Family Welfare, tends to be narrow in scope. There is a considerable bias in favour of sterilization, despite the professed "cafeteria" approach. Many aspects that are crucial for creating demand for FP, such as women's education, reduction of son preference, improvement in the status of women, poverty alleviation, reduction in the household's need for child labour to collect fuel, fodder and water are not included in the programme.

— Other ministries of the GOI and other departments of state governments administer programmes which can augment the demand for FP. However, there is little effective collaboration across these government agencies and the messages conveyed to people in the field tend to be truncated and, therefore, confusing.

— Women's groups have criticised the GOI's FP efforts for being excessive in magnitude and ill-conceived in design. These place disproportionate emphasis on contraceptives for women, provide inadequate medical after-care for women practicing contraception and introduce new contraceptives without adequate testing, according to women's groups. Norplant and "injectables" have been opposed by women's groups on the ground that they are "provider-dependent" and should be introduced only after there is a strong delivery system not only for administering the contraceptive but also for counselling and follow-up (Saroj Pachauri, 1993). The maternal and child health (MCH) programme is focused on maternal care and neglects gynaecological problems that are the cause of considerable morbidity and that impede the use of spacing methods of contraception.

There are no open and healthy debates around these issues in a spirit of "give and take". There is a great deal of resentment and plenty of sniping comments, however, that do not lead anywhere. The FPAI played an important role in the evolution of GOI's FP policy in the early days of the official programme. It is possible that it is still influencing the GOI behind the scenes. It has not, however, engaged the government in a constructive, open debate.

The state of Gujarat has a long tradition of voluntary work in the field of health. A study (Subramanian and Mehta, 1984) by the Indian Institute of Management in 1984 found that 70 per cent of the health volags were concentrated in four districts (Ahmedabad, Baroda, Kheda and Rajkot) of Gujarat. Three-fourths of these volags were in urban areas. One-third were sponsored by religious groups. The largest funders of these volags were private groups, followed by foreign agencies and the state government. More than half of the activity of these volags was maternal and child health. Family planning accounted for 10 per cent of their total activity.

The Government of Gujarat, today is very positive about the role of volags in the health and family planning sectors. As mentioned above, an entire block in the Bharuch district is being run by Sewa Rural. There are 20 volags operating Anganwadis (child centres) under the GOI's Integrated Child Development Scheme (ICDS). Sixty of the 173 Urban Family Welfare Centres of the Gujarat Government are being run by volags. In addition, government feels that volags can play a valuable role in the control of TB, Leprosy and AIDS.

The experience of Sewa Rural covering the period 1984-89, has been evaluated by a distinguished team (Khanna *et al.*, 1991). They conclude that the death rate and the infant mortality rate in the project area fell sharply. Equally remarkable was the rise of the CPR. There was an increase in the health awareness of the community. These results can be attributed, to a considerable extent, to a series of innovations carried out by Sewa Rural, including the manner in which it managed its cadre of workers and built up a congenial work environment. The review also concluded that the framework within which Sewa Rural collaborated with government made it difficult to focus on key health problems of the community and that too much time had to be spent on routine demands of government and on issues of lower priority.

Only scattered information is available regarding volag activity in health and family planning in Rajasthan. A directory issued by the Directorate of Medical Health and Family Welfare Services in 1989 lists 240 volags but it is likely that many of them are small and work only in limited areas of health education. Activities of some volags include information and education of FP matters. Very few seem to be active in providing FP services, however.

There are 25 listings in the directory compiled specially for this study, combining many sources. It includes BRS in Jaipur, Urmul in Bikaner and SM in Udaipur. To this list should be added the Parivar network which provides a number of common services to eight or nine constituent volags of very small size. These organisations embarked on a programme to create awareness of the need for FP in the context of a MacArthur Foundation grant. All four of these volags are part of the sample for this study.

There are 16 items in the Home Ministry and USAID print out detailing foreign grants to volags in the health area. The biggest recipient was the Social Work and Research Centre in Tilonia, followed by Bhoruka Charitable Trust in Churu and the BRS in Jaipur.

BRS received a grant of Rs. 2.8 million from the USAID in March 1988. The evaluation report completed in 1991 showed that immunisation rates which were very low at the outset of the project rose very rapidly in the population of 32,000 covered by this project. This was also true of antenatal care. The contraceptive prevalence rate increased from 10 per cent to 49 per cent. BRS obtained a second grant from USAID in 1991.

The GOR established a State Standing Committee, headed by the Health Secretary, for making grants to volags in the fiscal year ending 1991. Several meetings with volags have been held recently to explain government policies and programmes. A large number of volags have applied for grants but only very few applications have yet been approved. We attended a meeting in Jaipur at which some volags voiced their frustration with elaborate government procedures. At the same meeting, officials explained their plans for collaborating with volags in projects involving

(*i*) community-based distribution and social marketing of contraceptives;
(*ii*) training;
(*iii*) developing and pre-testing communication materials aimed at promoting FP and other activities.

AIDS CONTROL STRATEGIES AND THE ROLE OF NGOs

The global AIDS control strategy as endorsed by the World Health Assembly has proposed the following measures to meet the challenge of the AIDS pandemic:

1. Provide adequate and equitable health care to the growing numbers of HIV infected people falling ill;
2. Treat other STDs, as these increase people's biological vulnerability to HIV infection;
3. Reduce women's social vulnerability to HIV infection by improving their health, education, legal status and economic prospects;
4. Begin immediate planning in anticipation of the pandemic's socio-economic impact;

5. Enhance efforts to overcome stigmatization and discrimination.

There are three main objectives of the strategy:

1. to prevent infection with HIV;
2. to reduce the personal and social impact;
3. to mobilize and unify national and international efforts against AIDS.

NGOs have an important role to play in meeting many of these objectives.

Prevention of Sexual Transmission

Prevention of HIV infection requires making behavioural changes related to very personal and intimate practices, and bringing about these changes requires eliciting people's confidence and empathy. Awareness-generating activities alone are rarely enough to make people at risk take safety measures. Raising awareness is merely the first step; audiences must be motivated to examine their own risks and behaviours and to identify options of safe behaviours. They must also have the necessary skills to negotiate and feel capable of adopting these behaviours. Social, cultural, political and economic factors all influence risk behaviours, as they do also the ability of individuals to bring about changes.

While mass media and information campaigns can raise awareness, an ongoing, focused, interpersonal approach is needed to effect behaviour change. The role of NGOs in implementing interventions targeted at individuals with risk behaviour is, therefore, particularly relevant. Targeted interventions are those activities that are carefully designed to meet the needs and to fit with the characteristics of particular population groups. They are important in reaching marginalized groups such as IDUs, sex-workers, migrant workers and street youth. Peer education has been found to be a particularly effective approach including in Asia. *In order to ensure behaviour change, support services in the form of condoms, STD treatment services should be made available and accessible.*

However, many approaches which have worked in other parts of the world may not necessarily be applicable in the countries of South-East Asia. There are many social, economic and cultural issues that have to be considered. For example, prostitution is illegal in many countries, and yet it flourishes in the redlight areas or less formally among disadvantaged populations. Promotion of condoms is another sensitive issue in many countries in the region. Community-based organizations (CBOs) can often do a better job than others in resolving such issues.

Provision of STD treatment services is an important component of AIDS prevention. Recent research has established the interactions between STDs and HIV. Besides being transmitted through the same sexual behaviours, infection with an STD greatly increases the risk of HIV transmission. *It has also been clearly demonstrated that provision of STD treatment services at community level and educational programmes, which promote the use of such services, can reduce HIV transmission substantially (up to 40%).*

As condoms are the most cost-effective means of prevention of HIV transmission, promoting condom use, while simultaneously ensuring easy access to good quality and affordable condoms, is important. NGOs can help by promoting condoms and / or ensuring condom availability by adopting social marketing techniques or by linking up with ongoing condom social marketing programmes.

Prevention of Transmission Through Blood and Blood Products

Reduction of blood-borne HIV transmission involves strengthening the blood transfusion services and ensuring that all blood samples and commercial blood products used in medical settings are tested of HIV. *NGOs can reduce national dependence on commercial blood by popularizing the concept of volunteering to donate blood, carrying out effective blood donation campaigns and educating audiences about the importance of blood donation and the use of safe blood.*

Injecting drug use is a major mode of HIV infection in Asia. In this context, harm reduction approaches are crucial. *Harm reduction includes promoting a range of choices from not sharing needles to techniques for cleaning needles.* Some programmes provide bleach for cleaning or sterilizing needles. Also important are efforts to prevent injecting drug use and promotion of safer sexual behaviour among the drug users.

Providing Care and Social Support in Homes, Community and Health-Care Settings

AIDS is a chronic disease and the patients living with AIDS may have to move back and forth between hospital and home. In developing countries more of the care takes place within the communities and at home.

NGOs are able to relate to individuals and families, provide counselling to reduce the social and psychological impact of AIDS, and help family members and communities who are involved in the care of patients by improving access to medical services.

NGOs can act as advocates for provision of or access to care for people with HIV/AIDS similar to that available for people not infected with HIV. In this regard, referral mechanism to ensure continuum of care from the institutional level to community and home levels must be established through consultations among care providers and the health services.

Good basic care can be provided at home or by the community health workers if they have appropriate training and support and access to higher level referral services. Those caring for the sick in the hospital settings also need skills and knowledge to deal with all the problems and demands of assisting people with HIV/AIDS. NGOs can carry out educational activities focused on the development of positive attitudes and assist in the provision of home care by mobilizing community groups. They could, if possible, ensure that besides health and medical care, the daily needs of the sick could also be met.

As important as skills and knowledge are the workers' own attitudes, which will affect quality and access to services. Community workers and families providing care also need support and counselling by community-based organizations can help reduce the stress on people with AIDS, their families and the community. Effective counselling programmes can also assist families in making decisions and plans for dealing with terminal illness.

Advocacy and Countering Discrimination Against Persons with HIV/AIDS

Much work still remains to be done to change the hostile social climate that challenges those living with HIV and AIDS. Ignorance accentuates the discrimination, as most people wrongly believe that if certain population groups and infected people are isolated, the disease can be kept at bay. NGOs and community-based organizations can help to dispel such prejudices and misconceptions and to take up human rights issues on behalf of those who are discriminated against.

Policies such as those banning the entry or restricting the travel of HIV-infected people need to be opposed through the international mobilization of NGOs, governments, businesses and groups of people infected with HIV. NGOs can advocate policies against mandatory and routine HIV testing, particularly at work and in health care settings.

Building Alliances, Sharing Experiences

By building alliances with organizations and leaders, NGOs can create awareness about the social and economic impact of AIDS on communities and countries. NGOs working in the area of AIDS can find common ground with other NGOs, and private sector and other institutions, and persuade them to undertake HIV-related initiatives. Sharing technical, organizational and management skills can greatly strengthen those NGOs that have had little experience in the field of HIV/STD prevention and care. A greater level of communication among NGOs themselves and between NGOs and other actors would be mutually beneficial.

It is important that NGOs involved in AIDS prevention activities evaluate their specific strengths, interests and resources when selecting the interventions they plan to use. Seldom do NGOs in South-East Asia work exclusively on AIDS: most have added on AIDS/HIV prevention and care activities to their ongoing programmes or projects. It may not be possible for NGOs to provide for all components of priority interventions, or to reach out to all the risk groups. It is advisable that each NGO takes up one or two specific components or sub-components of the programme activities, leaving other components to be addressed through collaboration and development of referral networks.

WHO POLICY AND SUPPORT TO NGOs

WHO's collaboration with NGOs on AIDS is based on the World Health Assembly resolution WHA 42.34—"Non-governmental Organizations and the Global AIDS Strategy"—adopted by its member states in 1989. The resolution calls for governments, NGOs and the WHO Secretariat to work together by complementing each other's strengths and activities. From the very beginning,

WHO's global programme on AIDS promoted NGO involvement in the planning and review of the national AIDS programmes. WHO had also recommended that at least 15 per cent of the funds it provides should be made available to NGOs for AIDS activities. Additionally, WHO has had regular consultations with global and regional NGOs and had promoted their participation in the various steering committees and technical working groups. In collaborating with NGOs, WHO was guided by the following principles:

1. a commitment to create supportive environments globally and nationally for the contribution of NGOs;
2. recognition of the need to establish consultative mechanisms with NGOs as a prerequisite to partnership building;
3. recognition of the need to facilitate the government-NGO interface at both national and provincial levels in order to decentralize national AIDS programmes;
4. recognition of the contribution of NGOs to the national response, particularly in decision-making fora, policy development, planning, evaluation and in providing precise feedback, and
5. recognition of the need for mechanisms which will facilitate democratic representation of NGOs at decision-making fora at national and international levels.

DECENTRALISED HEALTH PLANNING

The basic goal of development planning is to eliminate poverty, ignorance and ill-health, improve the quality of life of the people and raise their standard of living. In this context, Article 47 of the Constitution states that, "the State shall regard the raising of the level of nutrition and the standard of living of its people, and the improvement of public health, as among its primary duties".

The Planning Commission was established on 15 March, 1950, to implement the economic and social policies of the government, as outlined in the Constitution.

The Planning commission functions as an advisory body at the highest policy level, without being involved in the responsibilities of day-to-day administration. The Prime Minister of India is the Chairperson of the Planning Commission. It has a full-time Deputy Chairperson, between five and seven full-time members and two or three part-time members *(such as the Finance Minister and the Agriculture Minister).*

The Planning Commission was constituted through a Resolution of the Government of India, which defined the scope of its work and assigned it the following functions:

- Assess the material, capital and human resources of the country, including technical personnel; and study the possibility of augmenting those resources which are found to be deficient, in relation to the nation's requirements.
- Formulate a Plan for the effective and balanced utilisation of the country's resources.
- Based on priorities, define the stages in which the Plan should be carried out, and propose a phased allocation of resources.
- Indicate the factors which tend to retard economic development and determine the conditions, which in view of the current social and political situation, should be established for the successful execution of the Plan.
- Determine the nature of the machinery which will be necessary for securing the successful implementation of each stage of the Plan.
- Periodically review the progress made and recommend necessary policy adjustments and measures.
- Make appropriate interim or ancillary recommendations.

Normally, policies are co-ordinated through mutual consultations between the centre and the states, based on overall national requirements. This system of consultation is an important and integral part of the process of planning and implementation. A National Development Council has been set up, with the Prime Minister of India as the Chairperson. It comprises of Central Ministers, Chief Ministers of all the States, Lt. Governors and Administrators of Union Territories, and the Deputy Chairperson and Members of the Planning Commission. This is the highest policy-making body, which considers and approves the policies and strategies of development planning in the country. It is serviced by the Planning Commission.

The Planning Commission aims at providing total and comprehensive socio-economic development planning, with major emphasis on policy planning. The Plan is usually formulated as a Five-Year Plan. Sectorwise working groups are constituted before each Plan period; their recommendations are considered by the Planning Commission while preparing the approach paper for the formulation of a Plan. Representatives from the Union Ministry and the state governments are actively involved in the working groups. The approach paper is later approved by the National Development Council (NDC). Guidelines are prepared on the basis of the approach paper and sent to state governments and central ministries; they then formulate a draft plan proposal. The proposal is then discussed by officials and members of the Planning Commission, representatives from state governments and ministries. The Plan is then formulated and finally approved by NDC.

A Five-Year Plan, however carefully formulated, is only an approximation for the Plan period. It requires adjustments and adaptations to changing conditions; these are inevitable and cannot always be foreseen or anticipated. Consequently, a Five-Year Plan is implemented through the mechanism of Annual Plans, which are prepared for each year, within the broad framework of the Five-Year Plan. This is done keeping in view the current situation and the likely availability of resources. Annual Plans introduce the much-needed flexibility in the implementation of Five-Year Plans by setting out detailed programmes of development to be implemented each year.

Mid-term appraisal is considered to be an important aspect of the planning process. Its purpose is to review the progress achieved in the execution of each stage of the Plan, and to recommend measures that may help in achieving targets and other objectives.

Historical Development and Planning Strategy

Although the National Health Policy in India was not framed or announced until 1983, directions on health issues were provided by the Constitution of India, the NDC, the Planning Commission, the Central Council of Health and Family Welfare, and Consultative Committees attached to the Ministry of Health and Family Welfare. The health care measures, formulated and implemented in successive Five-Year Plans, have been mainly based on the approaches recommended by the Bhore Committee (1946), such as the provision of comprehensive health services to the community. The First Plan saw the beginning of the development of rural health services and infrastructure in the country.

During the First and Second Plan periods only 3.3 and 3 per cent respectively of the total plan outlay was on health. This was well below the minimum of 10 per cent recommended by the Bhore Committee. Though the Indian government accepted the recommendations of the Bhore Committee, yet in the First Plan itself, 55-60 per cent of the budget was allocated to curative health services and medical education, and only a third of the funds available were allocated to public health. The major share was given to unipurpose vertical programmes—at this point, mainly for the control of malaria and smallpox. The Malaria Control Programme met with phenomenal success. In the Second Plan, the programme was converted into the National Malaria Eradication Programme. It was envisaged that malaria would be eradicated by 1966. This, of course, has not happened. Primary health centres were to be developed as part of the Community Development Programme.

Indian was the first country in the world to launch a family planning programme during this period. The importance of maternal and child health (MCH) was recognised; it was also made an integral component of general health services.

During the Third Plan, the recommendations of the Health Survey and Planning Committee, popularly known as the Mudaliar Committee, were implemented. The Mudaliar Committee noted that the primary health centre network that had evolved, bore no resemblance to that visualised by the Bhore Committee. Pleading a paucity of funds, the Committee suggested that additional PHCs should not be established; instead, the existing services should be 'consolidated'. This period also saw a great deal of activity in the health sector. Possibly inspired by the early successes of the National Malaria Eradication Programme—the National Smallpox Eradication Programme and the National Tuberculosis Programme (NTP) were initiated in 1962.

During the Third Plan, 2.63 per cent of the total allocation was for health. During this period, from a mere Rs. 63 lakhs in the First Plan and Rs. 5 crores in the Second Plan, the allocation for family planning shot up to Rs. 50 crores. In order to give the necessary thrust to the family planning programme, a separate family planning department was set up during the Third Plan. Alarmed by the results of the 1961 census, which showed a higher population growth rate than had been anticipated, the 'clinic approach' was abandoned in favour of the 'extension approach'. However, even before the extension approach could be properly established, it was also abandoned in favour of a target-based, incentive-driven programme, emphasising the use of IUDs and sterilisation. With the adoption of this approach, ANMs were made to concentrate on family planning activities, rather than their other responsibilities *(like maternal and child health, nutrition).*

From the Fourth Plan onwards, the budget for health shrank gradually, while that for family planning/welfare increased. The Fourth Plan document noted that since 1963, the Malaria Eradication Programme had received setbacks; the targets of the Smallpox Eradication Programme had not been achieved; and the Intra-Uterine Contraceptive Device Programme had met with a setback as a result of side-effects of IUD insertion, like bleeding and pain. Apart from epidemiological, technical and administrative reasons, one of the major causes for the failure of these programmes, was that by concentrating on vertical programmes, general health services had not developed. In 1973, the Kartar Singh Committee was appointed to consider the integration of vertical programmes. The Committee felt that integration would be both economical and feasible. It suggested that workers of only four programmes—malaria, smallpox, trachoma and family planning—be integrated and designated as multi-purpose workers. This vision of integration was seriously flawed, since it was confined to a few programmes only, and to the peripheral workers alone. At the more crucial, central and state levels, where priorities were set and financial allocations made, the programmes continued to remain vertical.

In the Fifth Plan, the outlay for family planning increased to Rs. 516 crores, while health was allocated Rs. 797 crores, representing 0.96 per cent and 1.49 per cent respectively of the total outlay. The primary objective of the Fifth Plan was to provide minimum public health facilities, integrated with family planning and nutrition, for the vulnerable groups. The Minimum Needs Programme (MNP) was introduced for the rural areas, under the outlay for total development—the rural health sector was also included in this. This Plan was committed to improving health care services in the rural areas by extending health infrastructure under the MNP and integrating the peripheral staff of all vertical programmes.

By the end of the Fifth Plan period, smallpox had been eradicated. However, the incidence of malaria increased, a modified plan of action was initiated to control the disease. The eradication of smallpox was possible because of foolproof planning, proper strategies for containing the disease, flexibility of funding, and day-to-day monitoring of the programme. The programme for the control of malaria did not yield any results other than bring down the reported number of blood-slide positive cases from 6.47 million to 1.66 million in 1987. However, the number of such reported cases gradually increased to 2.80 million in 1995. Of these, more than one-third *(i.e. 1.09 million)* were *Plasmodium falciparum* cases. The failure of the programme is mainly due to the pattern of funding, i.e. 50 per cent by the Central government and 50 per cent by the state government. It has been seen that often the share of the state is not forthcoming. The pattern of funding for the National Tuberculosis Programme (NTP) is similar.

While the Constitution of India requires the states to improve public health as its primary duty, it has been seen that state governments do not provide for public health programmes from their own funds. State funds are almost exclusively spent on curative services.

It is unfortunate that inspite of the fact that the Planning Commission was established more than 45 years ago, three glaring limitations are still evident:

- Insufficient and unreliable data at both the national and state levels, particularly at the district and sub-district level. This data is essential for local, area-specific decentralised planning.
- Gross under-estimation of the number of personnel required to be trained
- Lack of evaluation and research mechanisms to support planning.

It will not be wrong to say that health planning at the national level tends to be ad hoc. The trend is towards incremental planning *(increasing resources and outlays for allocation to different programmes, on an incremental basis)*, rather than on emphasising need-based planning, problem solving, and local priorities.

Another constraint is that major national institutions, like the Indian Council of Medical Research, New Delhi (ICMR), National Institute of Communicable Diseases, Delhi (NICD), National Institute of Health and Family Welfare, New Delhi, (NIHFW), and All India Institute of Hygiene and Public Health, Calcutta

(AIIHPH), which should play a decisive role in policy and programme planning in the health sector, have hitherto played a very passive role. There are only a few instances where these institutions have worked on national health issues and given a sense of direction to programme planning on specific health and population issues.

Another important issue concerning health planning in India is that the Ministry of Health and Family Welfare and the Directorate General of Health Services have very weak health policy planning and programme development divisions. At the state level, health policy planning and programme development divisions are either weak or non-existent. The most pressing and urgent need of the day is to establish and strengthen health policy planning and programme development divisions, both at the National and State Health Directorates.

Working groups are constituted by the Planning Commission before formulating a Five-Year Plan. Around eight working groups are set up for the health sector, covering major areas of health and population planning. At this stage, the quantity of resources earmarked for the health sector as a whole, or for the sub-sectors, is not specified. Therefore, the exercise tends to be need-based, and the outlays recommended by the working groups are usually much higher than what is ultimately available. This leads to great distortions when final outlays are fixed, as pro-rata reductions are usually made in the different programmes. What is really needed is a more realistic, need-based and resource-based planning exercise, emphasising proper priorities.

State Level Health Planning

Health is a state subject. Hence, the state should assume the major responsibility for health planning. Unfortunately, this has not happened. With excessive centralisation, states have become passive associates in planning. Even central guidelines are taken as directives, and no initiatives are visible. Only a very cursory and casual exercise takes place at the state level to formulate state health plans, inspite of the fact that most of the major states have State Planning Boards/Commissions. However, not a single State Planning Board/Commission has a worthwhile health planning division. It is important to realise that for meaningful socio-economic planning and development, health development is essential. This requires a separate socio-economic development division, within a state health planning unit. Health and health-related state institutions, like state institutions of health and family welfare and medical colleges, should be actively involved with state health planning units, in the formulation of realistic and relevant sub-district level, district level and state level plans.

Despite the fact that there is a Planning Commission at the central level and State Planning Boards/Commissions at the state government level, there is hardly any interaction between these institutions. It is strongly recommended that a half-yearly meeting of the Planning Commission and State Planning Boards is held regularly to discuss issues and problems related to development planning, including health planning. Moreover, the subject divisions of the Planning Commission should continually interact with state health planning subject units.

Decentralised Planning

The Planning Commission is supporting a project to develop models for district level planning in the Eighth Plan in three states—Andhra Pradesh, Maharashtra and Rajasthan. Enough data is now available from these states, as also from Tamilnadu and Orissa, about district level planning. It would be worthwhile to initiate decentralised planning from the bottom, since the Panchayati Raj system has already been introduced. Indeed, decentralised district planning should become the sheet-anchor for health planning during the Ninth Plan.

The Five-Year Plans of the central/state governments reflect the government's concerns with the macro perspective. These plans provide general directions and the necessary means for action; these need to be translated into micro-level action plans, so that the goals outlined in the Plan can be achieved. Moreover, centralised planning often does not take cognizance of the vital differences between health problems and health service delivery facilities existing in a given area. Uniform goals, solutions, targets, organisational framework and service delivery approaches are not suitable while addressing area-specific problems.

Although the district is the administrative unit for the implementation of all health programmes, its role in the planning of health services has remained limited. Traditionally, planning for health service development—both for the creation of a basic health infrastructure as well as for other programmes—has been performed at the national/state level. The development of a strong district health system, which can perform the task of need-based and resource-based planning, is a matter which requires the urgent attention of health administrators and planners.

At the state level, because of the fact that health is constitutionally a state subject, the planning and development of the state health services is supposed to be undertaken by the respective State Planning Boards/Commissions, within the totality of all the development plans of the state. However, this has not happened. The concept of district level planning exists only in policy documents. At the district level, the planning of all development activities *(including the health component)* should have been ensured. Unfortunately, this has not been done. A major gap in the effective implementation of primary health care, at the ground level, could well be the lack of decentralised health planning. A well-designed district health plan can prove to be an effective agent in the implementation of primary health care services and also cater to local needs and priorities.

District health planning should be emphasised for the following reasons:

- A district is an administratively manageable unit. It is small enough to be administered effectively and efficiently, and yet large enough to make it feasible to provide the components and technologies needed to support primary health care programmes.
- The district is the operational level at which government policies and strategies are translated into action. It is at this level that planning from the top and from the community can best be co-ordinated and integrated.
- The private sector is playing an increasingly important role in the delivery of health care, particularly curative care. Co-ordination between the government and private health care is possible and feasible at this level.
- In a district, it is possible to identify the population group which is at risk *(i.e. the underprivileged)* and decide on an action plan to support them.
- Communities can understand local problems and constraints at the district level. Appropriate action can be taken at this level to provide primary health care, and

match the available resources to the health needs of the community.

- Many key development sectors are represented at the district level; this facilitates inter-sectoral co-operation and the management of services.
- The district offers the greatest potential for developing balanced and appropriate intervention programmes.

Panchayats

Panchayats are an age-old institution. Recently, through the 73rd Constitutional Amendment Act, 1992, their powers have been considerably enhanced. One of the provisions of the Act is the establishment of a three -tier system of panchayats at the village, intermediate *(block)* and district level.

Panchayats have been assigned 29 rural development activities; some of these have a direct or indirect bearing on health. These include health and sanitation *(covering hospitals, PHCs and dispensaries)*, family welfare, drinking water, women and child development, the public distribution system and poverty alleviation programmes.

In states like Karnataka, West Bengal, Maharashtra and Madhya Pradesh, panchayats have already contributed immensely to improving health care facilities for the people. Such activities have received a further boost, as the Act now empowers village panchayats to prepare area plans for economic development and social justice (Jain 1993).

Various policy-makers and planners have attempted to identify the limitations of our earlier planning efforts. Kurien, for instance, observed (Kurien 1978). "A distinct failure of Indian planning is that it does not have links with the primary units. This does not mean that producer groups do not reach policy-makers. Some do... But Policy-makers have no way of reaching the 'target groups' among the primary units."

The working group of the Planning Commission on rural development, "keeping in view the potentiality of Panchayati Raj, (has) proposed that health infrastructure in the rural areas, is gradually but surely, made accountable to village panchayats, panchayat samitis and zila parishads" (Planning Commission 1996).

The focus has been on the strengths of panchayats. Their multi-faceted approach, individuality and problem-solving capabilities have been encouraged. The functions envisaged and performed by panchayats in the field of health and development are:

- Preparing area plans and allocating resources.
- Making the government health infrastructure accountable to panchayats.
- Empowering zila parishads to appoint *(and dismiss)* doctors.
- Involving and mobilising the community and encouraging community participation, in order to meet the health and development needs of the area.

If the first three above-stated functions of the panchayats are facilitated at the earliest, many of the health problems in the rural areas can be tackled at the primary level itself.

The Village Health Guide Scheme, which was introduced in 1977, has recently been reviewed. As per the recommendations, this scheme is being revived with certain major changes as the Panchayat Swasthya Sewa Scheme (PSSS).

The ultimate goal of the PSSS has been aptly summed up as "the first step towards enabling the people to organise and administer their own health services, with the active support of the government" (GOI 1995). The PSSS is to be administered, supervised and implemented by the village panchayat. It is envisaged that with the proper implementation of the PSSS, many of the existing health problems of the country will be addressed.

The development and growth of the PSSS have been proposed on the following lines.

> "In the Ninth Five-Year Plan, it is being initiated on a pilot basis in two districts of each state and one district of each Union Territory. The nucleus of the scheme will be a motivated social person from the village itself. She/he may be named the Panchayat Swasthya Sahayak (PSS) and should be selected by the village panchayat. She/he has to assist the panchayat in meeting the basic needs of health and act as a link between government health agencies and the people."

Various criteria have been laid down for the selection of a PSS. They should be local residents, socially acceptable and easily accessible. They should be motivated to provide social and development services in the area on a voluntary basis. Possible candidates include ex-army personnel, existing village health guides, retired government servants, post-masters and teachers, provided they are local residents. PSSs may be paid an honorarium and supplied with necessary materials—a durable kit and a manual. Supplies should be adequate, appropriate and available at all times.

There are many young women and men committed to improving the community, in terms of alleviating ill-health, poverty, illiteracy and fundamentalism. In Durg and Rajnandgaon districts of Madhya Pradesh, such committed people are known as 'janbhagidars' *(socially committed public participants or inside-change agents).* These janbhagidars have motivated individuals and groups *(like Yuva Mandals, Mahila Mandals and panchayats)* on issues like leprosy, iodine deficiency disorders, immunisation, polio, afforestation and literacy. Janbhagidars have also been able to destigmatise, demystify and demedicalise diseases like leprosy, by involving the entire community. In Maharashtra, 'Varkaree' as a group are highly socially motivated and active.

Community Participation in Primary Health Care

One of the key concepts of the primary health care approach in achieving *Health for All,* as expressed at Alma Ata in 1978, is community participation. The concept of community participation has now evolved to mean the process of empowerment of the people, by providing information, technical support and the potential for decision-making. This enables them to share the opportunities and responsibilities for action, in the interest of their own health.

Community participation does not imply that people respond to services which are planned and implemented from the outside. It means that people are fully involved in the whole process of planning, implementing, monitoring and reviewing health programmes. This is where the primary health care approach differs from traditional public health.

It is often asked: How can people participate in such a technical matter as health? The reality is that health ultimately depends on individual and community action. Almost 80 per cent of diseases are either preventable or are so simple that they can be solved without the assistance of a medical professional. No matter how good and efficient health services are, it is up to the individual or family to avail of health services. In short, people have to realise that they, rather than medical professionals, are the key actors in health. Moreover, medical professionals have to realise that health is a multi-professional discipline and depends on people's action. Adequate food, safe water, clean environment *(sanitation)*, good hygiene and health habits are the pillars of health. These are dependent on people—as individuals, families and communities. Therefore, *Health for All* cannot be achieved unless people are empowered and participate fully in health programmes.

Ultimately, community participation is about increasing individual and community control over people's own lives. Such an empowerment process is possible only if the health functionaries are empowered themselves, and do not see the village people or village organisation as a threat to their own power. Community empowerment, ultimately, is the devolution of power. Training health functionaries to share knowledge, in an empowering way, is important. Often health messages are restrictive rather than empowering. Medical and health functionaries often prevent the process of empowerment by mystifying information, or providing it only partially, so that people cannot process it themselves. To avoid this, medical and health functionaries need team training as facilitators.

It must be realised that community participation cannot be achieved quickly. Communities need to be developed and strengthened—this is a slow process. People also need to develop self-esteem and self-confidence. External facilitators need to encourage these traits.

For the sustainable achievement of *Health for All*, community participation is vital. It is also necessary as it lends itself to a dynamic process of development. In Jámkhed we have seen that, initially, communities addressed common issues such as immunisation, and emphasised maternal and child health services. As they continue to analyse their health situation, they have moved to newer areas such as women's health and cancer.

In terms of health, community participation means the ability to make informed health decisions and be an active participant in improving one's own health. It also means active participation in the health sector at the community and national level to create, influence and mobilise public opinion for improved public policy on health.

Role of Voluntary Organisations

Voluntary organisations have an important role to play in educating and sensitising the public in various aspects of health and sanitation. They can provide health services in areas where Government facilities are negligible.

While voluntary organisations can make the people realise the adage, *'prevention is better than cure'*, they definitely have an important role in lobbying for changes in health policies.

In rural areas, voluntary organisations can train local villagers as village health workers to provide basic health facilities.

Talking about the voluntary sector and health, Dr Mira Shiva says, "immediately after Independence, when the Government machinery was not even in place and meagre facilities were available for the health sector, a large number of voluntary efforts were responsible for providing basic health services. Of these the numerous Christian missionaries, Rama Krishna Mission and some Gandhian organisations provided the bulk of health services. There were also some charitable organisations who were involved in providing health care services."

With little state facilities, the organisations involved in providing health services had to face enormous problems in the early phase after Independence. With ignorance and superstition being the order of the day, many of these organisations had to tackle lot of challenges in motivating people in health care practices. This situation of having to make efforts to motivating the local community and even reaching out to them, sometimes in inaccessible areas, persisted for a long time.

The voluntary health effort has evolved in the following ways:

(a) Many organisations are running specialised community health programmes which include income-generation schemes for the poorer communities, for meeting their basic nutritional needs first and foremost.

(b) There are organisations running integrated development programmes. Health is taken as a part of these integrated development activities.

(c) Organisations working for the disabled are involved in rehabilitation programmes. Besides health care, the focus is also on education and empowerment.

(d) There are various groups which are involved in health research, critiquing Government policies, initiating

campaigns on issues such as drug policy, amniocentesis etc. and trying to make the people at large aware of various aspects of health.

One of the most successful campaigns initiated by voluntary organisations has been against baby food. "The campaign initiated by many voluntary groups in late 1970s has been considered most successful worldwide campaign. International organisations and also national organisations were intrinsically involved in this campaign and this resulted in the World Health Organisation formulating a baby food code. After a sustained campaign, the Government passed an Act regulating unethical marketing of commercial baby food," she informs. Organisations like consumer Guidance Society of India; Voluntary Health Association of India; Akash, Mumbai etc. were at the forefront of this campaign.

Another major campaign was against sex determination tests. Aminiocentesis had become one of the major issue by 1982. Patriarchal pressures had been the major cause of sex determination tests. In fact at a meeting convened in New Delhi in July 1982, a three-point position was arrived at wherein:

(a) the Government was requested to restrict the use of aminiocentesis to only teaching and research establishments;

(b) the Indian Medical Council was requested to take severe action against members indulging in unethical practices; and

(c) women's organisations were to remain vigilant against the spread of this practice for commercial purposes.

In fact many women were coerced into going for these tests.

The third major campaign initiated by voluntary organisations and health groups in the country was against use of irrational, hazardous and non-essential drugs. The campaign was focussed on use of rational drugs and strengthening of the quality control in medicines. The entire issue of combination drugs aimed to bluffing the people at large and the propaganda that certain brands are superior were the issues that were taken up by those involved in the campaign.

Another successful campaigns initiated by voluntary organisations and health groups was against the combination, 'hydrose-estrogenprogestrone'. The campaign initiated in 1982 was against the terotegenic effects of the combination in mothers. Use of this combination during pregnancy many a times resulted in congenital malformation. Also the same drug was being sold for entirely different cause.

Yet another campaign initiated was against the combination Chloramphenicol-Streptomycin which was administered to children for diarrohoea. The other campaign was against the use of the combination of vitamin B1, B6, and B12. A Public Interest Litigation was filed in 1993 and now the combination has been finally weeded out.

As part of its advocacy role, the voluntary organisations also need to work for changes in some health policies. For instance, the National Health Policy has not been reviewed since it was formulated in 1983. Also the voluntary organisations have a major role in exposing the scandals perpetuating in the health sector.

ENVIRONMENTAL SANITATION AND COMMUNITY WATER SUPPLY

Poor environmental sanitation and unsafe drinking water are major health problems in India. Water-related and sanitation-related infections account for between 60-80 per cent of all illnesses that occur in India. Moreover, many diseases like diarrhoea, dysentery, typhoid, intestinal helminthiasis, jaundice and cholera are endemic in various states of India.

The provision of safe drinking water and facilities for human excreta disposal were not priorities of national planning, especially in the rural areas, till the Fifth Five-Year Plan. Sanitation as a problem has not been tackled seriously in India; the rural areas have received very little attention.

Though a fair amount of progress has been achieved in terms of community water supply, health benefits have not been commensurate with the investments made, primarily because of the following three reasons:

- Community water supply projects have not been integrated with hygiene education and sanitation projects.
- Water quality surveillance has been totally neglected.
- People's participation, particularly that of women, has been lacking.

Historically, sanitation and community water supply have been given low priority by planners. Currently, less than 50 per cent of the urban population have a sanitary excreta disposal system, and less than 5 per cent of the rural population have safe excreta disposal facilities. Facilities for drainage, sullage and solid waste management are inadequate in urban and peri-urban areas, and almost non-existent in rural areas.

Over the years, the quality of these services has deteriorated due to the pressure of urbanisation, rapid population growth, mounting costs, the growing gap between the needs for these services and the resources of municipal bodies, and increasing managerial problems.

The sewerage services in urban areas are extremely poor. Currently, only about 200 cities and towns in India (out of a total of 3,245) have a sewerage system, and some of them only partially. Very few towns have sewage treatment plants. Most of these plants are badly maintained and are often out of operation.

In the rural areas, even elementary sanitary services are non-existent in most villages. Because of the extremely poor level of sanitation, it has been difficult to control infection, and soil-related and water-borne diseases, inspite of the substantial progress made in the area of water supply. For a majority of the rural population, defecation in the fields is the only form of sanitation. In 1990, it was estimated that less than 5 per cent of the rural population had access to sanitary facilities. Facilities for drainage and night soil *(foeces)* disposal are almost non-existent. As a result, there is large-scale soil and water pollution. This is one of the primary factors for the high prevalence of soil-related and water-borne diseases in rural areas.

Although the Rural Water Supply Programme and the Minimum Needs Programme were started during the Fifth Five-Year Plan period, the Rural Sanitation Programme was initiated only in the Seventh Five-Year Plan period (1985-90).

From 1985-86 up to the end of the Eighth Five-Year Plan, a total allocation of Rs. 29,774 lakhs was made under the Central Rural Sanitation Programme (CRSP), however, only Rs. 14,842 lakhs was utilised up to December 1995. During the same period, Rs. 41,416 lakhs was allocated under the Minimum Needs Programme, but only Rs. 30,625 lakhs was utilised. Mechanisms need to be put into effect to ensure that funds are released on time and fully utilised.

If the physical progress of the programme is viewed in terms of the number of latrines constructed, it can be seen that, till 1994-95, 22,32,167 latrines were constructed. Against a target of

7,60,187 latrines in 1995-96, till December 1995, only 3,15,325 latrines were constructed. These figures indicate that till today, the population covered by the government is less than 5 per cent. However, in actual terms, the total population covered by safe excreta disposal in the country is higher than what has been achieved through the efforts of the government. According to statistics on safe excreta disposal provided by the National Sample Survey, the population covered in various states is much higher. It ranges from 9 per cent in Bihar and Madhya Pradesh to 89 per cent in Assam in 1995 *(the all India figure is 21%)*. However, these figures are based on a very small sample size and cannot be considered reliable.

The present status of sanitation in the country, in the urban, peri-urban and rural areas, clearly indicates that the total coverage of the population in the country will remain a distant dream if the present government approach is continued. What is needed is a comprehensive community-based approach, with the total involvement of the people. As will be seen later, the mobilisation of funds and resources is not a serious problem, once the beneficiaries are made aware of the necessity and health benefits of sanitation facilities. A sustainable programme can only be developed with the active participation and contribution of the beneficiaries *(i.e. the people)*.

A considerable amount of funds would be required for the implementation of a rural sanitation programme which covers a major percentage of the rural population. Commission members are aware that one of the main reasons for the inadequate progress in this sector has been the lack of resource mobilisation. Perhaps the best option at present is to seriously consider the possibility of generation funds within the system. The details will have to be worked out, for example, who will provide these funds, how much and in what manner. The guidelines for monitoring and evaluating this new public investment pattern, in all its aspects, through well-established indicators, have also to be properly defined. Under the existing conditions, a realistic multipronged alternative should be considered. For instance:

- Substantial reduction in the cost of services through increased efficiency and the use of low-cost appropriate technologies.
- Mobilisation of additional funds from existing and new

sources, including the government, donors and users, and according higher priority to sanitation in the National Plan outlay.

- Incorporating user participation in cost sharing.

To make the programme a success there has to be a shift in approach to project planning. Because of financial constraints, there has to be a greater reliance on methods of cost recovery from the participating community. This approach is feasible because a number of users are willing to pay, provided the services are appropriate and even desirable, since it encourages the users to develop a feeling of ownership. It also brings into effect a system of decentralisation. The successful implementation of sanitation projects in Midnapore district of West Bengal has proved that the community can and will bear the cost of sanitation, if a sense of ownership is created in them through effective IEC *(information, education and communication)* intervention. This new concept of community management *(rather than just encouraging voluntary labour)* aims at assigning the role of controlling their own systems to the community itself; this encourages decision-making, creativity and builds self-esteem.

This obviously means that the community should be prepared to assume new responsibilities. In some states of India, where a three-tier system exists *(anchal panchayats, panchayat samitis and zilla parishads)*, the community is satisfactorily equipped with the required technical resources to take up this new challenge. Mobilising funds from the users themselves, rather than providing them from a Central government source, is seen to encourage a more effective and sustainable utilisation of resources. For example, because revenues are dependent on user payment, user cost recovery can ensure greater responsiveness to user preferences. There will, therefore, be a greater chance that investments will be more closely oriented to consumer demand, and the level of services chosen will be utilised by the communities concerned. However, the generation of resources under such conditions requires evaluation and finding lower cost options to suit the economic conditions of the people.

This, in turn, will increase the likelihood of long-term financial sustainability. Cost recovery from users can also be more effective in ensuring better operation and maintenance services than centrally-provided subsidies, since there is a closer match between the service provided and the revenue generated. As part of an overall pricing policy, user cost recovery can also ensure less wastage of resources.

It must be pointed out here that considering the extreme poverty of the weaker sections of the rural community, an element of subsidy/loan might be required. A rational cost-sharing and financial management strategy needs to be worked out, between the state government agencies, village panchayat samitis and the beneficiaries. The concept of a revolving fund could also be adopted, which could be operated through local voluntary organisations or panchayats. Rural co-operative banks can also play an active role in this programme.

It is now an accepted fact that the generation of funds alone will not solve the problem of running a sanitation programme. Appropriate low-cost technology must also be adopted. The choice of appropriate technology is crucial. Within the afore-mentioned framework, there is adequate scope of variations in design, materials and accessories to suit the financial capacities of different communities in various states.

One of the basic steps to improve rural sanitation is the proper and safe disposal of human excreta, with a view to controlling faecal-borne diseases which cause morbidity, debility and death. Inadequate and improper disposal of human excreta pollutes the soil, ponds, canals, rivers and wells. This results in:

- The increased prevalence of ankylostomiasis and ascariasis due to soil pollution.
- An increase in water-borne diseases like typhoid, dysentery, infective hepatitis, cholera and diarrhoea, because of the contamination of water supply sources.
- Greater incidence of fly-borne diseases due to the contamination of food by flies, which breed in and have access to open excreta.

The most satisfactory arrangement is to have a hygienic toilet system which does not allow the soil or the water source to get polluted or let vermin and flies have access to the excreta. A latrine is regarded as sanitary when the collection and disposal of night soil is done hygienically.

Planners, programme implementors and above all, users can choose from a wide range of latrines. The ultimate success of low-cost sanitation lies in its full utilisation. This largely depends on its acceptability by the users. At the same time, the system should be technically sound and dependable. The main considerations for identifying the right latrine are:

- The system should be liked by the community.
- The system should be in harmony with the social habits, local culture and customs of the community.
- The system must be affordable for the users *(low-cost for the poor)*.
- Technology should be user friendly and local materials and artisans should be optimally utilised.

Recently Sulabh Shauchalayas have become extremely popular as community latrines. Once they have been constructed and commissioned, they are self-sustaining. Sulabh Shauchalayas are suitable for both rural and urban areas.

Industrial Waste: Industrial waste is usually disposed or drained out of the factory area without being properly treated. Consequently, the land on which it is disposed can no longer be used for any kind of agricultural purpose; it also becomes a health hazard for the local population. Industrial waste gradually permeates into the soil and contaminates the ground water. When such water is drawn out and supplied to the public as drinking water, it causes health problems. In many areas, industries are located near rivers, and industrial wastes are discharged directly into the river. All effluents and industrial wastes must be treated before being removed from the factory area.

River Pollution: Human habitations are usually found near rivers. Many cities, small and medium towns, usually discharge their sewerage and other waste water into the river directly, without any treatment. People throw solid waste, half-burnt dead bodies and animal carcasses into rivers. These practices pollute the water and are a health hazard. They should be vigorously discouraged.

When Rajiv Gandhi was the Prime Minister, the Ganga Action Plan was taken up to cleanse the Ganga river water. The Centre provided funds to the state governments of Bihar, Uttar Pradesh and West Bengal *(states through which the river flows)*, and to the municipal corporations and towns situated on the banks of the Ganga. The cleaning operations started well but slowed down later due to various reasons, like delay in the release of funds, fund diversion and improper programme planning and implementation.

Hospital Waste: Huge quantity of hospital waste are accumulated by hospitals and nursing homes in urban areas, rural hospitals, community health centres, primary health centers, sub-centres, etc. Hospital waste is a potent source of infection and hence, should be properly disposed of.

Waste Water: The disposal of waste water is a problem in slum areas of cities and towns, and villages. In these places, stagnant pools of waste water and garbage around huts and houses are a common sight. They provide a breeding ground for mosquitoes and flies. Very little has been done to alleviate problem, either by educating the people or by showing them how to hygienically dispose sewage water and domestic garbage.

There is an urgent need to take up these problems and demonstrate the advantage of soakage pits, the proper use of waste water in kitchen gardens, composting, etc.

Present Status of Community Water Supply

Presently, although more than 90 per cent of the population have community water supply facilities, health benefits have not been commensurate with the investment made. The main reasons for this are—the desired standard of personal hygiene has been adequately maintained, lack of water quality surveillance, poor maintenance and lack of community participation.

Rural Scenario

India has one of the highest coverage figures for rural water supply in south-east Asia. However, because of its huge population, India accounts for 60 per cent of the total number of unserved people, in terms of water supply, in the region. Globally, 13 per cent of the total unserved population of the world is in India.The statewise figures for villages not covered, partly covered and fully covered by community water supply. As on April 1, 1995, out of 13,18,699 habitations, 8,18,130 were fully covered by community water supply, 3,83,140 were partly covered and 1,17,429 did not have any community water supply. This means that more than 90 per cent of the rural population have access to clean water. According to the projected figures of the Ministry of Rural Development, by April 1, 1996, only 64,987 habitations are expected to remain uncovered (*i.e. almost 95 per cent of the rural population will be fully or partly covered by community water supply*).

It is heartening to note that the basic norms for defining the desirable distance from a safe drinking water source are being revised. It has now been stipulated that a water supply source should serve a maximum of 150 people. The maximum distance that people need to travel for water has now been reduced from 1.6 km to 1 km in the plains and 50 metres in hilly terrains. The quantity of water being supplied remains the same, at 40 litres per person per day.

However, the statistics and figures of population coverage are often misleading. Many of the tubewells and handpumps constructed under government programmes breakdown or remain out of operation for very long periods. Consequently, people are forced to obtain water from unsafe water sources. Moreover, even where a handpump is functioning, the present norm of one handpump for 250 people or within a distance of 1.6 km, cannot ensure adequate water for a family. Often water for most domestic purposes, except drinking, is collected from grossly polluted ponds. As a result, the endemicity of diarrhoeal and enteric diseases and other water-related infections continues unabated. Epidemics now occur almost annually. A study conducted by UNICEF in 1992, covering 15 districts of the country, reported that handpumps and borewells are the primary source of drinking water for 40 per cent of the population. While traditional open wells served about 27 per cent of the people, 5 per cent were still collecting drinking water from exposed sources like rivers, lakes and ponds.

As in most developing countries, in India too, it is the women who are responsible for collecting water and managing its household use. According to a study conducted in 1989, women in rural India spend between one and four hours a day collecting water. On an average, they make nine trips to water sources, and collect 192 litres of water for a six-member household. The impact of carrying water on the health status of women could be very serious, especially during pregnancy.

Public water supply managed by municipal bodies caters to the urban population of most cities and towns. However, the amount varies widely, from 40 liters per head per day to 200 litres per head per day. Even within municipal towns, the population living in slums and some of the poorer sections do not have access to adequate water supply. In cities like Calcutta, Delhi and Mumbai, the affluent sections have the luxury of multiple taps; the slum population struggles to fetch water from street water taps that are inadequate in number and unevenly distributed. Most urban water supply systems, except in the metro cities, do not have any system of water quality monitoring or surveillance. As a result, water distribution systems are often a potent instrument for carrying pathogenic micro-organisms. In cities with intermittent water supply and underground sewerage, the water distribution system is often contaminated with faeces, and results in the spread of water-related and excreta-related diseases like hepatitis, typhoid and diarrhoea.

While all surface water sources (*like rivers, lakes and ponds*) are highly polluted with faecal matter, the ground water in many parts of the country is contaminated with fluoride (*Andhra Pradesh, Gujarat, Maharashtra and Rajasthan*), nitrate (*Rajasthan*) and arsenic (*West Bengal*). The increased use of pesticides and fertilisers in agriculture and the indiscriminate discharge of toxic effluents and hazardous solid wastes are increasing the danger of ground water pollution. In the absence of essential facilities for water quality monitoring and surveillance in rural areas, the population is seriously exposed to the risk of ground water contamination, with resultant impact on community health. Arsenic poisoning has been reported in West Bengal.

In India, financial and technical support to the urban and rural water supply systems is provided by the Central government, through the Ministry of Agriculture. However, the planning, design, construction, operation and maintenance of urban and rural water supply systems, (including laboratories for process control) are undertaken by the Public Health Engineering Departments (PHEDs) and the Water Supply and Drainage Boards of the respective state governments.

The metropolitan cities have their own water supply system and laboratories for testing and monitoring the quality of water. However, no institutional framework exists for the Water Quality Surveillance Programme (*incorporating different components, like continuous monitoring, sanitary surveys, data processing and evaluation of intersectoral co-ordination*), either in urban or rural areas. Even rudimentary facilities for water quality monitoring are not available in peri-urban, suburban and rural areas.

Unfortunately, the importance of this vital function in the overall management of drinking water supply systems is often not realised by concerned authorities and beneficiaries, the reasons being—administrative limitations, lack of government support and public apathy.

Under the National Drinking Water Mission, water-testing laboratories are being established at the district, state and regional level. The function of the regional centres is to provide guidance to PHEDs on various important aspects. However, progress has not been satisfactory. There is an urgent need to expeditiously establish laboratories at all levels to perform the following functions:

- Identification and assessment of existing laboratory facilities and needs.
- Strengthening existing laboratory facilities at different levels.
- Establishment of new district level water quality testing laboratories and the procurement of hardware.
- Water quality surveillance.
- Organising programmes for manpower training and awareness campaigns.
- Co-ordination with the PHEDs, water boards, zilla parishads, primary health centres, research and development agencies and university departments.
- Motivating people's participation through schools/ colleges, national social service organisations, and national and local voluntary organisations.

The strategy adopted for the speedy and systematic implementation of the programme is through the establishment of state level, district level and village level centres, each entrusted with well-defined activities. So far, however, the progress of these schemes has not been satisfactory.

The organisational set-up and routine water quality monitoring and surveillance should ensure the supply of safe and protected water to the community in urban, peri-urban and rural areas. The cost involved in routine surveillance and quality control would be a fraction of the capital and maintenance costs of big urban systems, where the existing laboratories can carry out the programme. The situation in peri-urban and rural areas is different.

In these places, there are a large number of small systems spread over large areas, which are often remotely located.

The universal goal of water quality surveillance is to safeguard and protect public health, through the supply of safe and protected drinking water to the community, at all times. Implementation, operation, maintenance and surveillance are different functions, which are generally undertaken by separate agencies of the government or autonomous bodies. In allocating responsibilities to the various agencies, the needs of the community should be kept in view. Operation and maintenance should be entrusted to an engineering agency, such as the PHEDs or Water Boards; water quality monitoring should be under the Public Health Department; the surveillance programme, as a whole, should be managed by inter-sectoral co-ordination.

In view of financial constraints, it would be prudent to begin with a basic level surveillance programme and establish its utility and acceptability at the administrative and community level. The programme should develop from a modest but effective and useful service to the community, and grow alongwith other activities. As was the case in many of the developing countries, it should not begin as a lofty scheme with sophisticated laboratory facilities, only to be abandoned later.

While surface water sources like rivers and lakes are serving big cities and towns through a distribution network, most rural habitations depend on ground water sources like handpumps, tube-wells and open wells. Ground water is not readily available in many parts of the country due to the presence of hard rock.

In the north, below the Himalayas, three large rivers—the Indus, Ganga and Brahmaputra—supply a vast alluvial plain with an abundance of water. The central and southern part of the country consists of a peninsular slab, where the surface water is scarce or seasonal, and the ground water is deep and difficult to reach. In recent years, the ground water levels have been further affected in drought-prone areas and in places where there has been over pumping for agricultural and industrial needs. Some of the states where severe ground water depletion is reported are Andhra Pradesh, Gujarat, Madhya Pradesh, Rajasthan and Uttar Pradesh.

UNICEF has provided substantial help to the Indian government for drilling wells in hard rock areas and developing appropriate handpumps. However, a proper maintenance system for these handpumps needs to be organised.

The present level of community water supply in urban and rural areas suggests that India might achieve the goal of assured access to safe water supply by the year 2000 AD, in terms of population and habitation covered by the Community Water Supply Scheme. However, a great deal of work remains to be done before everyone has access to adequate safe and clean water, close to their home. It is necessary to bring the water point closer, reduce the number of users per hand pump, and make more water available for sanitary purposes. It is also necessary to implement the Community Water Supply Scheme with active community participation, through panchayats and village level voluntary organisations, and train the villagers in village level operations and maintenance.

Human Resource Development

Although much of the earlier scepticism about the drinking water and sanitation programme was focussed on the question of availability of adequate funds the experience of many of the developing countries suggests that the greatest impediment to progress is not so much the lack of funds as the ability to utilise them properly. The efforts required to train sufficient manpower to design and construct necessary facilities, and to operate and maintain them, is no less challenging than generating the financial resources required. Equally challenging is the task of securing the support and participation of the community in the programme.

Human resource development activities which support the National Sanitation and Water Supply Programme should have two basic elements:

- A long-term educational programme for the community in general. It is necessary to inform the people about the demerits of bad sanitation and unsafe drinking water, as well as the merits of personal hygiene, good sanitary facilities and the consumption of safe drinking water.
- A short-term training programme, particularly for the staff of implementing agencies.

The success of any national programme depends largely on how well education and training needs are anticipated, and how well the authorities manage to impart appropriate education to a sufficient number of its citizens and specific training to the required number of programme implementors. The critical role that an effective educational and training system plays in sector development is substantiated by the experiences of a number of countries.

It is amply clear that the educational and training needs of a National Sanitation and Water Supply programme must take into consideration the strengths and weaknesses of the existing local educational system, and its institutional capacity for training. Formal education in schools and colleges, technical education at the graduate and postgraduate level, job-specific continuing education etc., have to be planned to take care of the needs of the sector in a complementary way.

Social Mobilisation

The problem of rural water supply and sanitation is further complicated by a number of social and attitudinal problems. A large percentage of the rural population is economically poor, educationally backward, and socially unorganised. One of the fundamental reasons for the failure of the rural sanitation programme in the past has been the failure to involve the people and design a system in keeping with their attitude and customs.

Water and sanitation schemes can no longer be viewed simply as engineering projects; they must be considered as projects in social intervention, requiring co-operation and counselling of the intended beneficiaries, particularly in unserved areas. Women need special consideration in the planning of water and sanitation projects. Local customs governing their position in the home and society, and their relative seclusion are factors that need to be taken into consideration.

Water, Sanitation and Health: Need for an Integrated Approach

When addressing the problem of improving sanitation and water supply in the villages, one must first establish the basic objectives of such activities. The primary objective is, of course, to raise the health status of the community. In purely scientific and technical terms, it has been amply demonstrated that the installation of a water supply mechanism in a community only partially improves its existing health status. If the full benefits are to be realised, then sanitation, hygiene in the home, changes in attitude and health education are also necessary. Almost all diseases in the water-borne category depend on exposure of human waste to water and food. Hence, the rate of infection may be reduced by improving waste disposal measures and water supply. A 1964 report by the Ministry of Health clearly indicated that the installation of water supply, without waste water disposal, merely results in a shift from one dominant set of diseases to another. It would be counter-productive, from the point of view of community health, to increase the community water supply level, without simultaneously improving environmental sanitation facilities, particularly human excreta disposal and drainage.

Based on the foregoing analysis, it is recommended that human resource development activities in support of the National Sanitation and Water Supply Programme should be an integrated package. It should cover community water supply, sanitation *(human excreta, waste water and garbage disposal)* and personal hygiene.

ECOLOGICAL DEGRADATION AND HEALTH

It is a well-known fact that poverty and ecological degradation coexist. In places where ecological degradation has set in, one usually finds a large section of poor in the society. Accumulation of wealth in areas marked by a poor natural resource base is usually based on capital input from the outside. So where there is little external input and high dependence on a degrading natural eco-system, poverty is extensive and consequently, ill-health common. Ill-health and ecological degradation lead to a downward poverty cycle. These relations are ubiquitous in South countries and India is no exception.

It is difficult, however, to link ecological degradation and ill-health in conventional research, because of a lack of consistency in distribution of income in any given geographic region. However, it is fair to say that where ecological health is poor, there is general ill-health. For example, in the case of flood-prone areas *(like parts of eastern India)*, there is a high degree of water inundation and waterlogging *(high water-table)*, leading to conditions resulting in high morbidity (Sen and Kirkos 1995). Even in epidemiological studies of flood-prone areas, these relationships are generally not brought out clearly, inspite of recent advances in environmental epidemiology and medical geography. It is self-evident to those familiar with these communities that inner health conditions and outer enviornmental conditions are related. One can observe seasonal variations in health. It is important, therefore, to adopt a new analytical understanding of the linkages between environment and health on an individual and community basis (South-South Solidarity 1996).

Research on the subject has tried to prove the spread and extent of ecological degradation through a large number of case studies, situational analyses, environmental studies, etc. (Carr-Harris 1992). Some of these studies are summarised here.

Broadly, three different archetypes can be drawn from different development strata:

- In remote tribal areas, where large-scale deforestation has taken place, ill-health of the tribal community is usually related to malnutrition, on the one hand, and pollution, on the other. Malnutrition can be directly related to poor ecological health (Menon 1994, Sen 1995, Chatterjee). High levels of tuberculosis, for instance, is found in the Shivpuri areas of Gwalior district. The majority of tribals are landless and have also been denied access to forest produce—their survival base. Malnutrition of this kind also exists in Orissa and has been documented extensively (Ali and Das). These conditions of ill-health are shown to be a direct result of the lack of access to land and forests and the inability to capture water resources. In addition, the industrialisation taking place in rural areas because of available resources, cheap labour, etc., often goes unmonitored, resulting in high levels of pollution. Malnutrition, compounded by pollution causes a tremendous imbalance in tribal populations.
- Small-scale farming in non-productive areas of the country, which can adequately produce food at or above subsistence level, face two kinds of environmental hazards. These are either from external sources *(i.e. the contamination of water resources by factories)*, which affects their cropping; or through the extensive use of pesticides/chemicals, introduced with intensive cropping. Both degrade the soil structure and destroy the land's productivity.

- In an urbanised setting, the environmental hazards faced by the inhabitants are related to population density, lack of sanitary conditions, excessive pollution generated by small factories/enterprises within the slum, etc. It is the poor that often live close to the most hazardous factories. This has a cumulative effect, which is compounded by ill-health owing to the general quality of life. Unlike middle class communities, poor people have no buffers against a hazardous enviornment (Basu 1992, Carr-Harris 1994, D'Silva 1993).

These three archetypes provide us with an understanding of the relationship between environmental degradation and ill-health, and illustrate the magnitude of the problem.

The environmental policy and programmes being implemented today, have not adequately considered health and other social costs. Whether this is the result of the inherent bias among our policy-makers, who believe that the environment is merely an external, physical entity, with only a functional or economic bearing on people, is a matter of debate. What is important is that infrastructural projects that are sanctioned, even after impact assessment studies, might actually be leading to an increase in morbidity and mortality in the area. To counteract these shortcomings in environmental policy and planning, many green activists and ecologists are calling for an entire new thrust to India's development. They cite the example of costly catastrophes like Bhopal and Chernobyl, to justify the need to curtail India's industrial growth, in favour of a more long-term and sustainable production system.

Obviously, these macro-changes are complicated by India being a newly industrialised nation, which must follow a path different from countries at the peak of industrial growth. With an abundance of raw materials and cheap labour, India can ill-afford to exclusively regard the Western brand of environmental measures as beneficial, for instance, introducing high technology equipment into industrial processes, so as to decrease waste. This may, in fact, have a negative effect on employment and overall productivity. Environmental health must safeguard against the deleterious effects of industrialisation on the people, without compromising the imperatives of India's economic development. Another shortcoming of the current environmental perspective is the tendency to look upon the environment as a set of finite natural resources rather than an integrated, physical and social setting in which people live. This bias is the result of the reductionist approach to environmental sciences. Over the last decade, we have been fortunate in witnessing the emergence of an alternative school of environmental thinking in India, which has raised the notion of the 'sociology of the environment'. This has enabled us to gain a better understanding of the environment's effect on the changing health status *(although little work has been carried out so far),* specifically on the impact of degenerating eco-systems on people's health.

Health Perspective on Environmental Hazards

There is ample literature on the social and cultural aspects of a 'demedicalised health system'. This notion became commonplace after the promotion of community health in the South countries in the seventies. However, limited attention has been paid to the environmental aspects of health promotion and preventive health. Generally, health sociologists tend to view the 'environment' as either synonymous with 'sanitation', and so can be easily 'managed'; or with the 'physical condition of poverty'. The latter view results in their limiting the options available to the poor and subsistence level people, thereby restricting possible changes in their environment. Both these views of the environment projected by health specialists need to be explored and reviewed.

If health planning is to include certain environmental hazards, it cannot continually reduce 'environment' to the physical condition of a particular disease. We have learned, for example, over the past three-and-half decades, that the elimination of malaria cannot be achieved by the annihilation of pest carriers and parasites. Had that been the case, the serve outbreak of more virulent strains of malaria *(post-1977),* would not have occurred, even after two decades of systematic spraying of DDT and other organophosphates. Instead, we have to view the environment as an 'eco-system' or 'habitat'. It was with this in mind that in the eighties, the Vector Control Research Centre in Pondicherry was able to pioneer methods in the area of bio-environmental control. These methods were successful in reducing the endemic malaria population.

Another lesson learned in our review of the health perspective is that the environment should not be equated with 'a set of unhygienic practices'. This view has gained ground as a result of increasing collaboration and technology transfer between Western countries and India, particularly programmes concerning water and sanitation. With regard to cleanliness, purification and hygiene, there are age-old beliefs in Indian tradition and culture which must be perceived in their proper socio-cultural context. A healthy environment involves not only hygiene but an integrated system of physical and social relations.

Because our health conditions are an integral part of our environment, we cannot always assume that ill-health is manifested by disease. Rather, ill-health is usually a condition of weakness or stress, and regardless of the symptoms, there is an accompanying loss of 'balance' owing to the change in the environment. It is important to diagnose and reverse this weakening process before serious consequences follow. With an understanding of a person's changing environment, the risk of health hazards can be significantly reduced.

New Dimensions of Eco-health

As indicated above, the environment in which we live is an eco-system or an integration of physical and social relations. Therefore, the conditions of ill-health are usually the result of a multiplicity of events; a correlation between the 'environment' and 'ill-health' is not easy. Scientists determine environmental factors through clinical testing of the disease and its casual agents, but this is only half the story. What is necessary is to look at some of the social and physical dimensions, in order to establish preventive health measures. It is through such an exercise that we can identify some of the environments that are directly related to ill-health.

The magnitude of the pollution problem in the country has compelled the Central Pollution Control Board (CPCB) to involve voluntary organisations and other citizens' groups in its planning and monitoring programmes. There is an implicit recognition that both the CPCB and the State Pollution Boards have been ineffectual. Efforts are being made at handling out water-testing kits and other devices. Although this may be a useful intervention, it is not in itself sufficient. Unless people are activated to seek redressal on urban pollution, the magnitude of the problem will become greater.

The only way to get advocacy started on industrial pollution is to relate the hazard to the people's eco-system. Once the people are convinced that their eco-system has a value, i.e. it is their own, they will be able to perceive the value of an eco-system's health as a campaign issue. In general, people are motivated to redress pollution, if it impinges on their family's well-being or on their livelihood; and they if can relate environmental hazards, not only to the results of industrialisation but also to the effect it has on the eco-system, which gives them succour and life.

Popular action must be accompanied by interventions from voluntary organisations, labour leaders, researchers and government officials. These groups need to give importance to community-based education that emphasises environmental hazards in the community. If we continue to focus on the effects of occupational and environmental hazards on organic species alone, we may miss some of the most devastating hazards.

The worst environmental hazards of the next few decades can be respresented not as events, rather, they will be related to the lowering of the productive capacity of any given ecosystem to regulate itself. This type of destruction needs to be considered at every stage of policy planning, particularly in the planning of India's industrial growth.

In adopting eco-system health practices, it is necessary that environmental hazards are equated with a population, in terms of local environmental conditions as a reference. This will mean that reconstructing an eco-system will be in complete consonance with the majority of people's needs. There are already many campaigns against pollution around the country that are not linked up or properly documented. Two examples of these are the leather tanneries in Kanpur and the Dhenkanal thermal *(coal)* power plant. Each of these require different advocacy programmes.

The Indian government is gradually accounting for the environmental damage being wrought by infrastructural development projects. In the last decade, the costs to the environment have been factored into the cost-benefit analysis in the planning system. This is based on the recognition that deleterious effects to the environment may result in the loss of human lives and immense destruction of the resource base on which most industrial production depends. Consequently, before the construction of factories, thermal power plants, dams, mines or stone quarries, or prior to any development which might affect forests, the Ministry of Environment and Forests must give its sanction. Yet, this does not sufficiently consider the impact, social costs or the adverse health conditions, created by large-scale infrastructural development projects.

In the Narmada case, for instance, the assessment of the health aspects was marginal. If a large-scale impact assessment study gives scant regard to public health, then the fate of lesser known and more poorly assessed projects can well be imagined.

When in the mid-eighties, Dr. S. Moudgal, Director of the Impact Assessment Division of the Ministry of Environment drew up guidelines on impact assessment of river valley projects, he described health problems as the outcome of changes in water velocity, temperature and other physical properties. No mention was made of the social, cultural or economic impact, except with respect to some of the relocation requirements. When one considers the dimensions of the Narmada river valley project, it is surprising that the impact of the changed environment in altering household economics, and hence the health status of individuals, was not considered at all. Village Parveta in Gujarat, where rehabilitation has taken place, is a case in point. Thirty six deaths were recorded over a period of two years, attributable to the unusually high incidence of diarrhoea, dysentery, nutritional deficiency, etc. this, perhaps, was in part due to the fact that the community had to adapt to an area where cultivation was more difficult.

In sum, environmental impact assessment does not sufficiently take into account the social costs *(including health)* of infrastructural development projects. Nor have we reached the stage where we fully understand the irreparable damage that such projects can cause to the environment and long-term health status of the people.

Over the past two decades, the government has launched a large number of environmental health programmes. Although a vast amount of financial resources have been allocated, the schemes are usually not well-executed unless local groups and voluntary organisations are involved in mobilising the people and assisting in their awareness programmes. Some examples are:

- Ganga Action Plan—reducing water pollution in the Ganga.
- Malaria Control Programme—using bio-organic techniques in malaria eradication.
- Water Technology Mission—providing safe drinking water to water-scarce villages, etc.

4

NGOs and Environmental Protection

MAINSTREAM AND GRASS-ROOTS ENVIRONMENTAL GROUPS

There are many types of environmental groups working at the local, state, national, and international levels. These groups generally fall into two categories: mainstream and grass-roots.

Mainstream environmental groups are active mostly at the national level and to a lesser extent at the state level. Often they form coalitions to work together on issues. Mainstream groups do important work within the system and have been major forces in persuading Congress to pass environmental laws. However, if they become too dependent on high salaries, large budgets, and donations from Earth-degrading businesses, they can end up spending too much time and money on fund-raising (in competition with other mainstream environmental groups). They can also have their goals corrupted by lobbyists and lose touch with ordinary people and nature.

The base of the environmental movement in the United States and in other countries consists of thousands of grass-roots groups of citizens who have organized to protect themselves from pollution and environmental damage at the local level. The motto of such groups is *think globally and act locally.* They take to the streets, forests, oceans, and other frontline sites to stop environmental abuse, make harmful activities economically unattractive, and raise public awareness about environmental abuse and the need for change.

Many local grass-roots organizations are unwilling to compromise or negotiate. Instead of dealing with environmental goals and abstractions, they are fighting perceived threats to their lives, the lives of their children and grandchildren, and the value of their property. They want pollution and environmental degradation stopped and prevented rather than merely controlled. They are inspired by the words of eco-activist Edward Abbey: "At some point we must draw a line across the ground of our home and our being, drive a spear into the land, and say to the bulldozers, earthmovers, and corporations, 'this far and no further.' "

Scientific groups and non-governmental organizations (NGOs) have played a major role in the environmental movement from its start. Scientists have served society by their contribution to the development of agriculture, forestry, public health and other measures that have improved the human condition. They were also among the first to point out evidence of significant environmental risks and changes resulting from the growing intensity of human activities. Interactions between scientists, citizen groups and other NGOs, and the media, created an increasing public awareness of environmental issues. This, in turn, created political pressures that stimulated Governments to act.

There are many types of environmental groups. Small ones are organized locally to fight local problems, often environmental distruption—immediate or potential—from pollution or some apparently inappropriate form of development. Others deal with a special issue, but on a national scale. There are many examples in developed and developing countries. Some now enjoy great public credibility. Groups objecting to the construction of nuclear facilities in their neighbourhoods or countries have been active in the United States of America, the United Kingdom, the Federal Republic of Germany, Austria, Sweden, and other countries. In India, the Kerala-based People's Science Organization Kerala Sastra Sahitya Parishad (KSSP) blocked a hydro-clectric project in the Silent Valley, one of India's few remaining rain forests. The *Mitti Bachao Abhiyan* in Central India raised questions about the ecological and economic usefulness of canal irrigation in raising food production. Relief efforts after the 1984 Bhopal tragedy engaged the talents and resources of a wide variety of non-governmental groups, among them KSSP, the Delhi Science Forum, the Medico

Friend Circle, and the Lawyers' Collective. A by-product of citizen activism in Bhopal is a new appreciation among those groups of the need to combine technical, political, and legal strategies in fighting for a cleaner and safer environment. In India, there are more than 350 NGOs working in the environmental field.

Other national NGOs are primarily concerned with the use of the environment and who should benefit from it. Some have been described as "sustainable development" or "appropriate technology" groups. Women have played a particularly important part in many of them. The Chipko Movement in India, is one important example. Historically, philosophically and organizationally, it is extension of traditional Gandhian non-violent protests that took place to protest against villagers being denied access to the forests and their products, under the Forest Acts imposed by the British in 1878 and 1927. The link was provided by two remarkable women, Gandhi's close European associates, Mira and Sarla Behn. They made a major contribution to the growth of ecological consciousness and to raising the status of women in the hills of Uttar Pradesh, and generated a new brand of Gandhian activists. Throughout the 1970s, local people—largely, but not exclusively, women—stopped the felling of their forests by outside contractors, often by hugging the trees ("chipko" means "to embrace"). Chipko's demand that the Himalayan forests should be declared protected forests was recognized at the highest level. Mrs. Indira Gandhi recommended a 15-year ban on commercial green felling in such Himalayan forests in Uttar Pradesh. Unlike the original protests against the Forest Act, Chipko has an ecological base: it arose from alarming signals of rapid ecological destabilization when water sources dried up, landslides increased and food production fell as the trees were cut down, and it has evolved into a demand for ecological rehabilitation. The Movement insists that producing "soil, water and oxygen" rather than timber or resin is the main purpose of the forests. But it has shown that, under proper popular control, they can also provide fuel, fodder, small timber and fertilizer for local people while being preserved.

The Green Belt Movement was set up by the National Council of Women of Kenya in 1977. Identifying forest losses as among the most serious causes of soil erosion and land degradation in the country, it helps communities to set up "green belts" of atleast 1,000 trees each. There are now more than 1,000 green belts and some 20,000 "mini-green belts" in farmers' fields and about 65 community tree nurseries run by women's groups. There are similar movements in a number of countries, such as Mexico, Sri Lanka, Indonesia, and the Philippines, all supported by people struggling for their livelihoods and linked to sustainable objectives.

In developed countries, women have often been the first to lead protests against air and water pollution, the dumping of wastes and the establishment of some industrial installations in their neighbourhood. For example, in Sweden more women than men are against nuclear power. Women in the United States, Federal Republic of Germany and other countries have participated actively in campaigns against nuclear power. the dumping of hazardous wastes and the use of some chemicals. Women have also played an important role in environmental education and in increasing public awareness of different environmental issues. Actresses, writers, politicians and scientists have led campaigns for wildlife conservation and environmental protection.

Many countries have influential broad-interest NGOs, which campaign on many separate environmental issues, as well as single-issue groups. Among the better known are the Natural Resources Defense Council and Environmental Defense Fund in the United States, Sahabat Alam in Malaysia, Grupo do los Cien in Mexico, Bund in the Federal Republic of Germany, Italia Nostra, and the Danish Nature Protection Society. During the 1970s and 1980s, there has been increasing co-ordination among national NGOs (in some cases even the merging of NGOs or the creation of coalitions, such as Wildlife Link in the United Kingdom to tackle important national problems.

There is similar co-operation across international boundaries to deal with regional or global issues. This may be said to have begun in 1948 with the foundation of the International Union for the Protection of Nature (later the International Union for Conservation of Nature and Natural Resources (IUCN), which is unique in having a membership comprising over 60 Governments, 130 government agencies and 350 national and international NGOs. Several NGOs, such as Friends of the Earth, Greenpeace, and World Wide Fund for Nature (WWF) comprise many national affiliates. The Nuclear Free Pacific Movement has been an umbrella under which many groups have met and taken steps to halt nuclear activities in the Pacific. Their activities were instrumental in accelearating the conclusion in November 1986 of the Convention on the Protection of the Natural Resources and Environment of the south Pacific Region within the framework of the UNEP regional seas programme: the parties to the Convention agreed to prohibit the dumping or disposal of radioactive wastes in or under the ocean, as part of a wide-ranging agreement to protect the environment of the region. The European Environmental Bureau (EEB) brings together NGOs from all over the European Economic Community (EEC) to work with the European Commission and member Governments, while the recently established African NGOs Environment Network (ANEN) co-ordinates the activities of African NGOs Environmental protection and conservation of natural resources in the wake of the first session of the African Ministerial Conference on the Environment, held in Cairo in December 1985. A global network for information exchange and joint action is provided through the Environmental Liaison Centre (ELC), based in Nairobi, which has over 230 member NGOs and is in contact with about 7,000 more. There is also a welcome and increasing tendency for environmental NGOs to work and campaign with NGOs primarily concerned with development issues and vice-versa. Meanwhile, the work of several non-governmental international and regional scientific institutions has provided valuable intellectual and practical underpinning to the work of NGOs and Governments alike.

In parallel with—and linked to—the great expansion of the NGO movement since the 1960s, there has been a marked increase in the number of governmental institutions established to deal with environmental issues. Today, nearly all countries have environmental machinery of some kind. At the regional level, interest in environmental issues has culminated in joint action in many areas. Inter-governmental organizations (bilateral or multilateral) have been established to deal with specific problems. Intergovernmental organizations like the Organisation for Economic Co-operation and Development (OECD), the Council for Mutual Economic Assistance (CMEA), the European Communities, the Association of South East Asian Nations (ASEAN), the Gulf Co-operation Council, the Arab League, and others have established special offices or units to tackle environmental issues. A number of development banks have divisions, units or advisers. At the international level, several activities have been undertaken by different United Nations bodies especially since the 1970s. The Global Atmospheric Research Programme (a joint effort between WMO and ICSU), the World

Climate Programme, the various projects of the ICSU Scientific Committee on Problems of the Environment (SCOPE), the Unesco Man and the Bioshpere programme (MAB), and several projects by FAO, WHO, IAEA and other United Nations bodies are examples of these activities. The establishment of UNEP in 1972 marked the significant commitment of the world community to the environmental cause. Since its establishment, UNEP has worked to co-ordinate the activities of the United Nations as a whole and rendered support to many national and international organizations. For example, UNEP has been supporting and working together with institutions like IUCN, the International Institute for Environment and Development, the World Resources Institute, regional inter-governmental bodies and others. UNEP has also acted as an important catalyst in bringing together different groups to discuss environmental issues and develop plans of action and promote international conventions. The Stockholm Conference itself led to the 1972 convention on the Prevention of Marine Pollution by Dumping of Wastes and Other Matter, and UNEP has brought about plans of action and international conventions for regional seas, the 1985 Vienna Convention for the Protection of the Ozone Layer and the widely acclaimed 1987 Montreal Protocol on the Substances that Deplete the Ozone Layer. UNEP co-operated with IUCN and WWF in formulating the World Conservation Strategy launched in 1980, and has convened, in partnership with other bodies, international conferences like the 1984 World Industry Conference on Environmental Management, the 1984 Inter-Parliamentary Union Conference on Environment, the 1985 Global Meeting on Environment and Development for NGOs, the African Ministeral Conference on Environment, which met in 1985 and 1987, and others. UNEP has also worked closely with the World Commission on Environment and Development and supported the recommendations of the Commission as outlined in its report *Our Common Future,* published in 1987.

Since the 1970s, the size, commitment and dedication of the many non-governmental groups and organizations that make up the environmental movement have made a significant impact in many countries. But today the environmental movement is so diverse that a question arises as to whether it is really proper to give it a single name. Environmental organizations and their members often differ in their concern over particular environmental issues, in the values and attitudes advocated, in the goals and objectives to be achieved, and in the types of strategies and tactics. Yet what is shared by all these organizations is a concern about socio-environmental relationships. UNEP has responded to such diversification by its "outreach" policy of opening up a dialogue with industry, parliamentation, relief, women, youth, religious and other groups that are receptive to the environmental message. The message is being accepted and adopted by more and more sections of society, and by more and more of the people, in both developed and developing countries. The environment is still becoming an ever more popular issue. Perceptions and attitudes are changing, and the changes are proving remarkably widespread and robust.

INTERNATIONAL ORGANISATIONS DEALING WITH ENVIRONMENTAL MANAGEMENT

There are quite a few international organisations which, if known, can be very useful for an environmentalist approach to business management.

Here we will know about selection of *(i)* governmental organisations and *(ii)* industry-based non-governmental organisations. The year of establishment, the main goals and activities and the most important publications of the various organisations are indicated as well as their current executive secretary (on July 1, 1988) and their address. The lists of organisations are in alphabetical order and do not claim to be exhaustive.

(i) Governmental Organisations

1. European Economic Community (EEC)
2. Food and Agriculture Organisation of the United Nations (FAO)
3. Organisation for Economic Co-operation and Development (OECD)
4. United Nations Economic Commission for Europe (ECE)
5. United Nations Environment Programme (UNEP)
6. United Nations Industrial Development Organisation (UNIDO)
7. World Health Organisation (WHO)

(ii) Industry-based Non-governmental Organisations

Overall organisations :

1. Bureau International de la Recuperation (BIR)
2. Business and Industry Advisory Committee to OECD (BIAC)
3. International Chamber of Commerce (ICC)
4. International Environmental Bureau (IEB)
5. Union of Industrial and Employees' Confederations of Europe (UNICE).

Organisations for a special branch of industry :

6. European Confederation of Pulp, Paper and Board Industry (CEPAC)
7. European Council of Chemical Manufacturers' Federations (CEFIC)
8. International Group of National Associations of Manufacturers of Agrochemical Products (GIFAP)
9. International Iron and Steel Institute (IISI)
10. International Petroleum Industry Environmental Conservation Association (IPIECA)
11. International Primary Aluminium Institute (IPAI)
12. Lead Development Association (LDA)
13. The Oil Companies' European Organisation for Environmental and Health Protection (CONCAWE)

Partnering with NGOs

Many of our examples involve partnership between business and NGOs. This may seem surprising, for the two are often at odds. But while there will always be some areas of disagreement, experience shows that they can work together successfully as long as each side trusts and respects the other. Eastman Kodak and WWF, for example, have worked in partnership on an environmental education programme. Hayes Bell, vice president and director of EH&S at Eastman Kodak, believes that:

> Even though the WWF and Kodak are partnering on an education program and not a program dealing directly with our operations, it was critical that WWF become familiar and comfortable with Kodak's past and current environmental issues. No company is perfect, and the environmental group

> needs to come to terms with the fact. However, they do need to believe that the company is giving environment (and health and safety) the proper level of attention. It is also important that the group is proud of their alliance with the company.

One important factor in making such partnerships possible is the realization of many environmentalists that, while protest has its place, the growing acceptance of an eco-efficiency philosophy within business makes collaboration a more fruitful strategy than confrontation. Paul Gilding, former executive director of Greenpeace International, is

> convinced that the real leadership in the 21st century will come from the business community. This may sound strange coming from someone who has spent most of his life facing down businesspeople . . . (but) . . . the environment has become a mainstream issue, from living rooms to corporate boardrooms. People's minds have been changed. The task now is to change their behaviour.

WBCSD executive director Bjorn Stigson welcomes such changes of heart and believes that green NGOs

> must get involved in helping to find solutions that work, and cooperate with industry in implementing them. The days when NGOs could ramain on the outside looking in—like theatre critics on opening night—are gone. Now, they must join the cast of the play in helping to put on an award-winning performance.

The logical end of this process is partnership at the heart of the business, with the entry of environmentalists into the boardroom. This is starting to happen. The U.S. environmentalist John Sawhill is now a member of the Procter & Gamble board. The U.S. hydrocarbons and chemicals producer Ashland Oil has also appointed Pat Noonan, former president of the Nature Conservancy, as a non-executive director. Paul Chellgren, Ashland's president and CEO, believes that this represents

> a major commitment by Ashland to consulting with and trusting those whose primary interests and expertise are in the environmental field. This example is being repeated throughout industry. What makes this partnership viable today is the emergence of the next generation of leaders in the

> environmental movement. They understand business strategy, budgets, resource allocations, priorities, and choices. Moreover, their knowledge and understanding of the environment is vital to industry's future. . . . In co-operating with industry this next generation of environmental leaders is taking a certain risk. They may be censured by their more ideological colleagues who may think it is a mistake for the lead of an environmental organization to sit on an industry board. But the willingness to take that risk distinguishes those leaders who will see us into the next century—a century we trust will be cleaner and healthier for all.

This emerging rapprochement between at least some environmental NGOs and business is symbolized by a remarkable multi-stakeholder partnership in the United States—the previously mentioned President's Council on Sustainable Development. Their 1996 report, *Sustainable America,* stresses the need for America to meet Agenda 21—and to do so in a way that maximizes eco-efficiency. In some respects the council's conclusions are merely importing to America concepts that are widely understood and beginning to be implemented in other countries. But it is distinctive for the breadth of its vision, its emphasis on the need for partnership between business and other elements in society—and the way in which it implemented this ideal in its own membership and processes.

The council was unusual, if not unique, in being co-chaired by a business leader and an environmentalist. The business leader was David Buzzelli, vice-president and corporate director of EH&S, public affairs, and information systems at Dow Chemical. The environmentalist was Jonathan Lash, president of the World Resources Institute, a leading NGO research and advisory body on poverty, development, natural resources, and environmental quality. Other members were from a wide spectrum of American society, including federal and state government, business, NGOs, unions, and minorities.

Remarkably, this diverse collection of Americans reached a consensus about the need for, and characteristics of (eco-efficiency and sustainable development in the United States. They identified ten goals for a sustainable America—most of which relate to broader social rather than narrowly environmental issues. They also identified five practical ways of achieving them:

1. Building a new framework for environmental protection
2. Informing and educating U.S. citizens about sustainability
3. Strengthening communities
4. Developing an ethic of natural resources stewardship
5. Limiting U.S. population.

The council also specifically endorsed the ideas of eco-efficiency and established an eco-efficiency task force to examine how they can be further encouraged in the future.

Voluntary Action

The number of voluntary groups in India actively interested or involved in environmental issues today is larger than in any other Third World country and probably matches the numbers found in Western countries, where the environmental movement had its beginning. Except for certain conservation-oriented groups and groups interested in protecting the urban environment, it would probably be accurate to say that most groups in India cannot strictly be called environmental groups in the Western sense. This is particularly true of grassroots voluntary groups in rural areas, whose existence and number lends a distinct character to the voluntary movement. Most rural grassroots groups have begun to take up environmental issues in addition to their long-standing concerns for rural and urban poverty, social justice, inequality, civil liberties, rural development, approapriate technology and health. Their perspective embraces not merely an understanding of the human impact on nature but sees this impact as arising out of the complex web of social and political relationships between human beings: what humans do to nature is essentially born out of what humans do to each other.

Harsh Sethi of the Indian Council of Social Science Research says in an article published recently in the 'Economic and Political Weekly' that this increase in interest in micro-organisations has grown out of the failure of the established macro-organisations—political parties, kisan sabhas, trade unions and the government—to do anything about growing poverty, inequality, landlessness, unemployment and centralisation of power, and to bring about positive developmental and participative trends within society. On the other hand the voluntary agencies often concentrate on these problems; they are where the action is, from remote villages to urban slums, dealing with local problems, with local populations.

These organisations are definitely non-political in the sense that they do not participate in electoral processes. But most such groups do have a political perspective of the society and its growth, which is sometimes clearly articulated, but more often not.

Broadly speaking, most voluntary groups—in all, they must run into thousands—especially those working in rural areas, can be divided into four major groups : charity and relief groups, development groups, action groups—some more openly political than others—and support groups—lawyers' collective, alternative professional associations, groups publishing journals, documentation centres, theatre groups. Charity and relief organisations have been forced to ask themselves whether charity can deal with social problems, and this internal questioning is pushing them towards long-term developmental activity, like Oxfam on a global scale and the Ramkrishna Mission on the national level.

Development groups, in turn, are being pushed towards action-oriented work. They often begin by taking up programmes to help the poor increase their social status, incomes and self-reliance in basic needs like energy and health services. In many cases, these groups supplement official efforts for development. Often they consist of middle class professionals who have opted out of lucrative careers to undertake rural development work.

But no matter how committed or innovative they may be, they face serious limitations. Most of them are small and operate in restricted areas. While this facilitates flexibility and a deeper knowledge of the local area and people, it also limits the range and type of activity. Moreover, local bigwigs, bureaucrats and politicians often frustrate attempts at honest work. Local vested interests become hostile as they sense that the organisation will no longer toe their line. The more politicised of the group members see their activity as futile and become cynical and disheartened or leave for a more explicity political group, or continue ineffectually where they are. The 'technicists' too, lose out in the process, and very often return to more conventional jobs. This loss of cadre finishes off most organisations. Some make fervent attempts to replace the external middle class professionals with local cadres. But such cadres fail to attract funds from external sources to continue the programme, and programmes of this sort, with salaried personnel can rarely be funded out of local resources.

The Dahsoli Gram Swarajya Mandal in Gopeshwar, which

pioneered the now world-famous Chipko movement, is a group which progressed from development work to activism, and typifies the story of most development groups.

Disturbed by the increasing poverty in the hills and the steady migration to the plains, a few young men of Chamoli got together in the early sixties to organise a co-operative labour society so that hill labourers could not be exploited by unscrupulous contractors. They started seeking contracts with the public works department and were able to double the wages of their members. In 1964, they formed the Dahsoli Gram Swarajya Sangh (DGSS) to start cottage industries based on the natural resources of local forests. Together with eight other local village co-operatives, they set up a factory based on the use of pine resin with the help of the Khadi and Village Industries Commission, but the forest department refused to supply these factories with enough pine resin. Even the price was higher than the price at which the state government's own massive factory at Bareilly got pine resin. Village factories, thus, lay idle.

DGSS workers soon realised that they had no rights or control over local forest resources, even though they could see their unscrupulous exploitation by rich contractors in collusion with the government. They also witnessed the massive over-exploitation of the herbal wealth of the region in which contractors were not only driving herbal plants to extinction but also cheating the people by paying them a petty fraction of what they would themselves earn from the market. DGSS workers went from village to village telling people about the right prices of these herbs. Remembers Chandi Prasad Bhatt, who gave up a clerical job in a bus company to found DGSS: "All during the 1960s we would run from the hills to the state capital Lucknow to plead our case before government officials there. But finally we saw the futility of this exercise. It would take years to convince an official and then he would get transferred. We would begin afresh with the new one."

Soon, the DGSS became more militant. The revolutionary spark came when the forest department denied the people the traditional ash wood for making the yoke for bullock ploughs but readily allocated it to a sports goods manufacturer. The events that followed are now well-known as the Chipko movement, which got ready support and participation of almost all sections of the hill population.

However, this trend towards activism amongst development-oriented voluntary agencies does not mean that development work by itself is useless. In fact, voluntary agencies have made significant contributions in working with neglected sections of the population and neglected issues, in responding to problems faced by local populations in local situations, and in developing new and democratic methods of operation. The latter contribution is probably the most important. These groups have shown the way towards experimentation with alternate ways of doing things like organising cheap and people-oriented health services. The successes of groups working in the field of health care, appropriate technology, water management and afforestation have forced professionals in these fields to debate their own approaches and soultions. The Medico Friend Circle, a coalition of highly innovative groups working in the field of health care, has tried to generate a major debate within the medical profession. In the field of environment, the afforestation work of the Chipko movement is today noted at all levels of government.

But even though the innovative work of voluntary agencies gets widely noticed, the ensuing debate has usually not lead to any major change in the ways of the government or of the major professions. The World Health Organisation, for instance, picked up the concept of primary health care from the work of some excellent grassroots health groups, but its programmes have not yet gone much beyond lip service. Even the few government programmes modelled on the concept of primary health care remain riddled with inefficiency, contradictions and inadequacies.

But what this publicity does do is to attract many more middle class professionals to development work and sometimes to development activism directly, leading to a growth in voluntary activity itself. It is no longer rare to find many students from premier institutions like the Indian Institutes of Technology or the Indian Institutes of Management keen to work with voluntary agencies on development activities.

The highly publicised success of voluntary agencies on the one hand and the trend towards activism on the other has resulted in a double-faced government response. While on the one hand government agencies have been showing increasing interest in involving voluntary agencies in development programmes, on the other they are wary of them and want to bring them under control, specifically by regulating their sources of funds. In October 1982,

Prime Minister Indira Gandhi had sent out a circular directing government agencies to involve voluntary groups in anti-poverty and minimum needs programmes. She suggested the formation of consultative groups in all the states, to be chaired by the state's chief secretary or development commissioner. In April 1983, the National Development Council, which consists of senior Central ministers and chief ministers, accepted a paper on public participation in development programmes which recommended the involvement of voluntary agencies as the eyes and ears of the beneficiaries of poverty-oriented government programmes.

The Planning Commission has hired a leading figure in the voluntary sector to work as a consultant on the involvement of voluntary agencies. A meeting called by the Planning Commission of select voluntary groups pointed out that voluntary agencies have a crucial role to play not just in traditional areas of social welfare like disaster relief and child care but also in professional areas like forestry, agricultural research and education, rural development, alternative sources of energy, non-formal education, housing, urban development, water supply and sanitation, women's development, development of scheduled castes and scheduled tribes, science and technology, environment and ecology. There is also a move to include an entirely separate chapter on the role of voluntary agencies in the Seventh Five Year Plan document.

Within the Department of Environment, the Rashtriya Paryavaran Salahkar Samiti (National Environmental Advisory Committee), set up to replace the former National Committee on Environmental Planning, consists mainly of representatives from voluntary agencies to keep the government informed about people's problems and emerging issues. The department has also published a theme paper on India's Action Plan for Wildlife Conservation and Role of Voluntary Bodies.

But not all voluntary agencies are happy with being the ears and arms of government agencies or their more efficient extensions. Their activisim bothers the government which wants to control their funding sources. In early 1983 income-tax concessions given to industry to support rural development work by voluntary agencies were withdrawn. Instead of direct donations from industry to voluntary groups, the Central government set up a National Rural Development Fund under its control, through which all industrial donations had to be routed if industrial firms still wanted to avail of the tax concessions. To date, that body remains a non-starter. While the government argued that industries were misusing these tax concessions to siphon funds for other purposes, many in the voluntary sector saw in this merely a step towards taming them.

In late 1984, the government took another step to tighten up the provisions of the Foreign Contributions (Regulation) Act, 1976. Sevanti Ninan and Kalpana Sharma pointed out in an article in the 'Indian Express' that though the amendments to this act appear to be aimed at political parties and to have arisen from the situation in Punjab, where large quantities of funds have been coming in from foreign sources for anti-national activities, "on a closer reading it is clear that the action is also aimed at the voluntary sector". All organisations receiving foreign funds were earlier expected to inform the Home Ministry about each foreign contribution they received and its origin. But the new rules make it mandatory for all organisations receiving foreign funds to first register with the Home Ministry before they receive such funds or, if they are not registered, to seek prior permission before they accept any foreign donation. The changes also bring within the ambit of the act smaller voluntary groups which were not funded directly by foreign donors but by intermediary voluntary organisations situated in India which were receiving foreign funds; they will now have to get registered with the Home Ministry if they wish to continue receiving these funds.

These changes have many voluntary agencies worried. As the head of one apex body of non-governmental organisations puts it: "today we may be in their good books, tomorrow in their bad books. Registration is only the first step in extending control." These steps lay the recipients open to constant harassment by district-level authorities and provides a handle for criticism to vested interests in their area of operation.

The worst affected will probably be those very small, localised development groups, often working in inaccessible areas, whose only source of funding so far has been through intermediary voluntary organisations who in turn get it from donors abroad. These groups neither have the inclination nor the physical and administrative capacity to deal directly with the Central government or foreign donors. This level of voluntary work could dry up completely because of the new restrictions. A member of the Kerala Sastra Sahitya Parishad (KSSP) though wary of the motivation of the government, expresses happiness over the new controls on inflow of foreign funds. "The voluntary sector must be forced to look at indigeneous sources of funds," he says; the KSSP accepts no foreign money.

The relationship of the government with environmental groups tends to vary with the groups. Generally, conservation-oriented groups, information and education-oriented groups and even some grassroots development groups, particularly the more well-known ones amongst them tend to get more funds from the government than those opposing government policies and projects. The creation of the Department of Environment (DOEn) at the Centre has provided some, albeit extremely limited, entry into the government for those groups which oppose specific government projects or policies on strictly environmental grounds. The DOEn, for instance, has tended to support those groups who are fighting the environmental degradation caused by limestone mining in Mussoorie. But those groups who have been opposing certain dams mainly on the grounds of displacement of people, a largely social issue though with some environmental implications, do not find much entry into the government through the DOEn.

This is also because DOEn's own limited clout with other government agencies means that it cannot push any broad concepts of eco-development other than those issues which are strictly environmental in nature. Several voluntary agencies and environmentalists had participated in the DOEn's exercise to draw up recommendations for the new Forest Policy. Several recommendations were accepted by the department but they did not find much favour with the Agriculture Ministry which is responsibke for forests. Arguments on the new Forest Policy continue.

Environmental activities of voluntary agencies can be categorised into three main areas : environmental education, data collection, analysis and information dissemination; mobilising and organising the public directly or through courts and the press to oppose public or private sector policies and projects that could be harmful to the environment or to people dependent on the environment; and activities directly aimed at the amelioration of environmental problems, which in some cases leads to highly innovative models of resource management and popular participation.

Interest in environment now cuts across the entire range of

relief and charity groups to development and action groups. Eco-development is of interest to many action and development groups bacause almost all such grassroots groups are in their own ways searching for an alternative to the present model of development.

Voluntary environmental groups work with a series of constraints, most of which they share with the voluntary sector as a whole. *Firstly*, there is a lack of trained personpower to carry out in-depth technical and economic analysis, though as far as social and political analysis are concerned voluntary groups are often better than even most academic and highly specialised institution. Certain individuals from support voluntary groups, universities and certain scientific and other specialised institutions do help the voluntary sector occasionally. But it is still very difficult for a voluntary group opposing a dam in a remote area to find an expert who can carry out an independent environmental impact analysis of the dam which would give their campaign a sharper edge.

Lack of access to authentic data from official sources on projects and programmes with environmental implications is a second important constraint and, once again, the gap is bridged to some extent by smaller voluntary groups seeking the support of voluntary groups respected within government circles or of sympathetic government officials and journalists. A third constraint is the lack of statutory support and judicial sympathy for efforts of non-official groups willing to fight against agents of environmental destruction. Judicial interests in environmental issues is definitely growing and is providing an avenue for environmental firefighting. But, definitely, there is still a long way to go before this interest percolates down to the lower courts.

By trying to work together more and more, especially on specific issues, when networks tend to get formed more easily, the voluntary groups have ocassionally been able to get over their smallness and have succeeded in getting their voice heard. The successful campaign against the Forest Bill is a good example of such coming together. Current efforts to get groups working with slum dwellers is another example. In sum, it can be said that the environmental issue is now definitely on the agenda of the voluntary sector and if it continues to grow at the same pace, despite all the existing constraints, it cannot but become a key issue on the national political and developmental agenda. If that happens, the voluntary sector will definitely have been the lead promoter.

Acute scarcity of water, lack of sanitation, deforestation, the rural energy deficit and soil erosion are the main environment problems under the heading of environment. Population pressures are adding to these problems which are already acute. India has a very large population of cattle and goats making it difficult to provide enough food for the livestock. Meanwhile, the acerage of grazing land is diminishing as a result of population pressure that reduces land holdings and compels people to encroach on forests and pastures. The scarcity of land and fodder is increasing. Declining land holdings also means reduced capacity on the part of farmers to invest in "bunds" and other works aimed at arresting soil erosion. Very frequently, the encroached land is on hill slopes or other terrain unfit for cultivation. Growing crops on such land leads to soil erosion. Nearly half of the total land area is now classified as uncultivable degraded land (Phadke, 1993).

Collecting water, fuel and fodder is becoming increasingly time and energy-consuming for rural women who are held responsible for assuring supplies for all household members and animals. In many parts of Rajasthan and Gujarat, people and animals have to leave their homes in the dry season and migrate long distances in search of water, food and fodder. These recuring migrations involve many people and have high costs in terms of sickness and death (Centre for Science and Environment, 1982, 1985).

Only 22 per cent of the total area is under forests. The total area remaining under forest cover, with a density above 30 per cent, is only 11 per cent of the total land area, compared to a norm of 33 per cent under the National Forest Policy. The rate of deforestation in Rajasthan and Gujarat is very high. The Rajasthan situation is particularly bad. The 16 districts in the Aravalli hills system are specially vulnerable. Productivity of forests is low in both states because of illegal felling, overgrazing and burning. A severe shortage of fuelwood, fodder and timber leads to premature cutting of trees.

The wasteland is estimated at 129 million hectares and it increases by more than a million hectare annually. A large part of Rajasthan, 16 per cent of the total land area, is classified as cultivable wasteland. The bulk of the wasteland in this state falls in the "upland" category. In Gujarat, the proportionate share of "upland" is much smaller. Also prominent in the latter state are sandy, desertic coastal lands, degraded forests and degraded pastures.

There is a chronic shortage of water in both states, partly related to the degradation of forests. Access to drinking water in the villages of Rajasthan is very low. Although the need for irrigation facilities in the two states is much more than in many other parts of India, the proportion of cultivated area that is irrigated is below the national average. The Rajasthan canal has greened parts of the Thar desert but hard layers of gypsum have caused waterlogging over a large area. The following illustration of water scarcity from Saurashtra is very pertinent:

> The grasslands have disappeared, mainly under the plough. The thorn forests have been felled. Now when it rains the water swiftly flows over the surface, causing erosion, and is swept into the sea. The rivers and streams are dry throughout the year. There is little ground water recharge, but irrigation-based agriculture, dependent on percolation wells and tube-wells, has caused so much drawdown that there is virtual exhaustion of groundwater. Saurashtra has now become a waterless desert in which even drinking water is hard to come by.

Government did not recognise the gravity of the rural environmental issue till recently. It did not have a headstart in this sphere as it did in the family planning field. Some progress has been made in chalking out policies and programmes but there is not yet in place a coherent, overall strategy aimed at sustainable development that is sensitive to the environmental dimension.

Many observers claim that the process of environmental degradation in India was greatly accelerated by the state taking control of natural resources in colonial times. Till this takeover, it is claimed that vital resources such as water, land and forests were managed by village communities in an ecologically sensitive manner (Shiva, 1991 and Saint, 1993). After losing control, local people no longer have a stake in maintaining these assets. The bureaucracy, the contractors and the people themselves began to misuse and over-exploit available natural resources. The government of independent India justified state management of natural resources in the name of socialism but it proved impossible to stop the continuing environmental degradation. Groups that lost the most from the new natural resource regime were those who were politically weak and disorganised.

The year 1988 saw a radical change in the government's forest policy. It was recognised that a major reason for deforestation was the alienation of common property resources, both forests and pastures, to private commercial interests and state departments. Instead of regarding forests as a source of revenue for the state, the new policy aims at providing fuelwood and fodder to local communities living in or around forests. The right of the people, particularly scheduled castes, tribals and the poor to minor forest produce was recognised.

The newly established Ministry of Environment urged state governments in 1990 to promote the idea of Joint Management of Forests (JMF) by the forest department and by villagers living near forests. Ownership rights, under certain circumstances, can be vested in village communities organised as panchayat or a co-operative. Committed volags were expected to motivate and to organise the local people in this context. Ten states have adopted the scheme so far, including Rajasthan and Gujarat.

The National Wasteland Development Board (NWDB) was established in 1985 to put wastelands to sustainable use, to increase the availability of fuelwood and fodder and to elicit the co-operation of the people in this endeavour.

The government announced a National Water Policy in September 1987. It recognised that water was a scarce resource, that past water development projects had experienced substantial time and cost over-runs, that a serious lag had emerged in the utilisation of the irrigation potential, that problems of water-logging and soil salinity had arisen and that volags should be enlisted in educating the farmers in the efficient use of the irrigation potential. Very little has been done so far to operationalise the water policy.

The current strategy for water resource management, focuses on large and medium projects and neglects rainfed agriculture. Governments' multi-purpose and major irrigation programmes have proved to be very controversial. Actual benefits from such schemes have fallen far short of projection (Chopra and Sen, 1992). Other issues relate to the displacement of people or the manner in which they are to be resettled. Examples are the storms over the Silent Valley scheme in Kerala, the Tehri Dam in UP, and the Sardar Sarovar and Narmada Sagar projects in Madhya Pradesh and Gujarat.

Government recognises that the problem of resettling people displaced by the construction of high dams has become complicated as land has become scarce. Nevertheless, according to Chitale (1992) "... compared to the number of people who derive benefits from water storages, the number of people required to be resettled is relatively small, say about 5 per cent". In the case of Sardar Sarovar, for example, Chitale reports that project beneficiaries will be 334 lakh people, compared to one lakh who will be displaced.

An alternative strategy would focus on the development of rainfed agriculture, involving water conservation and cultivation of crops that need relatively less water. Such a strategy would require working with very large numbers of farmers spread across a large territory, compared with the present approach that is based on a centralised model of economic development, according to Chopra and Sen (1992).

The electrification of villages is much higher in Gujarat, while biogas has been developed much more in Rajasthan. The installation of improved chulhas (mud stoves for cooking) is much further ahead in Gujarat. Government is subsidising private investment in non-conventional energy. According to R.K. Pachauri (1992) little progress has been made in defining a meaningful energy policy. He says:

> Numerous committees and bodies have in the past developed the elements of an energy policy for India, but their reports have gathered dust in the corridors of power and a short-sighted fragmented approach merrily pursued by a variety of departments all of whom are vital players in the implementation of energy policy.
>
> The result is a wasteful use of energy irrational pricing of power and neglect of programmes to develop renewable energy, particularly for rural areas.

The Fifth Plan recognised the need to minimise environmental damage while pursuing economic development. Government investment was subjected to an environmental impact assessment (EIA). However, there was no similar screening of private investment till 1990 (Muralodharan, 1994). Even now there is no provision requiring the active participation of the population directly affected by a project in the environmental assessment process. Muraleedharan also points out that the quality of these assessments suffers from the fact that they are the responsibility of project sponsors rather than of an independent institution.

The origins of the contemporary environment movement can be traced to the Chipko (literally means cling to the tree and oppose/felling) movement in the 1920s (Radha Kumar, p. 183). It was adopted by Sarvodaya workers in Garhwal and became a watershed in the history of the Indian environmental movement. The tempo picked up considerably during the last two decades and involved people as well as intellectuals. An important part of the women's movement, the Eco-Feminists, added their strength to the environmental movement.

The World Wide Fund for Nature, New Delhi, lists 895 volags throughout India doing environmental work in 1989. Out of these 41 are in Rajasthan and 72 in Gujarat.

Environmental volags are engaged in three types of activity. The first is ecological restoration. The second is location-specific ecological conscientisation that can spark popular movements to restore ecological balance. The third is advocacy *vis-a-vis* the government or the corporate private sector.

The issue of sustainable development is now on the national agenda. The mainstream development paradigm of the government and international agencies such as the World Bank, has been challenged. The forceful and vibrant environment movement has successfully opposed many government and corporate sector projects in the field of irrigation, industry and mining that were thought to have a deleterious ecological impact.

AVARD (1991) identifies the following ideological strands among environmental volags:

— Crusading Gandhians who favour the creation of close to nature village communities and oppose many sorts of modern development through fasts, *padyatras* (symbolic journeys on foot to make a point) etc. This strand is represented by the thinking of leaders such as Sunderlal Bahuguna.

— Appropriate technologists who are less opposed to modernisation but insist on a synthesis of old and new ways of doing things. They seek out more appropriate technological solutions than those adopted by conventional government programmes, for example. This strand is represented by Chandi Prasad Bhat. The emphasis is on participation and on how technologies impact on the poor (Gadgil, 1989).

— Ecological Marxists who oppose tradition, want to take science to the people and desire systemic changes prior to seeking ecological sustainability. Their posture is frequently confrontational.

The history of the Narmada Bachao Andolan (the movement to save the Narmada river) against the construction of the Sardar Sarovar Project (SSP) is an instructive example of government-volag relations. This projects impacts on Gujarat, Madhya Pradesh and Maharashtra. Disagreement among them on the master plan led the government to establish the Narmada Water Disputes Tribunal in 1969. The award of the Tribunal in 1979 visualised that the SSP reservoir would submerge 193 villages in MP, 33 in Maharashtra and 19 in Gujarat involving at least 100,000 people. Most of them are tribals. Since most of the benefits of the SSP accrue to Gujarat, the award insisted that displaced people should be settled in Gujarat on suitable land. In 1985, the World Bank lent $ 450 million to finance the SSP, subject to a number of studies, training and environmental clearances from governmental authorities. In 1987 government decided, at the highest political level, to proceed with the SSP project without any EIA (Bhaskar, 1994). Even today the EIA is not yet complete.

The implementation of the SSP has encountered formidable difficulties. From the outset, the Narmada Bacho Andolan has demanded a review of the project on a variety of grounds. In a memo submitted to government in June 1993, the Andolan listed 24 points that needed re-consideration including physical aspects such as the annual rate of flow of the river, the maximum probable flood, ecological aspects, cost and benefit estimates, displacement of the people, conditions of resettlement and economic viability of the project. Medha Patkar (1993), the celebrated leader of the Andolan, has demanded :

> We want the entire process of so-called development, which has proved disastrous for the people, to change. We are not for such piecemeal measures as reducing the height of the dam, or decreasing the submergence. We want an overhaul of the entire approach towards the exploitation of these natural resources.

Patkar is not alone in making these demands. She is supported by many intellectuals and volags. Bagchi (1993), for example, has questioned the government's latest estimate of the benefit-cost ratio. These estimates declined over time from 1.5:1 to 1.12:1. The estimate for the best possible ratio, according to Bagchi, is 0.8:1. He also points out that 13,744 hectares of forests will be destroyed.

The Andolan has attracted criticism in some quarters for romanticising the Adivasis (tribals) and manipulating Adivasi symbols. Vasudha Dhagamwar (1993), the Director of Multiple Action Research Group (MARG), is a strong opponent of the SSP but has criticised Patkar for monopolising the affected villages by excluding workers from groups other than the Andolan.

The Andolan is also criticised for losing sight of the larger environmental context in its single-minded campaign against the project (Baviskar, 1991). Many believe that Patkar overplayed her hand by going on a fast and, later, threatening to drown in the Narmada. And yet, it seemed that government responded much more to such acts, accompanied by dramatic media attention, than to rational discourse. In fact, some observers argued that government acted in bad faith at various points and did too little and too late when put under the pressure of public opinion. It was against this background that Patkar insisted on the participation of a group of "independent and eminent persons" in the negotiations between the government and Andolan.

Not all volags are against the SSP. Many volags and other independent thinkers believe that the trade-offs involved in the SSP are reasonable and that a superior way of solving Gujarat's acute water problem does not exist. What is essential, according to these observers, is to make sure that the government plan for resettlement of the tribals is fully implemented. History does not support the view that the governments concerned will keep their word. The Independent Review Commission, established by the World Bank, for example, concluded:

> The general Sardar Sarovar history of compliance is a history of omissions, unmet deadlines, extensions and ex-post-facto revisions (Morse and Burger, 1992).

Dhagamwar (1994) points out that another volag, Arch-Vahini, has taken positions very different from the Andolan:

> The Arch-Vahini holds that the Sardar Sarovar project will

bring the promised benefits to Gujarat, the oustees-will be given full and satisfactory resettlement with land compensation, and that reforestation will make up for lost forests.

According to Dhagamwar, neither the Andolan nor Arch-Vahini has taken a holistic view of the Narmada issue. They have not presented a credible alternative to the project. They have not tried to think out the meaning of tribal identity in a context that is undergoing demographic and ecological change, even if the dam is not built. They have not considered whether middle-class movements should take it upon themselves to articulate what the tribals want and secure it for them indefinitely.

Despite increasing concern for the environment and an increasingly pro-active role being played by various environmental movements in the country, the exploitation of our natural resources, pollution and deforestation hold major challenges for the coming decade.

It not tackled on an emergency footing, the quality of life of the people would continue to deteriorate and people living in cities would constantly be hounded by the ever-polluted air, while the people in the rural and forest areas face threat of fast depleting natural resources.

Reduction of land under tree cover, pollution of air and water that support all the life systems have posed the greatest danger to bio-diversity. Also with the rapidly growing population, more and more land is brought under cultivation. Craving for higher standard of living has given a boost to the production of all sorts of consumer goods and services. Most of the plant and animal species are interlinked for mutual survival and their destruction poses a danger to the protection of bio-diversity in general and survival of humankind in particular.

Role of Voluntary Organisations

The role of voluntary organisations in espousing the cause of the environment and playing a pro-active role in protection of the bio-diversity has become very important. In fact, the voluntary sector played a leading role in making environment a national issue.

A cursory look at the wide spectrum of organisations working in this issue reveals that many of them are involved in generating awareness, educating and sensitising people about environmental problems and bio-diversity; protesting against pollution from various sources like industries, vehicles etc.; protecting wildlife parks and sanctuaries from encroachment by industries, mining and tourists resorts; and protesting against forces leading to deforestation.

Voluntary organisations have played an important role in carrying out research in environmental education and research, be it in academic sphere or on policy interventions. One important role of the voluntary organisations have been to involve other sectors of the society in the environmental movement.

According to Prof. Shekhar Singh, environmentalist, it was with the Chipko Movement in the early 1970s that the country's environmental movement began taking shape. Men, women and even children from villages chained themselves to trees that were threatened by loggers during the Chipko movement. It was the beginning of the challenge.

The evolution of pani panchayats during the famines in Maharastra in the 1970s was a milestone in the environmental movement. The pani panchayats are people's institutions managing water resources in an equitable manner by ensuring that the community's grouping patterns matched the availability of water resources. The scheme was unique in the sense that water was not distributed randomly and the largest land owner did not get the lion's share.

Each land owner was allowed to irrigate only two acres of land, water was distributed equally after making calculations to ascertain how much was required to irrigate one acre. One trained person in the village supervised the distribution of water and ensured that no one was denied his share.

Prof. Shekhar Singh underscores that the intervention of the Kerala Sastra Sahitya Parishad (KSSP) in the Silent Valley Project in Kerala was also a turning point in the environmental movement in the country. After this campaign, the KSSP started campaigning in several other issues including industrial pollution, deforestation, rational energy policy etc.

Around the same time in mid-1970s, Mr Anna Hazare after retirement from the Army went back to his village in Relengan Siddhi and brought the villagers together to work for the development of the village. According to Mr. Hazare, when he came to Ralegan Siddhi, people were living in abject poverty. Due to little rain, agricultural output was low. After he undertook the project of watershed development using the local resources and technology to meet the water needs of the people, prosperity started coming to the village.

For initiating the watershed development project, it was necessary that a tree plantation programme was undertaken along with development of grasslands. Within a decade, Ralegan had become a model village, a classic case of striking ecological balance alongwith prosperity of the villagers. Later on a well-structured programme was initiated by the Government on watershed development.

Yet another interesting example of community land management is that of Sukhomajri village in Haryana. About two decades back, this village, located in the foothills of the Shivaliks was dry. After the intervention of one soil scientist, the people of Sukhomajri decided to rejuvenate the land themselves. The villagers reinvested their savings from the regenerated land for further ecological improvement through a cyclical mode of development. Sukhomajri is definitely a model village for sustainable development and success story for community forest management.

These are actually few interesting examples. A large number of organisations all over the country have been trying to evolve models of development for the community focussing on ecological balance. Many of these are being replicated.

According to Prof. Shekhar Singh, in the 1950s and 1960s, the major campaign by environmental groups was confined to wildlife protection. The Wildlife Preservation Society emerged during this time. This movement has taken a fillip in 1990s when the disastrous effect of the increasing depletion of biotic resources received wide national and international publicity.

Prof. Singh says that some voluntary organisations have also been campaigning against the destruction of areas in national parks and sanctuaries for cement factories and mining as well as for tourist resorts. A large number of organisations have been insisting that like joint forestry there should be some schemes of joint management of parks and sanctuaries.

Another critical issue is the antagonism between conservationists or wildlife officers on the one hand and social activists or communities on the other. This antagonism has always been in the interest of the powerful commercial industrial sector. Natural habitats are not only the home of wildlife and rural people but also the repositories of resources for our industries be it minerals, timber, water on hydro-electricity. The 'development policy' has served to exploit these resources for the enrichment of urban middle-classes and big rural landlords at the expense of wildlife and poor people.

The core point hence is the need of an alliance between local communities, voluntary organisations, concerned individuals and government agencies that can save natural habitats and wildlife from the clutches of destructive forces. Voluntary organisations have been making this point for a long time. In the mid-1990s a large number of voluntary organisations got together to work in this direction.

For instance in 1995, several groups jointly organised a *jungle jivan bachao yatra* (Save Forest Life Journey) through 15 national parks and sanctuaries, initiating a dialogue between forest officials and local communities. The same year, in October, a large number of voluntary organisations and conservation groups got together to initiate the 'Save the Tiger Movement'. Their memorandum to the then-Prime Minister stessed on the need to involve representatives of local traditional communities in the planning and management of wildlife programmes, to ensure their customary rights and access to essential livelihood resources which are in consonance with the conservation objectives of the area and to guarantee employment and other benefits to them.

The other issue which voluntary organisations have been assiduously taking up is pollution. Issues such as ozone depletion and green house gases have also been taken up by voluntary organisations. In this regard, the contribution of organisations like the Centre for Science and Environment (CSE) has been commendable. The CSE's, 'The State of India's Environment' report is considered one of the pioneering reports on environment in the country. Right from sensitising the people to the problem of pollution to making it a political issue, these organisations have been able to pitchfork pollution as a national issue.

Also many voluntary organisations have been taking up the issue of occupational health especially of the workers employed in hazardous industries. The concerted campaign by the voluntary organisations has resulted in increased awareness on environmental protection amongst the public at large. One often finds citizen's groups being formed for garbage clearance in cities or a pro-active stand being taken by these groups to shift factories from cities.

Then in order to safeguard the forest cover and environment, voluntary organisations have been working assiduously to form forest protection committees in forest areas. Villagers are encouraged to form these committees and zealously try to safeguard their forests.

According to Prof. Shekhar Singh, due to the Silent Valley Project intervention, the late Prime Minister Mrs. Indira Gandhi was forced to constitute the Tiwari Committee in 1980. The department of environment was also constituted as a result of this campaign. Subsequently, the National Committee on Environmental Planning and Co-ordination was set up.

According to a paper by Mr. Sharad Kulkarni, deforestation is another main cause of depletion of bio-diversity. "The National Commission on Agriculture in its report on forestry stated production for industry to be the main reason of forest depletion. Based on this the Ministry of Agriculture and Forests prepared a draft of forest bill to replace the prevailing Indian Forests Act of 1927. Voluntary organisations successfully protested against the bill which then could not be introduced in the Parliament. Later the Government adopted a Forest Policy Resolution in 1988 that stressed the maintenance of ecological conditions. Several organisations are now participating in the implementation of joint forest management projects. This will help to protect the bio-diversity in the country."

Prof. Singh points out that due to pressure by voluntary organisations working on environment issues, a lot of Government policies were shaped accordingly. He cites the case when the Department of Environment in 1985 constituted appraisal committees on thermal power projects. "Many organisations became members of these committees. As many of them had linkages with grassroot level organisations, they could give concrete inputs," he says.

He also cites the case of Environmental Protection Act and the changes in Wildlife Protection Act which were result of intense pressure from voluntary organisations. "In fact the whole environmental policy of India has been shaped by the pro-active work being done by voluntary organisations," he avers.

There have also been debates initiated by environmental activists that when the Montreal Protocol on phasing out Choroflouro Carbons (CFCs) and Halons was signed in 1987, as much as 88 per cent of the CFCs spewed into the atmosphere that year had originated from industrialised countries. The point put forth by the activists is why the third world countries be penalised when the industrialised countries were the worst violators.

One of the major contribution of various environmental groups have been in the field of legal intervention. Due to pressure from the environmental lobby, Green Benches are being formed in court and the number of public interest litigation on the issue of environment is on the increase.

According to a paper by Mr. M. C. Mehta, environmental lawyer, "Court orders have helped save the ridge in Delhi, shift hazardous industries from residential areas, activate authorities to keep the city clean, protect historical monuments like the Taj Mahal and protect rivers like the Ganges from indiscriminate industrial and domestic pollution."

While emphasising on the need to take both populist and non-populist measures as regards environmental issues, Prof. Singh opines that voluntary organisations need much greater co-ordination. A new mechanism needs to be brought about to bring in more linkages between organisations, he feels. Research capacities of organisations on environmental issues needs to be strengthened, he opines.

Conservation of bio-diversity has to be effected on a decentralised basis. While local communities will not be able to protect the biotic resources on their own and commercial forces are hell-bent on exploiting these resources by force or fraud, there is a need to develop a collaborative relationship between locals, government agencies and conservation groups. It is in this regard that voluntary organisations have to play a vital role. The voluntary organisations will, in the coming years, have to widen the scope of their conservation and regeneration of natural resources related activities and assume an even more vital role to meet the ever-mounting environmental challenges.

5

NGOs and Human Rights with Special Reference to Women and Child

NON-GOVERNMENTAL HUMAN RIGHTS ORGANIZATIONS

The development of international norms, institutions and procedures for the protection of human rights has gone hand in hand with the proliferation of non-governmental international organizations (NGO's) working in the human rights fields. On this subject generally, see H. Steiner, *Diverse Partners: Non-Governmental Organizations in the Human Rights Movement* (1991). As a matter of fact, as with the chicken and the egg, it is difficult to say which came first. Some NGO's played an important role in San Francisco during the drafting of the UN Charter. There they lobbied for the inclusion of human rights provisions in the Charter and for a system that would give NGO's formal institutional affiliation with and standing before UN organs. The result was Article 71 of the UN Charter, which provides that "the Economic and Social Council may make suitable arrangements for consultation with non-governmental organizations which are concerned with matters within its competence."

Article 71 was implemented in due course by ECOSOC. The subject is currently regulated by ECOSOC Resolution 1296 (XLIV) of May 23, 1968. It establishes a formal system that enables qualified

NGO's to obtain one of three types of consultative status with the Organization. The existence of this system has encouraged the creation of more NGO's, the adoption of similar consultative systems by other international and regional organizations, all of which has produced more NGO's. Today, as a result, there exist a myriad of these groups throughout the world. Some specialize in only one subject, such as human rights, health, or environmental matters; others focus either on more general interests and agendas or on particular issues of a given speciality.

Whether or not they have a formal affiliation with an intergovernmental organization, the NGO's resemble domestic pressure groups or lobbies. Human rights NGO's have played a particularly important role in the evolution of the international system for the protection of human rights and in trying to make it work. Governments which violate human rights are always eager to make sure that the applicable international human rights norms, institutions, and procedures remain weak and ineffective. The human rights NGO's provide a needed counterpoint to these governmental attitudes and deserve much of the credit for the progress that has been made in recent decades.

The functions human rights NGO's perform differ depending upon the purpose for which they were established, their resources, the geographic regions in which they operate and the nature of their membership. There are NGO's which are interested in the world-wide promotion of human rights. Others limit their activities rights problems in specific regions or sub-regions (for example, Central America, Africa, Asia) or to specific countries or issues. Amnesty International, the Lawyers Committee for Human Rights, the International League for Human Rights, the International Commission of Jurists, the Watch Committees, to cite but a few well-known NGO's, have world-wide interests. The Andean Commission of Jurists and the Washington Office for Latin America (WOLA), for example, are organizations with regional and subregional agendas.

The methods NGO's employ in the pursuit of their goals also differ from group to group. Some choose to resort to only one or a limited number of techniques or activities, be it the preparation of reports, the filing of complaints with international organizations, the promotion of international legislation, lobbying before national and international bodies, and so on. Others use all of these tools depending upon the circumstances. Some NGO's limit themselves to the protection of specific groups or to specific concerns. This is true of the Anti-Slavery Society, the Minority Rights Group, or the International Committee of the Red Cross. Others have much broader concerns.

All major human rights NGO's have consultative status of one form or another with the UN, the Council of Europe, the Organization of American States, UNESCO and other regional or specialized inter-governmental organizations. This status permits their representatives, subject to certain conditions and restrictions, to present reports to these organizations, to be heard by their committees and commission and, in certain cases, to affect the agendas of these bodies.

Many contemporary human rights instruments can be traced to proposals and/or drafts prepared by NGO's. The NGO's have on various occasions succeeded in getting the UN Commission on Human Rights, its Sub-Commission for the Prevention of Discrimination and Protection of Minorities and other UN bodies to focus on specific human rights violations, which they would otherwise not have done. The NGO's also deserve a great deal of credit for the creation by the UN and its Specialized Agencies of institutions and procedures for dealing with human rights violations. This has been accomplished by NGO's through their written and oral interventions in the proceedings of these bodies and by lobbying key representatives and delegations.

In recent years, some NGO's have also contributed significantly to the strengthening of the reporting systems that have been established under various human rights treaties. Thus, for example, the International Covenants on Human Rights and the International Convention on the Elimination of all Forms of Racial Discrimination require the States Parties to file periodic reports indicating what action they have taken to comply with their obligations under these treaties. These reports are examined by special committees which these conventions created. As a rule, these committees lack the power to investigate the varacity of the claims made in the reports which the states submit. They are usually also not empowered to hear witnesses or to request information from sources other than the state representatives, who are heard when their country's report is discussed by the committee. On that occasion committee members are permitted to ask the state representatives questions about the contents of their reports. The restraints under which these committees operate make reliable fact-finding difficult. This has prompted a number of NGO's to prepare their own country reports. Their findings are then passed on to any interested committee members prior to its meetings with the representatives of the reporting state. The information supplied by the NGO's enables the members to probe the veracity of the state reports and to get material into the record that does not appear in the state reports.

Over the past five decades, many inter-governmental organizations have established legal mechanisms that permit individuals, groups and non-governmental organizations to file human rights complaints. On this subject generally, *see* Shelton, "The Participation of Non-governmental Organizations in International Judicial Proceedings," 88 Am. J. Int'l L. 611 (1994). NGO's have invoked these procedures and filed numerous complains, particularly in cases involving allegations of massive violations of human rights. Here NGO's are often in a much better position than individuals to gather reliable information and to prepare the necessary legal documentation.

NGO's have filed many complaints with the Inter-American Commission on Human Rights, both under the American Convention and under the OAS Charter-based petition system. Thus, for example, a decision by the Inter-American Commission on Human Rights holding that the U.S. had violated the right to life by permitting the execution of minors originated from a complaint filed by the American Civil Liberties Union and the International Human Rights Law Group.

In three contentious cases that were referred to the Inter-American Court by the Inter-American Commission in 1986, the latter invited the lawyers of the NGO's which had originally filed the cases to join its legal team before the Court. These cases are interesting for yet another reason: they demonstrate how national and international NGO's can co-operate in certain circumstances. Here a national NGO—the Honduran Human Rights Commission —first brought the cases to the attention of the Commission. Thereafter the Honduran group asked an international NGO with offices in Washington—Americas Watch—to assist it. The latter's lawyers then stepped in to handle the cases before the Commission. When the Commission referred the cases to the Court, the Commission asked the NGO lawyers to join its legal team, which they did.

Human rights NGO's have also pioneered the practice of using distinguished foreign lawyers or judges as observers at trials of individuals who have been charged with or appear to be tried for political offenses. Amnesty International and the International Commission of Jurists try to make frequent use of trial observers in order to ensure due process of law for the accused. See, for example, the annual reports of Amnesty International. The mere presence at such trials of foreign lawyers acting as trial observers has tended to prevent some abuses; at times it has even produced acquittals.

A related practice, utilized with considerable success—particularly by the International Committee of the Red Cross—consists of inspections of prisons and detention centers for political prisoners. The ICRC attempts to ensure that those in detention are treated humanely and that they are provided with medical services and other basic necessities. Other NGO's have carried out important *in loco* investigations of human rights violations for use by inter-governmental human rights organizations and international tribunals.

The policies governments adopt in confronting specific violations of human rights being committed in other countries are made on the national level. The same is true of the policies that determine what powers governments are willing to confer on international organizations to enable them to deal with such violations. National political considerations also affect governmental decisions whether to ratify human rights treaties or what methods, national or international, should be employed to promote respect for human rights abroad. All of these and related issues must be addressed by a country's human rights foreign policy. Decisions affecting the formulation and execution of these policies are as much subject to various forms of lobbying as are other foreign policy decisions.

Human rights NGO's devote a great deal of time and resources to activities designed to influence the human rights policies and diplomacy of various countries. In the United States, for example, human rights NGO's are very active in promoting U.S. ratification of international human rights instruments. They advocate legislation to deny U.S. economic and military assistance to governments that engage in large-scale violations of human rights. They also monitor compliance with that legislation by the Executive Branch. To this end, they present evidence to Congressional committees, publish reports critical of Executive action, launch public information campaigns and institute legal proceedings.

The following description of the activities of one human rights NGO operating in the U.S. provides a good example of the different functions such groups perform:

> Amnesty International U.S.A. has developed an organization of legal workers, lawyers, and law students. . . .
>
> The Legal Support Network's activities include : litigation, public education, outreach, work for lawyers who are victims of human rights abuses, research and work for the ratification of human rights treaties.

Similar activities focusing on legal actions are carried out by other human rights NGO's including, among others, the Lawyers Committee for Human Rights and the International Human Rights Law Group.

Informal coalitions and relations between these groups allows them to speak with one voice on important human rights issues when that appears indicated, which gives them considerable political strength. At times they also co-ordinate their research and lobbying activities to avoid unnecessary duplication and to preserve scare financial and human resources. Most of these organizations derive their funding from private foundations, membership dues, and fundraising campaigns. To preserve their political independence and impartiality, which are their strongest assets, a majority of these groups refuse contributions from governmental entities or from sources that might have a political or ideological interest.

INFLUENCE ON INTERNATIONAL SOCIETY

NGO operations historically have been dependent upon inter-state organizations for the provision of channels of action. However, partly due to the limitations on participation and expression inherent when international arenas are controlled fundamentally by states, these NGOs have also devised new channels of action that allow them more freedom. International NGOs and only cross formal national boundaries—they also have created a direct and independent form of non-governmental diplomacy through networks of their own.

To return to human rights, NGOs have been involved at

crucial junctures in strengthening the expectation that states be held accountable for human rights practices in the 20th century, as international and regional human rights norms have been elaborated in response to problematic country cases, and states have been encouraged to create new inter-governmental reporting and monitoring procedures at the formal level. These changes have arisen not so much from enthusiastic state participation as from international popular and diplomatic pressure exerted on governments. Human rights NGOs, such as Amnesty International, have become skilled at mounting such pressure by feeding information into pertinent public and governmental channels for discussion, on the one hand, and distributing and promoting new human rights instruments, on the other. Further, it is often through such activity by NGOs that newly created norms become formalized and develop meaningful impact. This process changes the scope of state sovereignty as it, "reconstitutes the relationship between the state, its citizens and international actors."

Certain public goods such as communications, trade and environmental protection traditionally have been regulated by states at the domestic level. International exchange of goods and information also demands that states co-operate to establish mutually recognized regulatory standards in matters such as trade, monetary standards, communication and technology. As the legal, economic and ethical implications of such regulatory regimes cross borders, the issues themselves become internationalized, often coming into conflict with the goals of particular states. A growing literature on international governance documents the growth of international regimes that organize state practices in particular issue areas. Regimes are conceived of as tools for states' pursuit of self-interest, created and maintained in response to international demand for rules governing mutually beneficial international transactions. The concept of regimes, therefore, is fundamentally state-centric, although it can be inferred that non-governmental organizations also would cluster around international regime-based institutions, to exert influence on particular issues.

Although the regimes concept has been applied to human rights, the authoritative moral element in their enforcement is overlooked by the more state-centered theories of international governance. Human rights norms impose a duty on states to respect human dignity, both internationally and through the treatment of their citizens. Compared with the well-established sovereignty principle, codified in the Universal Declaration of Human Rights adopted by the U.N. in 1948, this duty to protect human dignity is a relatively new principle of international law. Human rights obligations potentially limit state policy choices in a categorical way, so that in practice, international demands that human rights obligations be fulfilled conflict with the older international principle of non-interference in domestic affairs. Thus, the moral component of human rights concerns, the idea that human rights should be a part of state practice under all circumstances, is at odds with a conventional interest-based explanation of regimes.

In the environmental field, the principles advocated by NGOs include humanitarian and conservationist concerns for the well-being of humans and the rest of nature. As with human rights protection, the potential conflict between international demands for environmental conservation and a state's claim to the right to control the resources within its borders touches directly upon state sovereignty. For example, the international community demands the preservation of Brazil's rainforest on the grounds that the rainforest is an international public good, while Brazil maintains that its right to exploit the rainforest for economic purposes overrides any international moral claim.

While the construction of any type of international regime can entail, to some extent, state concessions of sovereignty, environmental and human rights NGOs pose a particular challenge to states by calling for the universal application of certain ethical principles related to state conduct. Respect for human rights and environmental principles, however, requires not just verbal deference but concrete technical and procedural implementation as well. This often carries costly political and economic consequences for states reluctant to force changes either on themselves or on one another for fear of setting a precedent of intervention. For these reasons, states are likely to neglect the implementation of more restrictive standards of conduct unless pressed by third parties, and NGOs and private citizens, rather than states, have served as prominent conduits of pressure and influence on these issues.

NGO influence has grown in recent years precisely because they are different from states.

First, NGOs focus on single issues or sets of issues to the exclusion of others, while states must perform many functions, with national security as a top priority. The organizational mandate of Amnesty International, for example, commits it to an exclusive focus on promoting the Universal Declaration of Human Rights and related international legal instruments. Environmental groups as well, despite the complexity of environmental issue linkages, have limited policy concerns compared to states.

Second, in taking up principle-based issues, NGOs commit themselves to causes that states' priorities frequently subordinate to other foreign policy interests or ignore entirely. But international NGOs can draw on the activism of local memberships at the state level, in order to bring domestic public opinion into play. The involvement of domestic actors allows NGOs to bring pressure on states internally, based on domestic representation and legitimacy, as well as internationally, based on humanitarian principles and generalized public opinion. There is also evidence that most states care how they are regarded by others, suggesting that international pressure alone can affect state action under certain conditions. However, international NGOs are likely to be less successful in their attempts at influence if they cannot establish links with domestic actors. This problem is evident with regard to governments that repress domestic representation and civil protest or are too weak to be responsive to public demands.

Third, in contrast to states, the commitment of NGOs to their issues is intense. State and inter-governmental agencies deal with varied and competing policy concerns, while NGOs specialize on one or a few issues. This is not to say that NGOs do not have to balance their own priorities, but their scope is narrower and their membership is less ideologically diverse than the issues and citizenry to which states are accountable. As a result, NGOs can apply their resources of volunteer memberships and paid staff in a manner that is more focused than the attention and resources that state representatives may be able to devote to the same issues.

Today, NGOs face a choice of operating within arenas that are not necessarily mutually exclusive. The first is the inter-governmental realm. Inter-governmental organizations (IGOs), such as the United Nations, the Council of Europe and the Organization of American States, are the fora in which international legal norms are created, and NGOs seeking influence at this level must use such channels. However, because of their growing expertise and involvement in international issues, NGOs have earned a measure of authentic autonomy from states even within inter-governmental organizations. For example, human rights NGOs regularly lobby diplomats at the United Nations who, in most cases, are not experts in human rights or international law. To develop proposals and shephered them through the complex U.N. system requires experience and skill that take time to acquire. Further, although diplomats formally receive instructions from their governments, information also flows the other way, with the result that the lobbying efforts of informed NGO staff can have a significant influence on shaping government positions. Over time, NGOs are likely to possess more extensive knowledge and a more comprehensive view on their issue than any given diplomat. Overall, the neutrality of NGO faithfulness to principle, relative to particular state interests, when combined with the authority of their issue expertise, gives NGOs the potential for autonomous influence within inter-governmental arenas.

A second realm of activity is not directly related to inter-governmental fora. With increasingly dense networks of communications and informational exchange in the 20th century, international NGOs now also pursue concerns with other NGOs in self-created international arenas. In this respect, the interaction of NGOs might be said to form a nascent international civil society, which is independent of government policy making paths but brings individuals and grassroots groups together for informational exchange and political action. In these self-created arenas, where the agenda is controlled by the NGOs rather than states, there are fewer constraints on NGO expression.

The two channels of influence, inter-governmental and independent, correspond to two possible conceptions of NGOs. The first is the conception of the NGO as a third-party advocate within inter-governmental arenas. The second is the conception of the NGO as an organizational agent of social action outside traditional channels, or "the institutionalization of new populist movements." I address these two views of NGOs below.

In inter-governmental arenas, NGOs seem most threatening to states when they are most like them, that is, when they appear to be allied with identifiable state interests. A classic charge governments use to discredit NGOs is that they are front groups linked to particular nationalistic or ideological positions. Such criticism is often lodged against Amnesty International, for example. A collection of government and editorial responses to the group's work published in the 1980s shows a remarkable balance of accusations from both sides of Cold War ideology. In reaction to Amnesty International's 1976 campaign against torture in Uruguay, a Uruguayan newspaper editorial wrote, "Amnesty International has adopted virtually a unilateral position against Western countries and has remained almost totally silent on the subject of atrocities committed in the communist world." On the other hand, an excerpt from the Soviet newspaper *Izvestia* accused Amnesty International of being a tool of the West: "Even during its early years Amnestry International was in the keep of the imperialist secret services, first and foremost by the Americans, whose interests it serves:"

Historically, NGOs in the United Nations have represented humanitarian concerns. When NGOs were invited to consult with the U.S. delegation at the drafting of the U.N. Charter, their presence was understood to serve the interests of the U.S. government as much as those of the NGO consultants. The NGOs presence, nevertheless, enabled them to secure human rights language in the U.N. charter and continued direct access to the United Nations through the Economic and Social Council (ECOSOC).

The establishment of formal NGO consultative status in ECOSOC on 21 June 1946 was a calculated concession to U.S. NGOs, one which they used to advance human rights principles at the international level. NGOs with consultative status in ECOSOC are organizations "representative of major population segments... involved with the economic and social life" of the areas they represent, "having special competence in a few of the Council's areas of activity," or able to contribute usefully to the Council's work in some way.

An inevitable tension arises, however, when NGOs seek to change the behaviour of states through activity related to inter-governmental arenas, over which states exercise formal control. Ultimately, NGOs involved in domestic and international consultative and advocacy efforts are formally subordinated to state and inter-governmental administrative practices. The procedural tools available to NGOs through consultative status—preparation of reports, filing of complaints, promotion of international legislation and lobbying before national and international bodies—give NGOs limited procedural power relative to states. NGOs do not vote in ECOSOC, and they only observe proceedings in the General Assembly. When the U.N. Commission on Human Rights was set up, NGOs were "restricted, in formal terms, to stiff, cameo appearances." Indeed, until the late 1970s, "convention and habit ensured" that human rights NGOs would express their concerns in the United Nations "with circumlocutions, euphemisms, and evasions"—conventional diplomatic language, reined in by state practice.

Compared with states, NGOs may be limited in terms of formal participation within inter-governmental organizations (IGOs), but larger NGOs have evolved to rival state representatives in their effectiveness on certain issues. NGOs are motivated to make inter-governmental provisions for humanitarian concerns effective, and they can provide services that supplement inter-governmental resources as well as counterbalance the reluctance of inter-governmental bodies to monitor politically sensitive domestic state practices. NGOs acquire a substantive and historical expertise that may be unmatched even by government agencies. In the Human Rights Committee, the body that supervises compliance with the International Covenant on Civil and Political Rights, NGOs "supply information so that the members are better informed in posing questions to governmental representatives when they present their reports. The expertise supplied by NGOs extends to consultation on the drafting of particular texts formally advanced by states in inter-governmental discussions.

In addition to informational resources and expertise, NGOs tap into financial and volunteer resources that, as states grow stingy with resources devoted to international co-operation, can rival IGO budgets. While budgets and staffing levels may be constrained for inter-governmental organizations, NGOs can draw on their memberships for resources. Amnesty International's staff size and budget now stack up favourably against the proportion of U.N. resources dedicated to human rights concerns. The head of the U.N. Centre for Human Rights in Geneva commented that "at present, less than one per cent of the United Nations budget and less than 0.75 per cent of its staff are dedicated to human rights... We have less money and less resources than Amnesty International, and we are the arm of the United Nations for human rights. This is clearly ridiculous."

A further indication of the low priority that states give to issues supported by NGOs is the consistent lag in staffing and funding for the administrative unit of the U.N. Committee on

NGOs within ECOSOC. A 1992 General Assembly resolution passed in response to a report by the U.N. Secretary-General noted that, in contrast to the numerical increase of NGOs in consultative status and the increasing importance of their contributions to ECOSOC proceedings, "resources have remained at the same level since 1947, when the Unit was established.

The availability and size of NGO resources devoted to human rights, therefore, when compared with inter-governmental resources devoted to the issue, can be a source of advantage for NGOs, even in state-governed arenas. Still, in many cases, exerting NGO influence at the international level depends upon placing issues on the inter-governmental agenda, which requires securing co-operation from states and relying on their membership to take advantage of state representational mechanisms. NGOs may direct members willing to approach their own foreign policy-making bodies on behalf of the NGO, thereby effecting a two-tiered form of NGO influence: expert lobbying at the inter-governmental level, backed up by political pressure generated by citizen demand and awareness at home. Popular opinion thus plays a role in allowing NGOs the influence both nationally and internationally to capitalize on their memberships' purchase on representation before particular governments.

International and domestic NGOs can have great impact on government positions, in part because it is now "increasingly difficult for governments to stem the flow of information from local groups to international 'umbrella' human rights groups and international governmental monitoring bodies". This sharing of information is a key aspect in the growth of NGO influence, for NGO activity increasingly takes place outside of formal inter-governmental channels. NGOs are important members of issue networks, comprised by "a set of organizations, bound by shared values and by dense exchanges of information and services, working internationally on an issue."

In exemplary cases, NGOs complement each other's areas of expertise as they pursue a common goal. In a typical example in the area of human rights, a group of statisticians has formed a Committee on Scientific Freedom and Human Rights under the aegies of the American Statistical Association (ASA). The committee publishes an online informational newsletter that encourages its members to participate in the Amnesty International letter-writing network, Urgent Action. In this way, the statistician's group piggybacks on Amnesty International's area of expertise. In addition, by co-ordinating a pool of professional statisticians prepared to volunteer internationally for human rights monitoring projects, and by publishing a text-book on data analysis and human rights, the ASA committee offers another form of expertise in its reliance on already established professional networks to offer specialized services.

In fact, these newly dense networks of communications and informational exchange give international NGOs the option to choose between pursuing their own goals within international governmental arenas, recognizing that their autonomy will likely be limited or subordinated to state goals, and pursuing concerns with other NGOs in self-created international fora with fewer constraints on expression. Some do both, but the vision moving some newer NGOs dictates a link between methods and goals that eschews conventional politics and thus, state-mediated politics. This vision is that of the NGOs taking shape as "institutionalized representation of new populist movements." Indeed, while the focus here so far has been on the direct influence of NGOs in interactions with states, NGOs have also created their own system of activity and influence separate from the governmental sphere, referred to below as "parallel NGO activity."

The environmental movement is one is which a variety of approaches, including parallel NGO activity, has proliferated. Environmental groups at the national level in Brazil, for example, have approached environmentalism as a transformative social movement, emphasizing cultural politics (e.g., communicative activities aimed at reinterpreting politics by identifying and transforming what are understood to be social structures of domination) over formal political opportunities (e.g., influence attempts aimed at affecting policies and legislation through governmental channels and representative mechanisms). The Brazilian environmental groups have taken a broad view of environmental activism, forming alliances with non-environmental groups to address "green" concerns in varying social arenas and rarely mobilizing solely around specific environmental policy problems. By contrast, Venezuelan groups have concentrated on more narrowly defined political opportunities such as government-sponsored conferences to achieve influence on environmental issues, often in response to immediate threats. They too, however, began to supplement that activity with broader public appeals, such as use of the mass media to influence public opinion towards the end of the 1980s.

Brazilian environmentalists, accustomed to a grassroots approach to environmental activism at the domestic level, transferred this philosophy to the international level in 1992. Eager to facilitate interaction among NGOs, Brazilian activists sponsored a special assembly for NGOs to be held concurrently with the 1992 United Nations Conference on Environment and Development (the "Earth Summit"). Rather than being an organizing tool to achieve maximum influence at the inter-governmental conference, the parallel conference, dubbed the Global Forum, was intended to provide a more open venue for the exchange of information among NGOs. Many participants, according to Hochstetler, had come to believe that "official treaties and government declarations were less important than similar citizen commitments."

Some groups, however, did plan to pursue both strategies. The parallel venue was designed to attract the participation of a variety of groups, since NGOs with conventional inter-governmental orientations had access to participation in the Global Forum concurrently. As for the official U.N. conference, NGOs lobbied successfully for relaxed criteria regarding formal NGO participation at Rio and in meetings leading up to the conference. Thus, NGO participation in the official conference was not limited to those with ECOSOC consultative status, and a broader range of NGOs were able to participate.

The parallel approach benefitted both the Brazilian environmentalists, with their interest in social transformation, and groups with more pragmatic philosophies. The Brazilians set up the parallel conference as a potential launching pad for a global citizens' movement on the environment. This led them to approach the meetings as a prototype for what might be called a global civil society. To some extent, their idealism was rewarded. In the international encounters prompted by the Earth Summit, Brazilian were buoyed by the willingness of NGOs from the North to discuss structural issues, such as North-South relations, that governments were unwilling to address. In contrast, Venezuelan environmentalists, accustomed to working closely with their own governmental representatives, saw the parallel conference as a forum in which to "advance the agenda of the South." The Venezuelan activists' rationale was that their counterparts in the North could function as progressive influences among northern governments, advancing public opinion that sound international environmental policy should also address the developmental needs of the South. Both attitudes indicate that conferences like the Earth Summit provide significant opportunities for greater organization and linkage between international and domestic NGOs, whether the NGOs view the political opportunities available to them through a state-centric lens or in broader socio-cultural terms.

The parallel approach of the Brazilian domestic movement in the 1980s meant that the environmental groups in Brazil were not the primary channels for international funding and interest in the preservation of the Amazon river basin. It has been found that, throughout the 1980s, the holistic cultural emphasis of Brazilian environmentalists led them to focus on macro-level political and economic structures and to de-emphasize causes and solutions rooted in specific policies. International environmental lobbies, on the other hand, favoured applying pressure to change specific policies. In consequence, international sponsorship of efforts to preserve the Amazon basin harmonized more easily with non-environmental domestic political actors such as rubber tapper groups and indigenous activists, who also employed policy-specific tactics. With some exceptions, the ostensibly non-environmental groups that have participated in conservation efforts are "much more systematically integrated into international environmental networks than into their own national environmental movement."

The flow of international funding to the more project-oriented environmental groups is a trend that has been identified throughout Latin America. Specific environmental projects that fall under the rubric of sustainable development and are administered by regional or national NGOs, tend to attract a socially diverse, domestic membership. Thus, they are perceived as a safer avenue for international funding than older NGOs that were less guided by project-oriented ideologies. This suggests that the very shape of environmentalism, especially in developing countries, is decided by international funding trends. The typical stages in funding for Latin American environmental NGOs have been described as starting with money from international sources that favour grassroots action, then moving on to larger grants from private and governmental sponsors who favour sustainable development projects and large-scale environmental stewardship. Based on these trends, a change in how domestic NGOs define their projects is evident.

Similar forces appear to be at work regarding government environmental policy, as World Bank funding guidelines emphasize environmental sustainability for development projects. Here, lines between the governmental and the non-governmental grow blurry as NGOs assist with the administration of national projects. For example, a World Bank loan to Mexico in 1992 required collaboration between the Mexican government and Mexican environmental NGOs. A further example is the Brazilian government's protest that, despite its territorial sovereignty over the Amazonian rainforest, it cannot bear the costs of conservation on its own. The Brazilian government has maintained that if Brazil is to refrain from exploiting rainforest resources, it requires assistance from the international community in implementing conservation and development programmes.

The modern NGO has potential to increase its influence over the policy-making agenda in inter-governmental arena. The inter-governmental policy-making arena is likely to remain a central point for co-ordinating action on international issues such as human rights and the environment, but the NGO contribution to formal international aren as can turn them into organizational avenues for citizens as well as states on pressing global issues.

To a ceratin extent the prospects for increased authority of NGOs are positively linked to similar prospects for IGOs. Therefore, the shrinking of state resources devoted to IGOs, or the reluctance of states to participate in multilateral policy making can be expected to have a negative impact on overall NGO influence as well as on inter-governmental structures in the long run. NGO activity in parallel arenas also indirectly contributes to inter-governmental activity by helping to co-ordinate the positions of large international NGOs with domestic, indigenous or culturally specific understandings of issues, such as human rights, the environment and development. NGOs accustomed to consulting with governments may then carry such considerations into their inter-governmental work.

While NGOs' inter-governmental influence on human rights is earned by taking up causes states ignore or contravene and by mastering the intricacies of diplomacy to apply inter-governmental authority to humanitarian concerns, the challenge for human rights NGOs in actually changing state domestic practices remains daunting. It has been argued that repressive states can tolerate high levels of diplomatic and economic isolation for long periods of time. In this respect, the interchange between international NGOs and domestic groups becomes vital to NGO effectiveness. It is difficult for domestic NGOs to thrive under repressive governments, but international contact can foster their physical as well as political survival in a hostile environment. Domestic NGOs, for their part, help to provide information and lobbying efforts in support of NGO objectives at national and international levels. The challenge for human rights NGOs is not so much to develop international allegiances that compete with loyalty to the state as it is to increase popular demand that states respect principles of human dignity as a matter of practice.

The independent potential for NGO accomplishments outside of the inter-governmental realm, such as the use of transformative, citizen-based politics in the environmental movement, is more difficult to assess, in part because the history is brief. The Brazilian case suggests that domestic efforts to create other than state-centric, culturally based modes of activism on the environment are now at a disadvantage, in terms of recruiting international resources to their cause. However, it is possible to say that the interpretive activities of transformative movements, taking place alongside efforts focused on changing specific state practices, have the potential to strengthen ties between less-developed countries and the broader NGO networks, many of whose resources come primarily from participants in affluent countries.

In this respect the case of environmental NGOs seems to mirror that of human rights: Their memberships are motivated more readily by perceptible threats rather than pursuit of a comprehensive agenda rooted in structural change. Funding sources, as well, favour projects promising early and observable results. The seeming dichotomy between the principled and the pragmatic, evidenced in the international response to Brazilian environmental activism, suggests the potential for conflicts over NGO roles in the future. While investment in humanitarian values or moral principles virtually predicates dissatisfaction with the slowly grinding inter-governmental processes, funders' demands for effective practical remedies even when NGOs try to invoke broader considerations may lead to the neglect of the root causes of global problems. Still, as their capacities expand internationally, NGOs will likely be held by their members and by outsiders to progressively higher standards of effectiveness.

THE UNITED NATIONS AND NGOs

In the 1945 San Francisco meetings in which the United Nations Charter was drawn up and signed, 42 NGOs were invited to participate by the US government. They presented draft texts for the Charter, parts of which were eventually incorporated, including this passage from Article 71: *"The Economic and Social Council may make suitable arrangements for consultation with non-governmental organizations..."*. That laid the foundations for co-operation between the UN and NGOs. The Council granted consultative status to a limited number of NGOs, which meant that these NGOs could participate in some debates and, in some cases, place items on the agenda. Other NGOs, however, could co-operate in the field with the specialised agencies.

It was probably in the field more than anywhere else that the presence of NGOs began to be felt strongly. Specialised agencies and bodies such as the UN Development Programme and the UN High Commissioner for Refugees realised early on that NGOs offered them crucial resources and expertise. For example, without the co-operation of humanitarian organizations—ranging from CARE to Médecins Sans Frontières (Doctors Without Borders)—it would have been virutally impossible to meet the needs of refugees fleeing war. Many of these specialised agencies have their own relationships with NGOs; they can co-ordinate NGO efforts, provide funds for NGO projects or even receive funds from NGOs for their own programmes. The co-operation of NGOs has also furthered the goals of the UN in other areas such as disarmament, human rights, education, the environment and science.

Beginning with the 1992 UN Conference on Environment and Development in Rio de Janeiro, the broader participation of NGOs in addressing global issues became a fact. Over 1500 organizations were accredited to participate in the conference. In this and subsequent international conferences, such as the World Conference on Human Rights (Vienna), the International Conference on Population and Development (Cairo), the World Summit for Social Development (Copenhagen) and the Fourth World Conference on Women (Beijing). NGOs have shaped many of the points on the agendas some of which have already become law.

In short, NGOs participate in the UN system in four ways.

(i) They raise issues, such as women's rights and the environment, which then get placed on the world's agendas.

(ii) They shape decisions taken by the UN though it can be said that they are much less influential in politics than in the social and humanitarian fields.

(iii) They enter into partnership with the UN to help carry out its objectives and programmes in the field. and

Finally, they serve as important watchdogs of the UN, observing, criticising and reporting on its role.

PEOPLE POWER

The contributions of NGOs and countless individual lawyers, journalists and other activists have helped greatly to further respect for human rights throughout the world. To cite just one example: by 1990, some members of *Charter 77* in Czechoslovakia and of *Helsinki Watch* committees in several nations in Eastern Europe and the former Soviet Union were in power in countries where, just months before, they had been in prison.

Frequently, the fate of those who publicly denounce human rights abuses or work as human rights watchdogs is arrest, abduction, torture and worse.

- According to UN reports, in El Salvador in 1991 death threats were directed at several human rights activists, including the president of the *International Association Against Torture.*
- In India, the son of the president of the *Punjab Human Rights Organization* was arrested and executed in 1991.
- At least six human rights lawyers in the Philippines have been murdered in the past four years.
- In 1991 alone, the *UN Special Rapporteur on Summary or Arbitrary Executions* sent urgent appeals to 49 Governments on some 4,200 cases of death threats levied against persons who sought to cooperate with UN human rights bodies or who sought protection.

To protect the human rights of NGOs and others who, in speaking out on behalf of human rights, become victims of human rights abuses, a working group of the *UN Commission on Human Rights* is drafting a *Declaration on Human Rights Defenders.* The document calls for guaranteeing the right to:

- Form, join and participate in human rights NGOs;
- Denounce human rights violations publicly;
- Communicate with international NGOs and inter-governmental organizations;
- Have recourse to effective means of legal redress.

The work of publicizing human rights violations and bringing pressure on offending Governments often falls to NGOs. Their credibility, like that of the United Nations in the field of human rights, stems from the impartial application of universal norms to all Governments.

- At the International level, NGOs such as *Amnestly International* (winner of the Nobel Prize for Peace for 1977), the *International Committee of the Red Cross* and *Human Rights Watch* (with its divisions *Africa Watch, Americas Watch, Asia Watch, Helsinki Watch and Middle East Watch)* conduct on-site investigations, disseminate detailed reports and wage advocacy campaigns in international and domestic forums.
- Operating with far less public awareness and physical protection than their transnational counterparts are domestic human rights organizations, which, where possible, monitor the actions of their respective Governments. Among these groups are the *Tutela Archdiocesan Legal Protection Office* of San Salvador (El Salvador), *Vicarfa de Solidaridad* in Chile and the *Free Legal Assistance Group* of the Philippines.

The success of the human rights movement is best measured by the extent to which some Governments have incorporated human rights concerns into their policy-making. In the United States, the State Department has for more than a decade been required to produce an annual survey of human rights conditions world-wide to help Congress assess how U.S. assistance affects the rights of people in recipient countries. And Amnesty International's 1992 annual report concludes: "Countries whose rulers would not even have paid lip service to human rights a decade ago are now declaring their importance."

The *UN Economic and Social Council (ECOSOC)* defines a non-governmental organization as "any international organization which is not established by inter-governmental agreement". This broad term encompasses private voluntary organizations, community groups, professional and trade associations, labour unions, academic and scientific organizations and others.

- Thousands of NGOs concentrate on human rights, dealing with human rights in general or with specific rights or issues such as torture or prisoners of conscience.
- Many NGOs focus on other issues but incorporate human rights into their activities. The *Latin American Adult Education Centre* handles human rights within its wider area of concern.
- Other groups, such as those offering legal assistance to mothers, workers or the poor, indirectly support the advancement of human rights.

NGOs vary in how they are organized. Some are made up solely of volunteers or staff members. Others have restricted membership, such as the *International Commission of Jurists,* which is made up of 40 eminent jurists from many countries and defends and promotes the role of lawyers and judges in the legal protection of human rights. Some NGOs have members who participate in or contribute financially to the organization's activities. Amnesty International is the largest organization of this kind, with more than 1.1 million members in 150 countries.

Information is by far the most potent weapon in the NGO arsenal. Once NGOs collect and verify information, they transmit it to the United Nations and other international organizations. They also make extensive use of the media to publicize individual cases or general country situations.

- Amnestly International, Human Rights Watch and the *International Federation for Human Rights* are among the many NGOs which produce surveys, newsletters and other valuable reports on human rights violations throughout the world.
- *Promotion:* Mainly carried out by NGOs in the legal field, which seek to prevent legal abuses, lobby for laws on human rights protection and work for ratification of international human rights treaties.
- *Information campaigns:* For the general public and targeted sectors of society such as Governments, lawyers, judges or police. *Human Rights Internet* is an international communications network and clearing-house for human rights information.

- *Education:* Teaching human rights or encouraging education ministries and universities to incorporate human rights material into their curricula. The *World Association for the School as an instrument of Peace* organizes an annual international training session on teaching human rights for teacher in colleges and secondary schools.
- *Studies and research:* Investigating themes such as administration of justice, links between drug trafficking and human rights or how law functions within indigenous communities.

Article 71 of the *UN Charter* provides for the participation of NGOs, on a consultative basis, in the work of ECOSOC. Among the 930 NGOs with consultative status are Amnesty International, the *International Federation of Red Cross and Red Crescent Societies,* the *Andean Commission of Jurists* and the *Regional Council for Human Rights in Asia.*

- The United Nations maintains contact with a wide range of NGOs through the *Department of Public Information* and the *Non-Governmental Liaison Service (NGLS),* sponsored jointly by several agencies and programmes of the UN system.

NGOs provide information to UN experts who monitor human rights and generally try to influence the decisions of the many UN bodies whose work touches on human rights.

- Participation by NGOs in meetings of the Commission on Human Rights has increased from 33 NGOs in 1970 to 62 in 1980 and 150 in 1992.
- The issue of torture was taken up by the United Nations in response to a 1973 NGO campaign aimed at abolishing the practice.
- NGO lobbying helped establish the *Working Group on Indigenous Populations* and the *Working Group on Enforced or Involuntary Disappearances.* Says Diego Garcia-Sayan, a member of the latter. "Little would be accomplished without the growing professionalism of human rights groups..... The NGOs present and follow up on information in a reliable, precise and careful manner. Without this painstaking work, the Group would not be able to function

as it does..... The Group, alongwith many intergovernmental organizations, relies basically upon NGOs and not the Governments themselves. The NGOs provide the Group with information, pressure it to act and clamour for results. This is true of all of the United Nations specialized groups."

- According to the *Special Rapporteur on Summary and Arbitrary Executions*, S. Amos Wako: "NGOs are the source of most of the information and allegations concerning arbitrary and illegal executions received by the Special Rapporteur. This information is indispensable to the effective fulfilment of the mandate of the Special Rapporteur."
- The human rights complaint mechanism known as the "1503 procedure" is kept going almost exclusively by information supplied by NGOs. The procedure authorizes the *Sub-Commission on Prevention of Discrimination and Protection of Minorities* "to consider all communications.... which appear to reveal a consistent pattern of gross and reliably attested violations of human rights and fundamental freedoms" in a given country.

The consultative status of NGOs permits them to participate (without vote) in the drafting process of UN conventions, declarations and other efforts to set international standards.

- During the drafting of the UN Charter, NGO representatives helped ensure inclusion of articles mentioning human rights, including one to set up a commission for promotion of human rights.
- Some 30 NGOs, among them trade unions and religious, women's and parliamentarians' groups, were instrumental in drafting the *Universal Declaration of Human Rights.*
- NGOs helped prepare the *International Covenant on Civil and Political Rights* and the *International Covenant on Economic, Social and Cultural Rights,* both adopted in 1966.
- The *Declaration on the Elimination of Discrimination against Women* (1967) and the *Convention on the Elimination of All Forms of Discrimination against Women* (1979) came about as result of substantial input from women's NGOs. In 1976, the *Conference of African Women* submitted a 25-article draft convention to the *UN Commission on the Status of Women,* a text which had a significant impact on the final document.

- Amnesty International, the International Commission of Jurists and the *International Association of Penal Law* helped draft the 1984 *UN Convention against Torture.* A group led by *Defence for Children International* helped draft the 1989 *UN Convention on the Rights of the Child.*

Government ratification of the Conventions they sign often proceeds slowly. Once instruments come into force, government compliance is often lacking. NGOs make their presence felt at both ends of this process.

- In an effort that required ten years, NGOs helped secure the 35 ratifications necessary for the International Covenants on Civil and Political Rights and on Economic, Social and Cultural Rights to enter into force.
- When States parties present their national reports to the United Nations, NGOs provide information on the country concerned to experts entrusted with considering those reports.

NGOs are independent and willing to take risks in areas which Governments and inter-governmental organizations consider too politically sensitive. They have, by their very nature, a freedom of expression, a flexibility of action and a liberty of movement which enable them to complement the role of the United Nations in the promotion and protection of human rights.

- Says Mr. Garcia-Sayan of the UN Working Group on Disappearances: "Anyone who has ever attended a session of the UN Commission on Human Rights has seen the caution—to say the least—with which the government representatives act...it would seem that there exists a policy of not criticizing neighbouring countries directly or harshly. Strange but notorious silences can be understood simply as indicating geopolitical interests. The 'prosecutors' in these circumstances, that is to say those who hold human rights above other concerns, are the NGOs. They are the fuel and the lubricant which allow the machine to function and speed the working up."

For precisely these reasons, NGOs are sometimes accused of being anti-government or of undermining public order and the stability of society. Yet it is Governments that commit human rights violations. because human rights are precisely limits on the exercise of official power, and human rights violations are transgressions of such limits. If NGOs are sometimes perceived as being nuisances to Governments, it is because that is their role.

Role of NGOs in Achieving the Goals of U.N. Decade

The most important recommendation of the World Conference on Human Rights held at Vienna, (Austria) from 14 to 25 June, 1993 was that: "Human Rights, Democracy, Rule of Law and development be included in the curriculum of all educational institutions". It was on January 1, 1995 that the United Nations declared the UN Decade for Human Rights Education. It is heartening to note that in the same year, the Asian Institute for Human Rights Education was established at Bhopal. The AIHRE has forged ahead with the formulation of curriculum and preparation of sample lessons with the collaboration and co-operation of SCERT, Madhya Pradesh and DIET, Bhopal. The Conference of 1995 (WCCI) could come out with a declaration endorsing these attempts. The Regional Conference of WCCI held at Palayamkottai, Tamilnadu has gone a step further in promoting Human Rights Education jointly with a sister organisation - IAEWP (International Association of Educators for World Peace).

We have in India a National Commission on Human Rights and several state level commissions. But how far these have succeeded in ensuring human rights to our citizens? Human Rights violations are taking place in most places. How many are brought to sight and grievances redressed? Only a few atrocities against women are on the increase. Child labour is another area. Rights of the girl child are not secure. The aged are neglected. Corruption is on the increase at all levels. Even people at the helm of affairs are booked, at least after their powerful days. People amass money through foul measures. The rich are becoming richer and the poor, poorer. Human Rights are there on paper, but in actual practice they are very much neglected. So commission and laws are not enough. Awareness should be created among the people. Citizens should become law-abiding. None should get exemption based on political, communal or money power. From the lowest class onwards children should study human rights, values, democracy and practice them. Even if it is not in the curriculum or text book, every teacher and educator also should try to understand and make use of the hidden curriculum. This will naturally lead to the establishment of a society, state and world order dedicated to peace, progress and prosperity. IAEWP is one such NGO which tries at International and local levels to build up a warless society, where we-feeling is dominant. Educators at all levels are the best persons to inculcate human rights education: theory and practice among the future citizens. Our formal system alone cannot attempt or succeed in this endeavour. The non-formal sector has to play an active and ever increasing role in conscientising the masses. Herein comes the role of NGOs. Name-sake interventions are not enough. Rapid Action Forces are to be formed along the lines of social action groups (Activists) to counter human rights violations, not through confrontation and conflict, but through creating awareness and ensuring wilful participation and adjustment. Peopel's Council for Social Justice (PCSJ) is one such working in India (specially in Kerala). They are educating the masses and organising Neethimelas, outside the courts. Family courts are also in operation . . . But many are afraid of approaching these courts and commissions. What is needed first is to inform the public of such organisations, their role and functioning. Folk art forms and modern media have to be fully and effectively utilised to create awareness among the people on human rights, democracy and development. Education and development are the two sides of the same coin. One has to lead to the other. But is it happening? People look upto others for achieving their goals and stating their needs and urges. Prioritizing development activities (especialy local) is the first step to be undertaken. Kerala has launched such an attempt in the preparation of IX plan proposals. From the rural village / ward upward, the exercise is in this direction of establishing and maintaining human rights. From the lowest level of self-government upwards, efforts should be made to involve every citizen in the nation-building work.

India is celebrating its 50th year of independence. Definitely we have achieved a lot during these 50 years. Quantitative expansion is visible. How about quality? There is difference of opinion. In many fields we are lagging behind. Even we have nearly half of our population embedded with illiteracy, poverty, unemployment, etc. We are trying to make education a right for all. Values are eroding. Western influence is affecting our youth in many ways. Our unique culture is being spoiled. How to overcome these.

The only way out is human rights education, direct and indirect for all—using formal and non-formal approaches. Multimedia approaches should also be used to preserve our Indianness, the heritage which our forefathers have builtup.

The role of the UN should also be subjected to careful analysis and necessary changes have to be effected (including increase of permanent membership in the security council). Declarations are not enough. They have to be carefully translated into action. We educators have to pledge to bring about such desired changes and work hard in that direction. GOS's and NGO's have a role in such areas. We should stop accusing each other. What is needed is co-operation and collaboration.

Human Rights NGOs in the Third World

"Non-governmental organizations" or indeed the "non-governmental sector" (within which most human rights organizations operate in the Third World) are not easily susceptible of definition. So large a variety of entities operate within the "non-governmental sector" that all one can say about the sector is that it isn't the private sector either (atleast not the private corporate sector). Non-governmental organizations (NGOs) are the product of social action, history and culture. There has been a growing perception (both managerial and political) among international organizations and among northern governments that NGOs have the potential of being more effective agents of development than governmental agencies, atleast when working with or attempting to reach the poor. Consequently, there has been a significant increase in the supply of funding available to support the work of NGOs. There has also been, in many parts of the Third World' the explosive emergence of NGOs as a major collective actor in development activities and on the public agenda in general. This is a significant political, social and economic trend. Within the traditional areas of encounter between the state and the people, a new actor (the NGO) asserts itself with increasing forcefulness. The NGO explosion in the Third world is both quantitative (in terms of the scale and pace with which new NGOs have been multiplying and expanding during the last decade) and qualitative (in terms of the concerns, functions and roles that the NGOs are either asserting for themselves or are being called upon to play by governments and/or the international development assistance community). One particular kind of third World NGO—"poor people' organizations"—have become internally more sophisticated and thus have increased their militancy and mobilization capabilities. While most of the Third World NGOs have not started with an explicit human rights agenda, they have tended to come rather quickly to activities involving the promotion and assertion of human rights. In order to further appreciate the significance of the above truisms, it is also necessary to debunk the myth of yet another truism represented by the motion that a single, unified Third World exists, country and intra-country contexts vary a great deal in the Third World, indeed. But certain common trends and insights emerge when one focuses on the experience in the different regions of the Third World: Latin America, Asia, Africa.

The Asian Case

At its inaugural and subsequent meeting, the Asian Coalition of Human Rights Organizations reached consensus as to the situation confronting Asia:

> In virtually every country in Asia, to greater or lesser extent, we witness today several alarming and intolerable trends:
>
> 1. The growing impoverishment, exploitation and powerlessness of a majority of the rural and urban population: the poor.
> 2. The growing incidence of malnutrition, hunger and starvation and growing permanent degradation of the physical environment for the production of food and the meeting of survival needs.
> 3. The worsening of already intolerable conditions of those subject to multiple oppression and exploitation such as women, children and religious or ethnic minorities.
> 4. The routinization of the debasement of human beings leading to the very devaluation of human life itself.
> 5. The increasing adoption, by the elites in such countries, of a life-style (aping Western models of conspicuous consumption) whose affluence can only be sustained by the pauperization and exploitation of others.
> 6. The growth of fundamentalist trends in religious revivalism making religion a divisive rather than a cohesive force.
> 7. The increasing incidence of ethnic violence and cultural genocide.

8. The growth of material and moral corruption among the bureaucracy and their virtually total lack of accountability.
9. The increasingly authoritarian nature of political institutions despite their virtually total lack of accountability.
10. The growing militarization of developing countries achieved through government expenditure on arms at the expense of programs to alleviate poverty.
11. The imposition of hazards and harms upon powerless workers and communities through indiscriminate industrialization employing hazardous technologies.

The human rights movement in Asia has emerged in response to these intolerable trends and conditions. But the response has led to the emergence of three strands within the Asian human rights movement:

(a) Responding to extremely oppressive conditions and repressive regimes (in the Philippines and Korea, for example), a category of human rights NGOs emerged at local, grassroots level to mobilize local communities for protracted political struggles. Often inspired by liberation theology (or secular variants thereof as in the case of Bangladesh), these NGOs saw the human rights struggle as being, initially, a struggle against the present political regime.

(b) Responding to the ineffectual nature of government programmes to deliver basic services to (and meet the basic needs of) the rural poor, a second set of NGOs attempted to deliver such services themselves while also embarking upon education activities to develop the communities capacities to meet their own needs in the future. Such NGOs turned to human rights to assert entitlements of local impoverished communities to resources from the state to meet such needs.

(c) A third strand of the human rights movement in Asia arose out of the disillusionment of significant sections of the educated middle-classes (the bourgeois intelligentsia) with the results and the direction of the development model adopted by the country. Thus human rights organizations who were concerned about subjecting national development projects and developmental decision-takers to accountability under international human rights law began to emerge. A

notable example of this is provided by NGOs working to asserts rights of indigenous people and other poor communities displaced by development projects of the state.

Today, there is a real sense of urgency underlying human rights activism in Asia. Both NGOs and grassroots organizations of the rural poor are turning to human rights as a means to :

1. *Empowerment.* It is increasingly felt that human rights can play a significant role in the empowerment of the impoverished. The oppressed can become more self-reliant through an understanding of their rights. Indeed, the right to organize and right of association are vital to impoverished groups seeking to mobilize and organize themselves and thus develop countervailing power.
2. *Securing Accountability.* Human rights can also play a significant role in securing the accountability of those who wield power and control resources essential to the satisfaction of basic human needs. Rights to secure mandamus or prohibition are important checks on abuse of power. Rights of access to information, rights to a public hearing and freedom of speech and of the press are crucial in checking governmental lawlessness and abuse of discretion or powers by bureaucratic and government officials.
3. *Participation.* Human rights have an important role to play in combating exclusion as well as in asserting the right to participate in key decisions affecting resource allocation or relating to technology choice.
4. *Assert Values.* Human rights are also being increasingly viewed as a means to express and reinforce social value and ethical principle which should underlie the much-needed restructuring of social orders.

The above survey of the social and historical forces leading to the emergence of the current NGO "explosion" in the third World suffers from many inadequacies resulting both from subjective biases of the author and the inevitably impressionistic nature of the survey. It is offered only to be suggestive of the richness of contexts and diversities that must inform and humble attempts at analyzing and classifying Third World human rights organizations and their functions. And such analysis and classification, in turn, is an essential first step before attempts to assist, support or link such organizations are undertaken.

In order to understand human rights activism in the Third World, one needs to take a closer look at the people involved in human rights organizations. Three main categories have been involved: intellectuals, professionals, and activists. Prominent among the professionals have been members of the legal elite—leaders of the legal profession, former members of the judiciary and prominent legal academics. Their involvement has been of a more conventional kind, helping provide legal services and legal representation to indigents, or to those whose civil and political rights have been violated, or in "test cases" and "public interest litigation." Their approach has been mainly to work within the existing law, using existing legal processes to enforce human rights or to help bring about incremental development of the content of specific human rights. There has been the conventional liberal approach to human rights which presumes that compliance with rights is the societal norm and rights which presumes that compliance with rights is the societal norm and rights enforcement is only necessary in a few deviant cases.

Professionals and intellectuals in the Third World have attempted to reach out to human rights activists through a variety of intellectual and professional movements:

The Regional Studies and Development Studies Movement in many Third World countries has helped reorient lawyers and social scientists to special problems of development and under-development and to the human rights implications of such process. This has helped forge a new sense of identity and solidarity around " Third World issues" and has helped sensitize them to processes of impoverishment, exploitation, exclusion, and dependency and to the roles of human rights theory and activism in fighting against such processes. Concepts of dependence, integration into the global capitalist system, and transnationalization have been thus brought into human rights thought and action.

The Critical Studies Movement has called attention to deep-rooted pathologies that exist in law and the legal profession in most Third World countries. The Movement has been iconoclastic: debunking legal sacred cows and myths by calling attention to the wide gap that exists between the law in the books and the law in action; between law and justice, the movement has worked towards securing fundamental changes in the legal system to make it more accessible, more indigenous, more just (by fostering notions of redistributive justice) and more supportive of social change.

The Alternatives Movement has challenged the "development models" adopted by Third World countries—models emphasizing modernization, industrialization, economic growth (without conscious policies of redistribution), and integration into the global capitalist system. The movement stimulate human rights activism in support of the victims (e.g., indigenous people, displaced people) of development policies and projects and has also simulated activism centered around formulating and implementing policies and programmes of "alternative development" which are built and the adoption of alternatives to Western consumer-oriented life-styles. "This movement has brought inter-disciplinary perspectives and skills into human rights though and activism in the Third World and a fresh "alternative" set of values. It has helped foster the perception that, "law is too serious a matter to be left entirely to lawyers; for the issue of human rights is not merely a legal one but a potent political and social issue." It has also helped stimulate the process of deprofessionalization of law through "bare-foot lawyers" and "community dispute-settlement mechanisms."

Participatory Action Research. By far the greatest impact of an intellectual movement on human rights in the Third World has been the movement towards participatory action research. The concept of participatory action research (PAR) originated in Latin America but soon gained acceptance in Asia and Africa. PAR emphasizes the importance of participatory development of knowledge, action strategies and human rights through close interaction with grassroots communities. PAR has fundamentally changed human rights thinking and activism in the Third World by broadening the base of human rights actors to include those who are victims of human rights violations.

Human rights activists in the Third World have also increasingly reached out to intellectuals and professionals as a result of a number of action strategies they have adopted. Originally, most social activists adopted an attitude of "legal nilhilism"; the less contact with the legal system (particularly the criminal justice system) as their work on grassroots conscientization and organization gathered momentum. They soon began to shed such an attitude. Contact between activists and intellectuals and professionals increased within the context of specific action strategies which necessitated new forms of association and organization:

Campaigns : such as the Infant formula Campaign.

Coalition : such as the International Coalition for Justice in Bhopal.

Solidarity and Protest Organizations : such as Greenpeace.

Lobby Groups : such as the Asia Pacific Forum for Women, Law and Development.

Regional Networks : such as the Asian Regional council on Human rights.

Social Movements : such as the consumer movement, the women's movement and the environmental movement.

To sum up, intellectual movements, social movements, and pragmatic-action strategies and campaigns have brought the main human rights actors in the third World—victims, activists, intellectuals, and professions—together in a variety of situations of intraction. As a result, human rights organization in the third World have become more interdisciplinary in nature and more broad-based in composition. They have also become harder to identify and define, A few Third World NGOs wear the label of human rights. But the vast majority of Third World NGOs, concerned primarily with education, or development, or delivery of support and services, have adopted human rights into their agendas and programmes of action. A broad definition of human rights organizations in the Third World would have to include all these "non-specialist" NGOs which are undertaking significant human rights activities.

It would not be possible, desirable, or sensible to attempt to construct a single, comprehensive, all-encompassing typology of Third world human rights organization. Rather, one might suggest the many ways that loose typologies might be drawn.

Governmental/Non-governmental/Inter-governmental. While the majority of human rights organizations in the third World are non-governmental, there has been the recent trend (especially in countries like the Philippines, which are undergoing a process of re-democratization) to establish governmental human rights commissions.

International/Regional/National/Local. In Asia, where the governments have firmly rejected any regional intergovernmental human rights organization, a number of regional non-governmental organizations have sprung up.

According to Membership. In Asia, a distinction is usually drawn between people-based organizations (PBOs) and participatory organizations of the rural poor (PORPs) on the one hand which are primary-level organizations (e.g. of small farmers, fisherfolk), and support groups which render services to PBOs and which are referred to as secondary-level organizations. Human rights organizations could also be classified on the basis of membership drawn on professional lines.

According to Victim-Group Served. Some human rights organizations serve only single target groups, e.g. women, children, indigenous people. Others serve a variety of victim groups.

According to Functions. Distinctions are being made between human rights organizations performing mobilizational roles, advocacy group; documentation center; forum; coalition; or campaign, are used to describe a range of human rights organizations in the Third World. Most of them tend to be multifunctional or, atleast bi-functional.

According to Category of Human Rights specialization. This Western categorization of groups focusing on civil and political rights and those focusing on economic, social, and cultural rights, is not much used in the Third World where organizations tend to focus on both categories of rights. However, because of the gravity of problem in some countries, human rights organizations have emerged focusing on particular sets of rights such as those relating to ethnicity.

Many third World human rights organizations did not start as explicit human rights organizations at all and may have been emergency—aid organizations, philanthropic, developmental, or environmental organizations. This fact is often reflected in the roles and functions they play once they begin to address a specifically human rights-oriented agenda. Third World human rights organizations are not a mirror image of their first World counterparts. Nevertheless, it is possible and useful to study Third world human rights organizations in terms of the conventional roles of human rights activism.

Promotion. Many third World human rights organizations do embark on typical human rights promotion activities employing locally appropriate devices such as comic books, folk theatre or folk music, poster competitions, etc. But often, the promotional work forms part of a rights awareness programme that is fostering rights assertiveness as a means towards conscientization, mobilization, and organization for direct action.

Standard setting. Third World human rights organizations are increasingly recognizing the importance of partipating in standard-setting work, both at the international level (e.g. in relation to the right to development, or the convention on the Rights of the Child) as well as at the national level (e.g. in the Philippines to develop, comprehensive national codes on agrarian reform and on fisheries' resources).

Monitoring. Third World human rights groups have been actively monitoring implementation of national legislation (e.g. dealing with women's rights and child labour in India) and are beginning to be concerned with international human rights law (e.g. by bringing complaints before the Sub-Commission on rights of Minorities and Indigenous People).

Enforcement. Impressive strides have been made here by third World human rights groups in assisting enforcement of rights through the courts (e.g. by adoption of metalegal tactics in the Philippines).

Lobbying for Law Reform. There has been a flurry of activity here, especially in countries like the Philippines where parliamentary, legislative processes have been restored after a long lapse of time.

In addition to these conventional roles, human rights organizations in the third World have also played unique roles which result from their human rights activism originating in community and victim-group mobilization and organization, thus they have acted to:

Help create grassroots organizations and help their organizational development. They have helped organize people to make better use of their own local productive resources, to create new resources and services, to promote equity and alleviate poverty, to influence government actions towards the same objectives and to establish new institutional frameworks that will durably sustain humane people-powered development.

Help act as an intermediary between local government and community organizations.

Help, where circumstances warrant, raise funding and direct it to local community organizations.

Help develop capacity for and strengthen community-based resources management with an emphasis on participation, equality and equity. Human rights organization working in neglected rural areas have helped set up local production-related organization such as water-user societies, pastoral-grazing associations, credit, production or consumer co-operatives, food-processing co-operatives, farm equipment purchase or lease associations, tree grower associations, fishermen co-operatives, etc. At first glance, these activities seem far removed from human rights work. But these kinds of organizations have proved critical instrumentalities, not only for participatory local development but also for grassroots realization of human rights. At times these organizations have averted serious denials of human rights which would have resulted had their efforts not prevented ecological degradation imperiling the very survival of the most depressed sections of the local community.

Help create not only the means for community organizing but also for community self-defense.

Help assert community rights and raise community awareness and expectations.

Help protect activities against reprisals from high-handed administrators.

Thus, human rights organization in the Third World have had to constantly undergo a process of self-development. There has been a need for constant reflection based on praxis to reconceptualize human rights concepts and theory. There has also been a need for a professional unlearning and relearning process accompanied by the development of genuine professional humility. So far as lawyers are concerned, there has been a need for new kinds of law-trained people to act as:

— *community workers* who help to organize and participate in collective efforts of people to identify their legal problems and appropriate strategies;
— *advocates* of collective demands and group interests both in courts and in administrative, legislative and other institutions.
— *community* educators helping to develop community knowledge of law and legal para professionals within the

community whose knowledge and skills are geared to community needs.

— *critics* of proposed or existing legislation and administrative actions which impinge on the rights and interests of impoverished groups;

— *law reformers* asserting the claims of rural communities for changes in legislation and state structures; and

— *jurists* seekings to develop new jurisprudential concepts needed, for example, to articulate new rights which will help to empower the poor in their struggle against impoverishment.

It has been a paradox that the greater their success and achievements, the greater has been the need for support for human rights organizations in the Third World. Below, we briefly identify some of these needs. To elaborate upon such needs would be presumptuous, that task would be better left to a consultation with the human rights organizations themselves. There is, of course, a perennial and chronic need of funding. This need will be addressed later in this chapter. Other, and often more important, needs include:

Defense: There is a crucial need to devise effective mechanisms at national and international levels, for the defense and protection of human rights activists, community groups and people's organizations which face reprisals because they are seeking to assert rights and secure remedies. Recent events in Malaysia and Singapore underscore the need for urgency for developing Amnesty International-type counterparts to protect Third World human rights activists — especially those working at grassroots level. There is also a need to develop national and regional mechanisms to deal with an allied problem. As human rights NGOs become more successful, some governments seek to close the political space for their continued operation by enacting a variety of legislative and policy measures which increase regulation and restrict the activities of NGOs. These are usually accompanied by attempts to co-opt, fragment, and divide the NGO community. Recognizing this danger, several Asian human rights organizations have recently formed a coalition to resist. While the coalition is still in its infancy, its work will be of interest far beyond the region.

Solidarity: Third World human rights NGOs have little opportunity for south-south exchange of experience and for solidarity building. Such opportunities are beginning to be created for development NGOs but usually permitting only limited exchange on only a regional basis. This world human rights activism has reached a level to well justify the setting up of mechanisms for exchange across the regions of the Third world.

Information sharing: Much of what has been said regarding needs for solidarity apply equally here, too. Existing systems for human rights documentation are indeed a valuable first step. But mechanisms also need to be devised to facilitate person-to-person exchanges and information sharing. The same could also apply to human resources development, for example, with regard to barefoot lawyers.

Linkages with International Human Rights System: It is increasingly being felt by Third World human rights organizations that they are now ready to press for enforcement of human rights, not only in national fora but also in the variety of interaction, leading to the development of more enduring linkages, between Third World human rights activists and the international human rights law community. Such interaction would doubtless prove mutually enriching and lead to more effective enforcement of human rights.

Organizational Development: For many Third World human organizations, and other NGOs twin profound processes are presently at work: an inner-oriented one by which NGOs are striving to overcome structural weaknesses, dispersion, amorphousness within their own house, and a concomitant outer-orientned process by which NGOs are learning to contribute more effectively to the broader, societal goals they pursue. They are facing a need for expansion in coverage and comprehensiveness (i.e. extensive development) as well as for strengthening the many fragile and ephemeral NGOs that risk disappearing without a trace (i.e. extensive development). There is a need for strengthening internal, organizational structures, fortifying their decision-making and reproductive processes. There are problems of need for scale-up and replication to achieve greater impact. There is a need for better and ongoing participatory evaluation. Sensitively provided support that enables access to modest resources (financial and human), coupled with autonomous and participatory interaction and consultation, will go a long way towards meeting these needs.

Research for Better Comprehension and Analysis. There is need, only partly met, for greater reflection, self-appraisal and critique of the third World human rights movement. The need is for research at conceptual, theoretical, and action levels. This research must largely be undertaken as a participatory process and the findings of the research need expression and dissemination through new channels to complement existing ones. The fruits of such introspection may well benefit human rights organizations not only in the Third World, but everywhere.

The specific mechanisms through which the above needs for external support can be addressed will need to be evolved through a partnership of equals and not by donor benevolence alone. Equally important is the need to devise effective participatory mechanisms whereby Third World human rights NGOs can make an effective impact upon the policy-making processes of government and development assistance agencies—be they bilateral or multilateral.

Third World NGOs have done some hard thinking regarding problems and dilemmas involved in funding, especially where funding is sought from an external source. They have identified opportunity costs, credibility costs, flexibility costs, and vulnerability costs that might result from funding. They have grappled with the struggle for self-reliance and autonomy on the one hand, and access to an adequate resource base on the other. They have experimented with a variety of funding mechanisms such as grants, endowments, and revolving funds. They have experimented with income generation which carries its own strengths and limitations. International NGOs have played a crucial role in raising private funds and channeling them to developing countries but there have been problems of NGO independence, geographical allocation of resources, interference in the NGOs own agenda, priorities and approach; and of NGO accountability. Third world NGOs have helped work out for themselves some of the problems inevitable in a donor/recipient relationship and have even begun to articulate the elements that help build up a good relationship: demand-led, honesty, commitment to values and goals, relevance, flexibility, confidentiality, partnership, long-term collaboration. They have even been able to soften donor insistence upon "projectizing" activities and have earned recognition of the principle that not only project but also processes are deserving of donor support.

Thus, over the years, Third World NGOs and donor agencies have been working seriously towards fashioning a truly rewarding "partnership of equals." This partnership is presently in great peril with governments in countries like Indonesia and India placing severe constraints upon the NGOs freedom to receive foreign funding. These restraints have also been accompanied by a variety of other restrictive or corporative measures which place in jeopardy the effective survival of NGOs as autonomous and independent entities. The NGOs are fighting back against their own governments' repressive policies. At this juncture, their most vital need for external support is precisely support in their present struggle for survival. Donors can, and should, exert influence over recipient governments to ensure that the latter maintain public policy and legislative frameworks that safeguard the role of NGOs —a role they have fought so hard and so long to get recognized. Similarly, donor agencies must be vigilant to ensure that NGOs win their struggle not only against repression but also against cooptation. The current flood of rhetoric from governmental and international agencies alike, looking to NGOs to perform a variety of functions and play a variety of roles that governmental agencies themselves cannot, must be viewed with healthy scepticism as a potentially co-optative ploy.

By and large, Third World human rights NGOs have tended to shy away from institutional relationships with one another. Attempts to coordinate have (often rightly) been peceived as attempts to control. NGOs cherish their autonomy, identity, and independence and therefore are willing to accept, at most, loose coordination within a membership organization (e.g. Thailand, Philippines). Other factors militating against formal institutional relationships involve "turf"; competition for scarce or limited resources; ethnic, religious, or other cultural diversity; different perceptions of mandate ranging from narrow civil liberatarian to broad empowerment focused. Different perceptions of mandate and different philosophies of human rights or of human rights activism also keep human rights NGOs (e.g. Amnesty International and, to a lesser degree, the International Commission of Jurists) have their own national chapters and these link together in their own international institutional form. But between countries, even at a regional level, there are few instances of institutional relationship between human rights NGOs but instead there tends to be regional human rights NGOs formed. Fresh problems arise in the relationship between Third World human rights NGOs and regional and international human rights NGOs especially in respect of division of labour.

Third World human rights NGOs are much more successful in their functional relationships. They have often come together in action campaigns. They have worked together on training programmes, on fact-finding missions and on election monitoring. Such situations do not endanger each NGOs independent identity, hence functional relationships have proved much more effective than institutional relationships.

Although there is much talk of the human rights community, at both national and international levels, there is much plurality within such community if indeed there be one rather than several distinct communities. Similarly, the phrase "human rights movement" is often used prematurely even in situations where there has been an upsurge in the volume of human rights activity but not yet the emergence of a movement.

Third World human rights organizations have brought fresh approaches, both theoretical and strategic, to human rights activism. On the theoretial plane they have focused attention not only on human rights but also on inhuman wrongs; not only on human rights but also on the right to be human. They have sought to address human rights violations resulting both from governmental lawlessness as well as human rights situations where vindication of right is essential for continued survival. Yet they have struggled to establish not only the right to survive but also the right to survive with dignity and equity. They have grappled with the violence, both of human rights violators as well as the violence out of which human rights are born. They have worked to generate not only a jurisprudence of rights but also to generate ruth, indignation and shame regarding human rights violations. They are constantly struggling to keep human rights truly a for all. They deserve fullest external solidarity and support in their times of crises.

Role of NGOs in Promoting Human Rights Education

The concern for human rights and fundamental freedom has assumed a global dimension and is of vital significance to the world community. Human Rights intrinsically and pervasively impact the quality and fulfilment of life of societies in all nations and ensure the prevalence of freedom, justice, peace and order in the world. "The task of the protection and promotion of Human Rights is a complex one and requires the co-operation of all sections of society, political parties, non-governmental organizations, lawyers, judges, public servants, teachers, police, media persons, and others. I appeal to all of you to observe human rights in your homes, at the work place, in your neighbourhood and everywhere. The goal is to create a culture of Human Rights across the length and breadth of the country."

There are certain minimal rights which have come to be accepted as basic freedoms of the individual. These rights are broadly classified into civil and political rights, on the one hand, and economic, social and cultural rights, on the other, and these are indivisible and inter-dependent. The aftermath of World War-II which caused unprecedented misery, death and destruction made the conscience of the world think of the ways and means to remove the violations of human rights and dignity practised by some nations. This concern culminated in the Universal Declaration of Human Rights on 10th December 1948 by the General Assembly of the United Nations. It sets forth the fundamental liberties and rights common to all people on earth. Since, the declaration, colonial people have been liberated, several conventions adopted and a United Nations High Commission for Human Rights established. The preamble to the Declaration records that recognition of the inherent dignity and of the equal and the inalienable rights of all members of the human family is the foundation of freedom, justice and peace in the world and their disregard results in barbarous acts which outrage the conscience of mankind. Therefore, human rights should be protected by the Rule of Law. The U.N. Declaration comprises of 30 Articles. To protect and implement these Articles there are other connotations of great importance, namely, the recognition for the international instruments adopted by UN, ILO, UNESCO and others and alongwith their recognition, also the adherence to them.

But the question remains, are we fully conscious of the ethical truth contained in the Articles of the HR Declaration? Do we recognize in our way of life and behaviour the implication of the fact that human rights belong within the common heritage of humanity? These rights reveal a purity of purpose. They demand urgent implementation.

Today the society is more or less violence striven. Concern with human rights cannot stop with the enunciation alone. There is need for more positive and operational steps. In order to carry the work of promotion of HR's various non-governmental organisations have started the work in every part of the world. NGOs are the voice of the people of the world. It is gratifying to note that inspite of sharp differences among themselves, the NGOs managed during the Vienna Summit to reach an agreement among themselves for their joint proposals. NGOs have made their impact on the civil society of Asia, Africa and Latin America in the preparatory conferences in Tunis, San Jose, Bangkok and the Asian Conference. Now the people in general no longer have their problems to Government alone to see the violence and injustice but depend on the NGOs. NGOs have a share in the responsibility of greater accountability to their own and their future generations.

The charter of the United Nations makes reference to human rights and fundamental freedoms in a number of clauses. In the preamble, the people of United Nations express their determination "to reaffirm faith in fundamental human rights, in the dignity and worth of human person, in the equal rights of men and women and of nations large and small".

The United Nations can only live upto the expectations which are raised by its charter and collective efforts are made by all of its organs as also by other organs of international and national society and Governments, inter-governmental and non-governmental agencies and organizations of the world and alongwith them the individuals share the responsibility of joining in a common human rights efforts.

In the initial stages, for achieving the goal the International Human Rights Organizations were founded by League of Nations and United Nations viz.; London-based Anti-Slavery Society for Human Rights in 1938, the International Committee for Red Cross in 1963, the French League for Human Rights in 1898, the larger number of NGOs at national, regional and local level emerged after 1970. Some of the significant NGOs are People's Union for Civil Liberties (PUCL) in 1974, the People's Union for Democratic Rights (PUDR) in 1976 and Centre for Democracy (CFD). These organisations have established their expert activity by investigating and undertaking on the spot studies and by publishing their observations. The activities and functions of the NGOs must be through their perception and action and the NGOs deserve to be recognized in the perspective of social, cultural and economical rights as the Fundamental Human Rights. Justice P.N. Bhagwati has rightly observed: "we can escape from this paradox and break the vicious circle by organizing the poor". Thus, the activists and the NGOs have greater opportunities to work but of course with greater professionalism to face greater challenge.

The Non-governmental organizations can play a very important role. The important functions may be,

1. Collection of information about the violation of HRs and monitoring the same.
2. Education.
3. Legislation.
4. Preventing HR abuses and rendering humanitarian help to the victims.
5. Solidarity.
6. Working in the areas of social right.

There is a very minor point of contention. NGOs in India suffer from non-cooperation, i.e., the consumers of NGOs help nurture, a feeling of hostility. Thus NGOs undergo a very tough time in convincing the people that their attitude is good and that they will help the deprived class. It is suggested that the NGOs may be given some form of Identity Cards which carry more weight. Or this is only with a view to carry out the promotional programme of HR awareness.

Human Rights and Voluntary Sector

Problems of poverty, under-nourishment and illiteracy are compounded by disparities among States. India ranks 138th out of 175 countries for which the Human Development Index (HDI) is computed. Kerala ranks first among the Indian states with an HDI comparable to that of China. At the bottom of the scale are Uttar Pradesh and Madhya Pradesh with a rank similar to that of Madagascar, Rwanda and Senegal. Kerala's Infant Mortality Rate (IMR) of 16 deaths per 1000 live births in 1995 was comparable to the average IMR of 14, among the industrialized countries. As against this, Orissa had an IMR of 103 deaths per 1000 live births worse than the average IMR of sub-Saharan Africa.

To mention these figures is not to decry the achievements since Independence. Life expectancy has nearly doubled from 32.1 years in 1951 to 60.8 years in 1991. Infant mortality for the country as a whole has been reduced from 146 in 1951 to 74 deaths per thousand live births in 1995. Literacy rate has risen from 18 per cent in 1951 to 52 per cent in 1991. Food grain production has more than doubled between 1951 and 1991 and famines have been virtually eliminated. But we need to remind ourselves that the pledges at the time of Independence are far from being redeemed for many in this country. Socio-economic disparities still exist not only at the regional or state levels but also among sections of the community. For instance, the level of human development among the Scheduled Castes and Scheduled Tribes which constitute a quarter of the country's population has remained low.

Deprivation and inequalities have given rise to discontent which often finds expression in acts of violence. This has led to greater stresses and strains on the administration of criminal justice. The law enforcement machinery is under greater strain in areas characterized by greater socio-economic disparities. A majority of the victims of delayed justice are members of the weaker sections of society. Though the economic profiles of people under custody are not available, one can, without much reservation, say that it is the poor who are incarcerated the longest, without trial, for their inability to secure bail or to engage a counsel to argue the case effectively in the court. This is true of people who die in police custody as well.

Going by the responsibilities voluntary organizations have chosen, I perceive a wide spectrum, at one end of which are those who perform watch-dog functions, who highlight human rights violations, attract the attention of authorities for punitive and remedial measures; while at the other end are those who equip and empower people to enjoy their rights. Given the nature of rights, such a wide array of roles is inevitable. Strong expressions of outrage following illegal arrests, detention, fake encounters or custodial deaths capture the attention of the people at large and of the authorities in particular, and create an atmosphere for prompt punitive or corrective action. Even though the role of voluntary organizations in such cases was earlier limited to articulating violation, there is a growing tendency, which is very welcome, to undertake inquiries and report the findings.

Recent years have witnessed significant developments in the understanding and interpretation of economic, social and cultural rights. New generations of rights are emerging. The right to a life with dignity is seen to bring to its fold a variety of rights which impinge on the quality of not only the individual but on the environment as well. Such terms as the rights of the working women or the rights of persons with disabilities are assuming increasing currency, signifying the need to address the special requirements of certain vulnerable sections of society. There is greater concern today about the right to safe drinking water or the right to pollution-free air. There are voluntary organizations working in those areas, engaged in the harnessing of resources, in terms of technology, material and man-power, and in the implementation of programmes which become models, capable of replication elsewhere.

The right to education is one specific area that comes to my mind here. In Kerala which is almost cent per cent literate, 61 per cent of the primary schools are in the private sector; while in Bihar which has a literacy percentage of 44, only 1.02 per cent of the primary schools are listed in the private sector. Educational institutions run by voluntary organizations have developed teaching techniques which are substantially cost-effective. There are voluntary organizations engaged in serious efforts at eliminating child labour. These efforts are multi-dimensional, the most basic being awareness generation at the family level and provision of attractive schooling facilities to the children.

Speaking of women's rights, there are a number of areas which cry out for attention. Let us start with the female foetus. The census data show a very sharp decline in sex ratio (male/female ratio) in India; it has come down from 1000:972 in 1901 to 1000:927 in 1991. These figures are a reflection of the staggering cruelty and violation of the rights of the girl child and the societal pressures and tensions in those parts of the country where the female child is readily aborted or killed. There are reports of alarming increase in child prostitution and the insensitivity of authorities to its prevalence. Despite the existence of the Child Marriage Restraint Act, 1929, child marriages are rampant in certain parts of the country. Experts have been publicly warning us of the disastrous consequences of the birth of millions of children in our country with an I.Q. level far below normal, only because of lack of attention to some very elementary, simple and cheap nutritional requirements of expectant mothers. Empowering women through the instrumentality of the Panchayati Raj institutions is one of the ways of dealing with women's issues. To achieve success it is imperative that the empowerment is meaningful and effective.

The issue of human rights is a very important component of the socio-economic development programme for the uplift of the dalits and the tribals. Basic to all the developmental efforts for the uplift of the dalits and the tribals is respect for their human rights, respect for their right to equality and equal opportunity, their right to a life with dignity, the right to enjoy the Rights guaranteed by our Constitution. Statutes and schemes are important, but they become meaningless in the absence of a commitment to enforce them and to implement them. The annual report of the Ministry of Welfare for the year 1994-95 records not only a higher incidence of poverty among Scheduled Castes and Scheduled Tribes, but also a slower elimination of the extent of poverty among them. The data available indicate that the conviction rate under the relevant Act has been very low. There is a need to look at a number of socio-economic factors which contribute to the continued ineffective enforcement of the provisions of this Statute. Voluntary organizations do have an important role in remedying this situation.

There are hundreds of voluntary organizations which work quietly among the less privileged, in the remote areas of our country, satisfied and happy with the changes they are able to bring about. They need to be brought into the national focus, for their work needs to be appreciated, emulated and rewarded. A National Assembly of Voluntary Organizations, such as this, can provide an opportunity for highlighting the good work that is being done, as much as an opportunity to learn from each other and to derive collective strength to undertake more challenging tasks.

This brings us to the role of the NHRC in supporting voluntary organizations. It is only appropriate to quote here the relevant para from the annual report of the Commission for the year 1994-95:

> The responsibilities entrusted to the Commission under the Protection of Human Rights Act 1993 cannot be adequately discharged without the development of close and co-operative ties between the Commission and non-governmental organizations— the eyes and ears of the people of India. For the Commission, it is not just a statutory obligation, under Section 12(i) of the Act, "to encourage the efforts of non-governmental organizations and institutions working in the field of human rights", but a necessity to do so, if its own efforts are to be well-informed and in tune with the deeper aspirations of the country, aspirations that find expression in

the courage and idealism of many non-governmental organizations and institutions working in the field of human rights". As the Commission noted in its first report, the cause of human rights has much to gain both from the practical help and from the constructive criticism that NGOs and the Commission can bring to bear in their mutual interaction and growing relationship. To this end, the Commission has, from time to time, invited leading human rights activists and NGO representatives over for discussions and advice and sought their help in practical ways. In addition, in every visit to a State, the Commission had made it a point to benefit from the experience and knowledge of NGOs, whose contacts at the "grass-roots" level give strength and meaning to the human rights movement where it matters most.

In the development of a working relationship with NGOs, the Commission has identified specific areas. These cover articulation of complaints of human rights violations; association in matters of inquiry into complaints; awareness creation through education and training; and joint action on issues in respect of which NGOs have specialized knowledge.

The complaints which the Commission has been receiving span from "custodial deaths to fake encounters and disappearances, from child labour to bonded labour and violence against women, from refugees to migrants from the rights of dalits to those of tribals, from complaints about the way in which TADA took its toll, to submissions questioning the constitutional validity of other Acts such as the Armed Forces (Special Powers) Act". These complaints display a remarkable degree of conviction, courage and dedication on the part of NGOs. In accordance with the provisions of its Regulation, governing the procedure of work, the Commission has associated NGOs for conducting inquiry into complaints. In many instances, NGOs have tendered evidence before the Commission, during its visits to states, on complaints made to it. In the matter of awareness creation through training and education, the Commission has associated itself with the effort of a number of NGOs in Delhi as well as in the states. The Commission has turned to NGOs having specialized knowledge, for taking up studies on such matters as child labour and prison reforms. It has benefitted from the reports of NGOs on such social issues as female infanticide and fake encounter deaths.

In order to be mutually more supportive, the Commission has taken up a programme of collecting relevant data on NGOs in a systematic manner. A questionnaire developed for this purpose was published in the Commission's newsletter some time ago, seeking information from such NGOs who may wish to work with the Commission. More than a 100 NGOs have so far responded. The data would be immensely useful to the Commission in identifying partners to work in areas related to the protection and promotion of human rights. The data would be useful to NGOs as well, in networking with each other to strengthen each other's capability and in avoiding duplication of work. This would also be useful to the Commission in advising potential donors on the location and capability of NGOs.

The Commission is firm in its belief that the protection and promotion of human rights in our country require the courage and commitment of NGOs, and their ability for sustained hardwork. The work of the Commission during the four years of its existence has convinced it of the need for working closely with NGOs. There will be a widening and deepening of the relationship in the years to come.

Voluntary organizations are watch-dogs as well as trend-setters; watch-dogs of what we must protect and preserve; and trend-setters of change and transformation.

WOMEN

The term Non-Governmental Organization (NGO) is to-day popularly used to denote associations working outside the formal administrative framework of Governments. From the socio-historical perspective the practice of formation of 'societies' probably evoled as a response to the need for individuals with common, non-commercial interests to come together voluntarily. It was a process whereby they could promote numerous charitable, religious and cultural objectives with some degree of formalization of association. The groups as legal entities could then collect, own and manage funds and activities systematically. A movement that began with *maths* and *ashrams* in the eighteenth and nineteenth centuries to promote religious, moral or social upliftment of communities has today become a central theme of development. NGOs are looked upon as important instruments for promotion of develoment activities particularly at the grassroots.

The Seventh Plan document on 'socio-economic programmes for women's has clearly stated that voluntary agencies are to be fully involved in launching an organized campaign against social evils affecting women. They have thus been given a prominent place in the Plan document.

In the Indian context NGOs are generally societies registered under the Societies Registration Act of 1860. This is applicable almost universally in the country with slight modifications in different states. The recognition is granted by issue of a Certificate of Registration by the Registrar of Societies. A society formed under this act though not legislative, is deliberative in character and must have a system of conducting its affairs alongwith rules for governing its practices.

Once a voluntary group registers itself, it has considerable flexibility of operation. However, all members are bound by the Constitution of their society.

As there has been a mushrooming of NGOs in the last decade there is also a movement to form national associations of organizations with similar objectives. These become fora for interaction and dissemination of information. Such associations may also, in the long run, prove to be regional linking mechanisms for activities in a particular field, for example, water resource development or promotion of primary health care services.

Recently, the Ministry of Home Affairs has made it mandatory that a society receiving funds from external donors be registered with them under the Foreign Contribution Regulation Act. This is a fairly simple procedure to comply with.

NGOs and Women's Development

The NGO focus on women-specific issues in programmes is still in its formative stages. So far, efforts have largely focussed on employment generation at the micro-level. In the context of development co-operation one of the major problems has been identification of suitable NGOs to participate in carrying forward programmes. This is an extremely difficult yet crucial exercise for donor agencies who usually have very limited staff to interact with appropriate NGOs.

It also requires great sensitivity to balance the policy needs of the donor, the Indian Government and the implementing agency. In this context, there is a need to expand the professional base for expertise in handling women in development issues and projects.

A certain amount of negativism exists in some NGOs about co-operation with the government structure. Some of these doubts are well-founded as the red tape, elaborate requirements for reporting and follow up of Government machinery for release of sanctioned funds has resulted in undue harassment, pressure and very often diruption of planned activities. However, one can hardly overlook the fact that with all its weaknesses, the Government structure is stable and has an outreach to all parts of the country, and that it aims at equitable distribution of resources. Funds can thus be rushed to difficult areas compulsorily. Further, the Government infrastucture (functioning with varying degrees of efficiency) is available throughout the country. It is a system of people but not a 'people's system'. Its continuity is not dependent on the motivation of individuals. Above all the system is highly accountable. The flexibility of NGOs on the other hand provides ground for experimentation and innovation. We may rush into a 'development disaster' if implementation of nationwide programmes is thrust on NGOs who are not ready to take the burden. Their role must be seen as more significant for conscientization at the micro-level, to initiate people's movements to fight for their rights in development. The motivation of workers in this sector is definitely of a different colour but co-operation with the Government system is inevitable and desirable. In our enthusiasm for a movement for the 'right kind development' we must not get carried away. The NGO/voluntary movement has to be nurtured and promoted but not pushed to take over development.

It is true that over the years the NGO efforts in India have grown in sophistication and professionalism. However, the real potential of the voluntary development community to be a major force for self-sustaining, broad-based development for the country has yet to be realized. Their role must be seen in the right perspective by the donor agencies, the Government and above all the NGOs themselves, then alone will we get the most fruitful results from the movement.

Suggested Role for Voluntary Organizations: Based on discussions with key persons in the three sectors, evaluation studies and literature on experiences with the voluntary agencies in other developing countries, the role of voluntary agencies has been synthesized as below.

(a) To Organize the Poor: The area where the voluntary

organizations have forged ahead to create hope is for development with community participation. There are innumerable examples where they have organized local communities to work for development or fight against anti-development activities. The most well-known of these is the Chipko Movement against indiscriminate deforestation in the hills of Uttar Pradesh. As mentioned earlier, the political will and creation of administrative structures for promoting women's development have, to a great extent, been realized in the first decade; the cue now is for the voluntary section to develop the recipient mechanisms or local organizations at the grassroots level.

(b) Demystification of Technology: Progress in science and technology at the macro level over the last few decades has led to a certain degree of alienation of the rural poor. As agricultural technology moves from the fields to university laboratories the farmer begins to become a dim figure in the picture. However, if the results of the work of scientists are carried back to the field it results in a healthy interaction which strengthens both the technologist's and the farmer's knowledge. Voluntary organizations working at the micro-level can promote this healthy use of technology in various fields.

(c) Professionalization of Voluntarism: The concept of unpaid services is based on the principle that *daan* (or voluntary contribution) is not enough to meet the challenges of development in a fast industrializing society with very clear systems of economy. Voluntary workers need to be professionals with skills for the management of complicated socio-economic situations in the field. To ensure a clear dialogue and understanding of an organization's proposals for development activities the donor and Government need clearly formulated proposals.

Violence Against Women: Implications for Civil Society

Gender violence is rooted in the socio-economic and political context of power relations. It manifests within class, caste and patriarchal social relations in which male power dominates. Today's escalating violence against women takes many forms; dowry crimes; witch hunting to wrest from single or widowed women the resources they possess; rape; amniocentesis or the sex determination test (advertised saying "Better pay Rs. 500 now than Rs. 50,00,000 later); violent eve-teasing often ending in heinous and lethal attacks on young women; the persistent onslaughts on the womb through repeated abortions; rising domestic violence within the family which seems to defy coverage by existing provisions of the law. Women' status continues to be plagued by inequality and gender discrimination. The relative degrees of advancement made in terms of health, literacy and education, employment, grassroots democracy with reservation for women in the panchayats are vitiated by the backlash to women's empowerment as a concept and objective of development. Mainstream society continues to resent these small gains in true patriarchal fashion and this collectively manifests as one form or other of violence against women e.g. Mishri Devi, a Scheduled Caste sarpanch in Thikri village, Rajasthan proudly raised the national flag on Independence Day 1998, little knowing the terrible consequences. Soon after she unfurled the tricolour, she was attacked by men from Other Backward Classes (OBCs) and stripped nude for "daring to raise the flag". Apparently a Scheduled Caste male is eminently more acceptable as President of the nation in K.R. Narayanan, but as a society we still nurture caste prejudices with perverse, diabolical consequences for women.

Indian civil society has been much more empathetic to the discourse on rape and dowry than expected. It has traditionally been the arena for struggle and conflict. However contemporary civil society is in a state of conceptual confusion and patriarchy fortifies itself in day-to-day relationships here. Paradoxes abound in state responses to civil resistance e.g. protesters resisting the double speak on development on projects like the Narmada and the Tehri dams have faced police lathis, even bullets, and oppressive bureaucratic responses. Thus it is true that the rhetoric of civil society allows for the rise and growth of all kinds of politics, but is all of this desirable?

Further civil society allows space for caste, class, communal and patriarchal projects as well as movements challenging them. So "If civil society is both communal and patriarchal, how can it be democratic? (Prof. Neera Chandoke). Thus democracy is under attack from all quarters and the rights debate is the only choice for those who advocate equality. The problem is finding sensitized officials in the enforcement authorities including the police and the judiciary to investigate and try these cases to deliver gender justice.

Women are subjects of familial terror including modalities of violence. Yet, the human rights discourse of protection has been denied to women. Thus, women are the paradigmatic alien subjects of international law. To be an alien is to be another, an outsider. Celina Romany finds thus that women are aliens within their states, aliens within the exclusive international society. (Romany: *"State Responsibility Goes Private")* espousing international Human Rights Law and its universality. Yet some critical questions need to be asked here: How can an inherently biased rights discourse become more responsive to the most basic rights of women? Can a human framework that construes the civil and political rights of individuals as belonging to public life neglect to protect the infringements of those rights in the private sphere of familial relationships? Can a universal rights framework be allowed to exempt the state from accessibility for those violations that result from a systematic failure on its part to institute political and legal protections necessary to ensure the basic rights of life, integrity and dignity of women? What kind of state are we dealing with? U.N. Special rapporteur on Violence against women, Radhika Coomaraswamy sums up that barriers to the consideration of women's rights as Human Rights in South Asia are rooted in ideological aspects, especially as they relate to the tension between the law and civil society, as well within the legal system itself. Given the fact that the liberal state is largely "Male jurisprudentially" it adopts "the standpoint of male power in the relation between law and society". (Catharine Mackinnon, *Towards Theory of the State,* Cambridge, Ma Harvard University Press, 1989, 163). Thus between a male oriented state, a civil society that is patriarchal and communal (Neera Chandoke) there appears little hope for womens' equality. Celina Romany confirms this: "The blown-up liberal state of international society, like its model, supplanted feudalism with democratic revolutionary struggles but nonetheless left women's human rights in the obscurity of medieval times". All of this leads to patriarchy and patriarchal attitudes being fortified on a daily basis. Violence against women helps maintain patriarchy. This is seen as largely falling within the private sphere; gender equality in the public sphere is marked by state duty stating its intent by law or otherwise, to treat women equally. "To punish disobedience—discipline, liberty, family tradition perpetuates a culture of terror that humiliates woman, teaches children to lie, and spreads the plague of fear. Human

Rights should begin at home"— [Eduardo Galeano, *The book of Embraces* (1989), 143.] The abuse of women by their male partners is among the most common and dangerous forms of gender-based violence. Largely considered as something that is located in the private realm of family relationships, domestic violence to date is not easily accepted as a human rights concern, or as a serious offence in the eyes of the law. The common experience of women is to be advised by the police personnel at the police station level or by officials, even judges in family courts, to go home and adjust to life with their tormentors. Society too shuns any outpourings of such experience and the traditional attitude has been if you close your eyes, the problem will go away.

Thus domestic violence against women is systemic and structural, a form of patriarchal control of women built on sweeping assumption of male superiority and female inferiority, sex-stereotyped roles and expectations, and economic, social and political predominance of men and dependency of women. Jealousy is a common theme in violent homes. The whore-madonna mystique alternates in the male psyche, now this, now the other. The power and the potential of the intimate setting underscore power on the one side and vulnerability on the other. Details only embellish the project-whether it is pregnancy, mothering, beauty or the sheer intimacy of the relationship; economic success, social relations, the vagaries of home management all make their presence felt. Despite modernisation of life across the globe, the basic patriarchal standard continues to express and replicate itself through gender and familial violence in the private realm. And most studies of domestic violence come from western societies mainly the UK and USA, where the patriarchal arrangements are thought to have been most challenged by shifting economic, social, political and ideological conditions, testifying to the extra-ordinary durability of patriarchy.

The mainstream international human rights discourse on women's rights has internalised the logic of state sovereignty, characterising both progress and challenges for international human rights in terms of and limitation of state sovereignty." ..... like Gulliver tied down by the Lilliputians, state sovereignty is to be limited by a multitude of international human rights norms" (Knop).

So then, is the system of sovereign states problematic for

feminist political and legal change? What is the alternative to working with state? Can civil society provide a stable alternative? While some may demur at this, I propose that women CAN work through the non-state groups and networks that make up international and domestic civil society and influence the development, interpretation and implementation of international law by states. Further, this suggests that women break down the monolith of the sovereign state to represent their interests directly in international law where the state would traditionally represent women's interests. Women's interests and concern are not defined by or even significantly in many cases by state borders; they are shaped by gender, sexuality, culture and other factors.

True women must traverse an unknown path, feminist discourse now needs to venture onto an untraced trajectory to forge their passage. What is called for now is creativity and imagination, judiciousness and wisdom to top all the pioneering forays that feminism has made over the better part of this country.

International human rights treaties such as the women's convention, and recognizing international customary law on human rights need to be developed further. While this is necessary, it is not sufficient to achieve women's rights but serves as a basis to build on. Treaties offer a framework which needs to be bolstered. They equally need effective monitoring and follow-up practices from the state to fulfill the obligations of international law. While this is well known the larger problems have been in ensuring women's participation in the drafting of such laws at the domestic level, and secondly in getting an extremely patriarchal state and society to radically change their attitudes towards women. Patriarchy is as ingrained as gender-bias and for the latter to lose prominence, the former will have to be dislodged.

Most follow-up actions of the state constitutes setting up committees of officials with a tokenist representation of civil society organizations (CSOs) that are politically in favour. Hence no meaningful debate is forthcoming.

Further official acts, even those which are part of follow-up procedure to international conventions, are cloaked in secrecy. Thus what has great potential for problematization within the ambit of civil society, is lost to civil society and the creativity of feminist critiques and analysis, thanks to the mystification of half of humanity's hopes and aspirations. Such culpability in state procedure is highly unacceptable to one and all in civil society.

Hence the path forward is by no means free or smooth. Obstacles lurk at every step, ambush, even sabotage is possible. The Indian women's movement, in anticipation of these and more, is now calling for the provisions of CEDAW to be used in dealing with gender violence and gender bias to establish equality once for all. However we have amply witnessed the propensity of bodies like parliament and legislature to violently oppose the Women's Reservation Bill to ensure more equitable participation by women in the political system and the politics of the day.

Models for Development

Gender equality is a multi-faceted concept which implies equality of opportunity in economic as well as socio-political and legal aspects. Gender inequality, therefore is not prerogative of women in economic poverty alone. There is a different and subtle version of poverty called socio-political poverty, which target 80 per cent women as victims globally, regardless of their economic status. Pre-designed "Poverty Alleviation" programmes have been found to address only economic poverty—a grave error as far as women's empowerment is concerned. Designed, planned and executed by "Specialists" alien to the women's neighbourhood, these poverty alleviation programmes actually ridicule the sense and sensibilities of women clientele.

Most so-called poverty alleviation programmes are not responsive to women's socio-political needs which is frustrating for both the women as clientele as well as activist groups. Many grassroot practitioners and community based women's groups often have ideological conflicts with the donor community (governmental and non-governmental) or their deputies who come with a pre-designed project and target approach where quality is flung out of the nearest window. NGOs who dare to question are normally "black-listed" or coerced into accepting the funding on the donor's terms. In the process the client communities are left with no option but to throw away the results of participatory micro-planning and are resigned to their fate, accepting one more top-down development plan and programme. The onus of participation is left to the clientele groups participating here implying that women remain beneficiaries in programmes pre-planned elsewhere. So much for the volumes on sustainable development and award-winning books of Indian economists, adorning prestigious libraries.

To all those who survive on poverty issues and development programmes, marginalized women are target "beneficiaries" and "consumers" of resources. We conveniently forget that these women are in reality our "clientele" who use our services and pay for them in more ways than one and "producers" who contribute to the larger economy thus entitled to have a say in its direction. The "development tourists" are the real "beneficiaries" of all development programmes in the country. We not only use upto 80 per cent of all development resources to cover our exhorbitant overheads costs, but also get paid to spend that targeted sum!!

And playing a facilitating role in this transition of women's communities, from being invisible to becoming invincible, has invariably been a small voluntary agency which understands and accepts sustainable development, genuinely believes in people's capabilities and facilitates qualitative changes, without feeling insecure and threatened about the transition. When women begin to move forward resisting patriarchy and subordination, their experiences inspire other women in the vicinity—for the simple reason that women in general are perceived by men as helpless humans who need to be patronized, subordinated and protected. Of course, those who try to convey to gender insensitive men that women could do better given the opportunities, are ruthlessly mowed down, in spirit and letter. Nevertheless, the few courageous women who have managed to find their rightful place in the sun soon become role models for others who were either conditioned to their own misery or resigned to their fate. Those concerned with women's empowerment are often faced with the dilemma of "How" and seek to replicate what we call "best practices". Can there be single method to women's empowerment? Well, after 22 years in the field I emphatically say "No". Programmes have to be geared to address the needs of clientele women and their families/ communities. A successful Gujarat experience can in no way be replicated in Tamilnadu nor a Karnataka experience could be replicated in Haryana, simply because there are countless intrinsic factors like the diverse nature of economic, socio-political and cultural milieu relevant to the areas which could impact the processes of change. India may be the largest democracy in the World—but she is definitely not a collection of cut and paste federal states with the same repetitive hues and depths.

It has been observed based on the themes of international conferences, atleast in India, that programme priorities of donor institutions and many NGOs (particularly the globe-trotting ones) have changed. Unfortunately priorities of people do not change so often. Small grassroots NGOs who attempt to work with the communities themselves normally seek support for low budget programmes. But the majority of donors are not interested in small budget and slow moving realistic programmes, because they feel it is not "viable". They demand results and reaching targets overnight, prefering to support the big "credible" and "well-known" NGOs who are over-saturated with foreign grants. Thus small initiatives which could facilitate genuine empowerment through community-owned interventions are marginalized. Donor agencies have gone to the extent of bull-dozing small NGOs to replicate gargantuan mistakes of larger NGOs, under the illusion that something that works in one geographical area should be adopted as a panacea of all women's empowerment projects across the country. Such an attitude and insensitivity in donors to community's needs are detrimental to sustainable development and stifling to activists groups who believe more in women's capabilities than their own.

Further it did seem to matter if the "poor" women themselves were conspicuous by their absence at these "intellectual" discussions and partying! None thought it relevant or significant to ask the women what their needs were. "Poor" women were forgotten till the second Summit, when again organizers hardly thought it apt to include grassroots women as participants. The Micro-credit Summit and several other similar Summits, have thus served only to add one more line to the overflowing curriculum vitae of many of the participants, and of course to sponsor government counter-parts who made no bones about the fact that they came only to shop!! For marginalized women and their communities at the grassroots, in the tens of thousands of villages and urban slums across the Indian sub-continent, there is no single answer to end poverty of an economic as well as socio-political nature. They know their problems, concerns, pains. But the solutions? When they do not know of choices how could they make a decision on what suits them the best? But if given information on what is available, given access to and control over all forms of productive resources and assets, and to decision-making process, they could easily and effortlessly make their choice.

The moment we think we know the answer required by a particular community, sustainable development inevitably takes a beating. When we modify our ideology and objectives to suit the needs and mandates of the donors, hypocrisy begins to lead us towards personal gains and this is a symptom that tells us we are in the wrong profession! Sustainable development will remain a much researched theory, if there is no ownership by clientele groups. The process of participatory micro-planning is even more difficult in programmes attempting to mainstream gender-simply because we are conditioned to believe that we need to dictate needs and solutions to the last "T" if women have to be "saved" from their pathetic plight. Not that we do not know about participatory processes. Participation be damned!! We are in such a hurry to fulfill projects and targets in accordance with our mandate and submit reports to the dictums of donor agencies to obtain more funds, that we totally forget the human nature of our work. Donors themselves are worried about public accountability in their respective countries—numbers and statistics matter—so also media hype. But what about the quality of our inputs and their impact on the economic and socio-political empowerment process that we are supposed to be working for? It is high time we did some introspection on whose sustainable development we are promoting. Why are there few examples of successful and sustainable development models vis-a-vis the figure of 30,000 NGOs in the country receiving foreign funds and probably another 50,000 registered NGOs outside the purview of the FCRA (Foreign Contribution Regulation Act) and the Ministry of Home Affairs, Government of India?

By simple logic, even if each of these 80,000 NGOs attempts to facilitate an empowerment process for 500 women per year, who are marginalized economically and socio-politically, less than a decade is required to cover the 35 per cent below the poverty line of the approximately 500 million women in the country. If Government interventions (which quantitatively account for three times of the inputs of all NGOs put together) could strengthen NGO efforts, the actual duration of a 100 per cent empowerment process should only be less than half a decade. The fact that the nation has left more than half a century of independent governance behind it and that we still have at least 35 per cent of our female population marginalized on all counts, speaks volumes about whose sustainability we are siezed with! To facilitate growth women need visibility, they need a hundred thousand opportunities to be seen and heard. How many of us are willing to rope in women from the grassroots to a forum where we rub shoulders with VIPs and VVIPs and jostle for media attention? Very often I hear a supposedly "intelligent" and "practical" reason for not inviting grassroots women to an international forum—(even if the issue being discussed centres around these very women)—that "they do not understand or speak English"! I think this is the most ridiculous reason one could think of. I wonder how many of the European participants at these Global Conferences speak English. How many of us have parents who are well-versed in the Imperial language? I think we are fortunate to have grown up and developed in an environment where we have never been resource-poor. If the illiterate little girl from Usilampatti (a village in Tamilnadu where female infanticide is rampant) is given the same opportunities that we had, she could probably be a 100 per cent better achiever than many of us. Is it that we are afraid of the consequences of empowerment itself? Do we feel threatened by the outcome where illiterate women, given access to information and knowledge, could uproot our very existence as minor kings and queens in our areas of operation? I think most of us do not welcome empowered women—especially those whom we feel should be grateful to us for doling out "benefits" and should never raise their voices against the many injustices we commit.

On the other hand, wherever the NGO has played a facilitating role encouraging women to evolve and grow into confident and capable collectives of SHGs to empower themselves and their communities, it is a joy to watch the transition and the women in action. It takes time, pain and selfless efforts and few NGOs have been capable of this "let go" attitude and commitment to sustainable development. But wherever it has happened, we have a ready model of women's empowerment to learn from. The document that the UN system, Swiss Development Corporation (SDC) and SPANDANA have jointly published throws light on some select examples of such empowerment processes, using micro-finance as a tool, where the NGO or an individual activist concerned has been a facilitator, NOT the owner of the processes.

If NGOs can now do some re-thinking on their approaches to women's empowerment and sustainable development we will surely have many more successful experiences to share and learn from as marginalized women break their silence and assume power.

Gender Sensitivity and Gender Justice

Gender sensitivity, is a bent of mind which may come through socialization by the family and/or other associations, educational institutions, etc. Alternatively, it may be the result of intellectual conviction developed at a later stage through the acquisition of certain types of knowledge and gradual extension of one's other social values.

The Committee on the Status of Women in India (CSWI) which too accepted the Constitution as its premise and goal. came to the conclusion that neither the Indian State nor the various subsystems of society had ever gone beyond the myth of legal equality (which too remained only notional rather than real). Hence, the utter failure on the part of policy-makers, the educational system, the media and most other social institutions to take effective measures to break the institutionalized subordination and inequality of women.

The CSWI also perceived both intuitively and analytically that gender equality could not be an independent value but was intrinsically linked with the achievement of human equality and the abolition of all institutionalized inequalities, and it believed:

(1) that equality of women is necessary, nor merely on the grounds of social justice, but as a basic condition for social, economic and political development of the nation;

(2) that in order to release women from their dependent and unequal status, improvement of their employment opportunities and earning power has to be given the highest priority;

(3) that society owes a special responsibility to women because of their child-bearing function. The safe bearing and rearing of children is an obligation that has to be shared by the mother, the father and the society;

(4) that the contribution made by an active housewife to the running and management of a family should be admitted as economically productive and contributing to national savings and development;

(5) that marriage and motherhood should not become a disability in women's fulfilling their full and proper role in the

task of national development. Therefore, it is important that society, including women themselves, must accept their responsibility in this field;

(6) that disabilities and inequalities imposed on women have to be seen in the total context of a society, where large sections of the population—male and female, adults and children—suffer under the oppression of an exploitative system. It is not possible to remove these inequalities for women only. Any policy or movement of the emancipation and development of women has to form a part of a total movement for the removal of inequalities and oppressive social institutions, if the benefits and privileges won by such action are to be shared by the entire women population and not be monopolized by a small minority;

(7) that if our society is to move in the direction of the goals set by the Constitution, then special temporary measures will be necessary, to transform *de jure* into *de facto* equality.

Conceptually, this required a major shift, from examining the conditions of the minority of women who had benefitted from the equality clauses of the Constitution, to the majority who, the Committee discovered, had become more marginalised, more unequal and less protected than at the time of Independence. Choosing macro-indicators like the declining sex ratio in the population, the widening gender gap in life expectancy/mortality, poverty, unemployment, and other forms of exclusion from social, economic and political opportunities for participation and survival, the Committee unhesitatingly reached the conclusion that social processes and institutions—some inherited from India's past and some unleashed during the colonial period—had continued unchecked and even accelerated in the quarter of a century after Independence, the adoption of the new Constitution and the introduction of planned development.

The members of a Committee in their indictment did not spare anybody, including themselves in this admission of failure. Policy-makers and planners, law-makers and law-enforcers, educators and opinion-makers, specialized agencies created by the State for different sectors of development, political parties, people's organizations, including women's organizations, trade unions and other occupation-based organizations—all came on the dock for the Committee's judgement. Social scientists and other members of the academic community (from which some members of the Committee had been drawn) came in for particular criticism for their failure, in their social research and analysis, to break through the social construction of gender and the urban middle class mindset which perceived all women as replicas of women in their own families or class, and contributing to the increasing invisibility of the overwhelming majority of poor working women in rural and urban areas.

The Indian women's movement which has grown, expanded and developed as a grassroots base during the last few decades, has unhesitatingly condemned the "co-optation" of terms like "empowerment" coined by the movement without substance, either as goals or as strategies.

It was only the pressure from the women's movement, especially the pioneers of the women's studies movement (which included both women and men), that led to the inclusion of the entire chapter on "Education for Equality" within the policy statement. Without that pressure (we have evidence from very senior civil servants responsible for the formulation of that policy) the word "equality" would not have featured in the Education Policy statement at all.

In answer to my critique of the 9th Plan draft, requesting that the last plan document coming out of the Government during the twentieth century should atleast try to preserve the conceptual advances that had been made during the previous decades, the Secretary, Department of Women and Child Development, asked me for a note reviewing the approach to gender equality over the previous Five-Year Plans. I was amazed to find that what I wrote as an aide memoir had been incorporated wholesale not only in the final report of the Working Group, but also in the draft first report by the GOI to the UN Committee monitoring the implementation of the Convention on Elimination of Discrimination against Women (CEDAW).

A current slogan coming from international donor agencies and even national governments is to step up investment in "gender sensitization". A number of donor agencies have invested a substantial part of their aid earmarked for women in having their own staff "gender sensitized" by some academic institutions in the North.

The CSWI had lamented that the process of post-Independence development demonstrated many features which showed "regression from the norms developed during the freedom struggle". The kind of response that the CSWI's negative findings evoked from the members of the freedom generation, i.e., those who were old enough to be thrilled and excited by some of the radical ideologies that the struggle threw up, was far stronger than that shown by the younger generation of political and bureaucratic elites. This included not only social scientists and civil servants but also many leaders of the Indian Press, which through the 70s and 80s remained a strong supporter of the women's movement, contributing through their investigative journalism, substantial evidence to strengthen the agitations against increasing violence against women. However, the impact of the new market ideology on the press, has made it increasingly difficult for the women's movement to depend on this erstwhile ally.

The hostile reactions to the women's reservation Bill only proves what many of us have been stating for the last two decades—the subordination of women is an advancing process whose roots lie both in the political economy of globalization and its supposedly hostile—but in effect most powerful ally—the politics of cultural, religious, or ethnic revivalism which seek to confine political, cultural and ideological identities by accidents of birth. For any such objective, the control over women's freedoms and rights is a logical pre-requisite. In addition fundamentalism of all hues—whether it is the theology of the free market or the orthodoxy of population control—has a long history of subordinating both human and democratic rights to other national or global objectives. People and children, and women because they have unfortunately been endowed by nature with the demonstrated dimension of reproduction, are increasingly viewed as "dispensable".

The Indian women's movement has consistently opposed all these forces and the various compromise formulae that they devise for women's "empowerment". The women's movement has, till date, opposed all attempts to use its demand for one-third reservation as a bargaining counter because any dilution now will ultimately be targeted at the Panchayati Raj provision, to which the movement had given first priority. Women's empowerment, like "national integration" (a phrase which has done more to damage the Indian polity than any provisions for reservation) is historically linked:

(a) with the end of "the sanskritisation process" which 50 years of "modernization" operating "democratically" has

not been able to weaken (and globalization has only enhanced and accelerated); and

(b) development of new social institutions and values which can challenge social hierarchy, patriarchy and the identity politics of accidents of birth buttressing the theory of purity-pollution, which has always haunted our history.

We know that in many countries, including India, there is a tendency to link the health and well being of women to the health of the children and the family. It is obviously important to address the health of women as mothers: women suffer enormously when their children have to face hunger, deprivation, illness and early death. The traditional definitions of women's health and well-being need to be broadened to reach beyond the reproductive and maternal, incorporating mental and physical well-being across a women's life cycle. An undue emphasis on women only as mothers, leads to the neglect of women who do not fall within the category of wives and mothers (or future wives and mothers). Women who are outside these well understood roles, such as widows, unmarried women, old women, mentally or physically handicapped women, become invisible to policy-makers and administrators.

It is now sufficiently clear that as far as women's everyday life is concerned, we are facing a massive failure of both, the promises of modernity and the promises of tradition. There is a need in many areas to break away from the traditional forms of agriculture since the traditional forms, much advocated for their "holistic" approaches, are unable to provide food security all the year around. Yet, unless proper methodologies for assuring that poor households get access to new opportunities and that within these households women can get access to food are put into place in each micro-region where such changes are attempted, women's empowerment will make little headway. Second, the hope that there are cultural life styles of communities (such as the tribal communities) which are inherently more just to women is belied when we study how households procure food and consume it all the year around.

In recent years one disturbing trend has been the appeal to tradition as a way of ensuring rootedness and meaning in life. Interestingly, it is not only the appeal from higher castes, those who want to create borders between communities by strictly controlling the sexual and reproductive bodies of their women, but also the practices of tribal groups, dalits and other backward castes which raise a profound concern for women. It is argued by some that tribal women must decide to marry only from the men of their own groups because other men cannot understand the tribal traditions and that marriages across different groups would lead to the disappearance of these traditions. There have been similar incidents of violent village "justice" meted out to women who dared to defy caste elders. When we add to this the incidents of rape that upper caste men have deployed to "discipline" women from other backward castes and the many judgments which simply disbelieve women, we can see new sites on which women's oppression is reproduced.

On the other side, there are the downsides of development and modernization which hit women particularly hard. Sexually transmitted diseases, including AIDS, may be viewed as a form of sexual violence since women have very little control over their sexuality. Violence against women may originate in State policies or in long rooted symbolic cultural practices. A gender sensitive understanding of this requires of us that we do not make the lives and well-being of women hostage to the passions of the State, the honour of the community or the means through which other agendas are fulfilled. It does not appear to me to be just, to appropriate the pain of any group or to inflict suffering in the name of grand projects of society. When it comes to women it is especially unjust to inflict such suffering upon them because traditionally they have borne the burden of extinguishing the self for the sake of an imagined future, for the community and the State. This is why a turning away from grand projects to the travails of everyday life seems appropriate, within a gender sensitive perspective.

Women's Development

Although women hold eminent positions in government and society, the vast majority live under conditions of great material deprivation and under very restrictive traditional norms. They are expected to produce or assemble whatever is needed for the home, children and cattle in rural households. Tribal women have to cut trees not only for domestic fuel and fodder but also to get cash to buy food.

The enforcement of a strict moral code has meant lack of

access of girls to education and skills, early marriage, burdensome outlays on dowries, *purdah*, strong son preference, female foeticide and infanticide.

The sex ratio (the number of females per 1,000 males), a summary indicator of gender differentials, captures the essentials of the present situation very well. The average ratio for India has tended to decline over several decades from 972 in 1901 to 929 in 1991, despite all the efforts made to improve the status of women. Mortality rates are higher for females than for males up to the age of 35 (Meera Chatterjee, 1990). These differentials are the result of the strong prejudice against females as well as the "triple burden" of reproduction, household work and work outside the home put on females. Infant mortality differentials have persisted and child mortality (0-4 age group) is particularly large pointing to the neglect of the girl child. Female mortality in the peak child-bearing years is 40 per cent higher than for males. Sexually transmitted diseases and reproductive tract infections are a major problem.

Malnutrition is common among girl children and, in later years, poor nutrition causes anaemia which affects nearly two-thirds of all women. Females in low-income families have an inferior nutritional status compared to males. The caloric intake of women during pregnancy and lactation is 30 per cent short of requirements. Maternal mortality accounts for 2.5 per cent of all female deaths and the risk of death related to child-bearing for Indian women is 200 times that experienced by their counterparts in industrialised countries.

The primary school enrolment ratio for girls (6-11 years) rose from 25 per cent in 1950-51 to 84 per cent in 1989-90. Nevertheless, it remains far below the male enrolment rate. The corresponding ratio for enrolment of secondary school for girls (11-14 years) rose from 5 per cent to 45 per cent. Girls in secondary school as a proportion of the total student body rose from 17 per cent to 32 per cent during the same period. Notwithstanding this progress, the secondary enrolment sex differential remains significant. Furthermore, nearly half of all girls enrolled at primary school tend to drop out of school. This female literacy rate at 39 per cent remains well below that of males. There are 197 million female illiterates above 7 years of age.

The average age at marriage has risen somewhat but even today 88 per cent of females in the 15-19 age group are married and face high pregnancy risks. Fertility rates for women up to 29 years remain very high.

According to the Census, women are "marginal workers", that is their economically productive activity, including unpaid work on the farm or family enterprise, is less than 183 days per year. Presumably, the rest of their time is spent on rearing children and other household chores. The vast majority of women work in low-paying, low technology, informal sector activities. Women have much less access to credit, technology and training than men. About 30 per cent of rural households are headed by women but few women have legal rights over land or property. Women contribute a substantial part of the incomes of landless households.

There is a rigid moral code which demands from females almost unqualified adherence to traditional male-oriented values and mores. Son preference remains a powerful factor influencing the treatment of the female infant and the young girl child. The prohibitive economic burden of marrying girls, involving dowries and feasting of relatives and friends, reinforces the strong demand for sons. It also makes early marriage on auspicious days, when various expenses can be shared or avoided, very attractive for parents. The custom of *purdah* remains very much in place. A host of fasts and rituals have to be performed by the wife to further the safety and welfare of her husband. The social esteem of married women depends on their producing sons. Wife beating, harassment about dowries considered to be insufficient, and sexual assault are common. Finally, there is the custom of *sati* (widow immolation) performed at the death of the husband. It seems that traditional culture views women only in terms of their relations with men.

Even though Gujarat is a relatively advanced state and women have made substantial progress in terms of education and participation in political and social reforms, yet the overall status of women in this state remains a cause of concern. There is a paradoxical dichotomy in the usual set of social and economic indicators as they apply to females.

The female literacy rate is relatively high in Gujarat but the sex-ratio is only slightly higher than the Indian average. The infant mortality rate for females remains at the level of the all-India average. At this level, it is comparable to the rate in Bihar which is one of the BIMARU (sick) states with a female literacy rate less than half that of Gujarat.

Infanticide, violence against women and dowry deaths are on the rise. Women tend to suffer during episodes of civil strife such as caste wars. Rajkot has one of the highest female suicide rates in the country. This is attributed to dowry demands and violence against women.

The Constitution of India prohibits discrimination on the basis of sex and insists on equality before the law as a fundamental principle. There are special provisions granting equality of opportunity for women who are treated as a minority group suffering disabilities based on sex.

This constitutional imperative has inspired a succession of governments at the centre and the states to design a variety of approaches, establish special institutions and implement programmes aimed at assisting women. The establishment of the Central Social Welfare Board in 1953 was a landmark, followed by the creation of comparable institutions at the state level to assist volags engaged in women's welfare activities. The premise was that progressive legislation, such as the Special Marriage Act, 1954 and the Hindu Marriage and Divorce Act, 1955, combined with programmes funded by the Boards, mentioned above, would suffice to improve the condition of women.

This approach was found wanting by the analysis in the report *Status of Women in India: Towards Equality* published in 1974 in the context of preparation for the UN's first International Conference on Women. Veena Mazumdar, one of the main authors of the report, found explosive evidence of increasing marginalisation of women. The report brought out the ineffectiveness of the legislative approach and questioned the basic development strategy of the government. Ironically, new laws, such as the Equal Remuneration Act, 1976, were passed in the wake of the report. Some new initiatives also emerged, such as the reservation in 1979 of Integrated Rural Development Programme (IRDP) funds for women to the extent of 30 per cent in 1979 and the launching of Development of Women and Children in Rural Areas (DWCRA) in 1982.

The Sixth Five Year Plan (1985-90) devoted a separate chapter to women's issues for the first time. It acknowledged that legislation had not proved to be an effective approach and put the emphasis on programmes to provide education, employment and health for women. A separate Department for Women and Child

Development was established in 1985 as part of the Ministry of Human Resource Development.

The National Commission for Self-Employed Women and Women in the Informal Sector, with Ela Bhat as the Chair-person, reported in 1987. The plight of such women was highlighted in the Shramshakti (Work Power) report and the need for them to organise themselves was demonstrated. This part of the labour force required legal protection and the report recommended the appointment of a labour commissioner for the unorganised sector. The Shramshakti Report did not influence government policy very much.

The same year, 1987, also saw the establishment of women's development corporations in 17 states, including Gujarat in 1992. The aim was to identify women entrepreneurs, establish women's co-operatives and provide technical assistance. It is too early to assess the impact of these corporations.

The Government of India prepared the National Perspective Plan for Women in 1988. The document acknowledged that government efforts on behalf of women had not been successful and advocated the implementation of recommendations made in the previous reports. The plan, ostensibly for 1988-2000, failed to assess resources required and did not provide operational details for implementation. The plan was roundly criticised by women's organisations for relying on old development models that were not valid.

The National Commission for Women was established in 1990 to review the implementation of legislation affecting women and to recommend new laws where necessary. It has the powers of a civil court and it can entertain complaints from the public.

A major criticism of these programmes is that they tend to operate piecemeal; they are not integrated either at the level of ministries or in the field. Frequently, their schedules do not take into account the compulsions of their clientele. In many cases government staff delivering the services are not adequately trained. Also, government has been criticised for creating specialised institutions for dealing with women's issues, such as women's banks or women's police stations. These are regarded as tokens. Instead, government is being urged to sensitise all its programmes and institutions so that the gender perspective is fully embedded in them.

Resources provided for women's programme were inadequate

even 30 years after Independence (World Bank, 1991). It is only in recent times that the bias against women in government development schemes has been recognised.

Many of the schemes mentioned above operate both in Rajasthan and Gujarat. In addition, a distinct scheme in Rajasthan must be mentioned. The state government initiated the Women's Development Programme (WDP) in 1984 in six districts, with the help of UNICEF. Its aim was to organise and empower rural women through communication of information, education and training. Only the guiding principles were formulated. A detailed blueprint was not prepared because the aim was to let the programme evolve participatively at the field level. Much emphasis was put on internal and external evaluation. Conflict is inherent in WDP. As women are empowered, they challenge the existing power structure, including the government itself.

The WDP was reviewed 18 months after its initiation (Jain *et al.*, 1988). They found progress to be slow at that time but concluded that it was generating self-confidence among those involved. Another report, (IDS, 1991), six years after the programme was initiated, identified some positive and some negative outcomes. On the positive side, it was claimed that *sathins* (village women volunteers) paid, trained and supervised by government had become leaders and were challenging injustice.

On the negative side:

(i) *sathins* had demanded to become government employees;
(ii) *prachetas* (responsible for 10 women's development centres) had become cynical;
(iii) the focus had shifted from process to results;
(iv) reporting had become routinised; and
(v) frequent changes of senior government officials had generated instability.

Clearly, WDP is an important innovation but it has not lived up to its early promise. It has over-invested in *sathins* and neglected organisational work at the village level. These *sathins* have not built up much support at the community level and they have become dependent on state functionaries. There are many vacancies in the WDP programme. The attempt of *sathins* to take up gender issue e.g., prevent child marriage) at the village level has generated a backlash which exposes them to considerable danger. Furthermore, the philosophy of WDP is not well understood by state and district officials who have used *sathins* to implement government determined targets instead of letting them catalyse the working out of the participative field programmes.

The women's movement has long history going back to the pre-Independence period. Early protagonists of the women's cause were men who had been influenced by western liberal values and who questioned child marriage, the low status of widows and the practice of *sati.* Women themselves played no part in these protests against traditional practices (Radha Kumar, 1993). Later, educated upper caste women joined the movement.

Gandhi's freedom movement brought women to the fore. He felt that women were uniquely suitable for non-violent protests. As women joined the political battle, they began to seek equality for themselves.

The women's movement today is an amalgam of several different traditions and ideologies, some indigenous (Gandhian, Sarvodaya), others foreign (Marxist, Western liberal). A series of mass campaigns on a large variety of diverse issues, including protection of trees (CHIPKO), protest against price rise, struggle against rape and dowry, against Muslim Personal Law ignited by the Shah Bano case, against alcoholism and against communalism after the events in Ayodhya in 1992, give some idea of women's concerns.

The All India Women's Conference (AIWC) was established in1927, inspired by both Gandhi and western liberal ideas. The main aim at that time was to promote the welfare of women and children. Today, AIWC has 100,000 members, 400 branches and their work consists of promoting literacy, family planning, child welfare, hostels for women and non-conventional sources of energy (AIWC, 1991). Clearly, the rationale of the organisation is now a mixture of welfare promotion and developmentalism. The aim is to help destitute women and to raise their status within the existing system without challenging its basic parameters.

At the opposite end of political spectrum, the National Federation of Indian Women, a Marxist group, came into being in 1954. Later, in 1971, the Shramik Mahila Sanstha was established under the auspices of the Communist Party of India. Marxists claim that the women's question is subsumed under the broader notion of class conflict and that women should attack class and patriarchy.

The 1974 landmark report on the status of women, mentioned above, became an inspiration for many volags in the women's field. It served to legitimise women's issues, to broaden the base of the women's movement to include not only elite but middle class women and to emphasise the need to improve the economic aspect of women's lives.

Questions are asked about unequal gender relations within various classes and communities, particularly in urban settings. The dowry tradition is one focus of attention in this context. Consumerism stimulates the demand for dowries and consumerism too is attacked by women's groups. Dowries accentuate son preference and female infanticide. These practices are also attacked by women's groups. Women's volags have broadened their work to address the issue of violence against women, including eve-teasing, rape and on so.

Many volags working in villages believe that emphasis should be put on community issues, such as health and education, rather than on divisive gender questions. The anti-men flavour of Western feminism never found widespread support in India. Such sentiments were confined to highly educated urban women.

The emphasis by environmentalists on the need to deal with deforestation, scarcity of fodder and the increasing difficulty of obtaining water in rural areas made a big impact on the women's movement. It became clear that these environmental issues had a particularly adverse impact on the work and lives of women. Thus Eco-Feminism was born. The question of gender inequality in the context of deteriorating environment came to the fore.

The confluence of the women's movement with the environmental campaign is a notable event. What is equally remarkable, however, is that the posture of the women volags on family planning is hostile. Many women's groups believe that the primary problem in India is poverty and inequitable distribution of income and wealth. Reducing fertility, according to them, is a second order issue which has attracted an excessive and ill-conceived effort by the government. The official family planning programme is perceived to be defective in the following ways:

— There is excessive emphasis on contraceptive techniques to be used by women and little effort to get men to bear part of the burden.
— The focus is on recruiting women acceptors and there is

inadequate commitment to provide the medical after-care that women need while practising contraception.

- New contraceptives are introduced for women without adequate testing under relevant social-economic conditions.
- Spacing methods not only prolong the child-bearing period for mothers but reduce the time available for young girls to attend school before they are married off, since girls are expected to take care of their siblings at home.
- Poor parents see children as additional earning units necessary for survival. The small family norm may mean an even lower consumption level for the household.
- The sex ratio of females to males is already declining. The combination of son preference and the adoption of the small family norm will depress this ratio even further, it is argued.

Gujarat has a strong tradition of voluntary work aimed at women's welfare. The All India Women's Conference had branches in the state since the 1920s. Many organisations of the Gandhian kind sprang up in the 1930s and 1940s. Among them was Putliba, a volag we studied. The Gujarat State Gazetteer lists 90 organisations which aim at increasing women's welfare. They were well supported by the Congress ministries. The split in the Congress and the choice these volags made to support Morarji Desai, rather than Indira Gandhi, lost them government patronage to some extent.

The Self-Employed Women's Association (SEWA) was established in 1972. It grew out of the women's wing of the Textile Labour Association. SEWA's aim was to unionise women workers in the unorganised sector. It deals with issues such as minimum wages, rights to land, occupational health, home-based workers and access to credit. SEWA combines three movements: labour, co-operative and development. SEWA has 30,000 members and it has organised 30 all-women co-operatives. In 1982 an attempt was made to establish SEWA BHARAT, that is women's groups all over India affiliated with SEWA, Ahmedabad. Many organisations were established but some have closed down and others claim complete independence.

SEWA has made a great impact on the voluntary sector. Its

contributions have been recognised the world over. Nancy Barry, the President of Women's World Banking, said that SEWA was a model at the global level. Kalima Rose (1992) concludes:

> Under SEWA, women have forged a new model of what a trade union, can be... SEWA organises women who work in their homes, in the streets of cities, in the fields and villages of rural India, with no fixed employer, carving their small niches in the economy, day-by-day, with only their wits to guide them against incredible odds of vulnerability, invisibility and poverty.

Although Rajasthan has made Mahila Mandals since the 1920s, there are few volags which focus exclusively on women's issues in Rajasthan. However, there are many who are multi-sectoral and who take on women's issues as part of a broader set of activities. Perhaps, the most important volag in the women's field is SWRC in Tilonia in Ajmer district, founded by Bunker and Aruna Roy which made a major contribution to the conceptualisation of the government's WDP, as mentioned above. Other prominent volags in this area are Sewa Mandir, Bal Rashmi, the Kumarappa Institute, People's Education and Development Organisation (PEDO), Centre for Community Economies Development Consultants (CECOE-DECON), Ajmer Adult Education Society, Tarun Bharat Sangha and URMUL. These organisations are working mainly to raise women's awareness, promote education and literacy as well as stimulate income earning activities. The Institute of Development Studies focuses on research and policy work. Ashta has helped organise tribal women so that they can get minimum wages for collecting forest produce.

Despite the much hype and hoopla over the new millennium when the world supposedly entered a new age, the condition of women in India continue to remain pathetic. The patriarchal society continues to throttle women's rights due to which they are treated as second-class citizens.

The President K. R. Narayan in his message on the eve of the 50th Republic Day had succinctly said, "The status of women and the status of the dalits are the greatest national drawback and the greatest national shame. 170 years after the abolition of 'sati', the practice still manages to raise its head and what is worse, even gets explained away as suicide are saintly sacrifice. The female-half of the Indian population continues to be regarded as it was in the 18th and 19th centuries. In parts of rural India, form of sadism seem to be earmarked for dalit women...it has been extended as one of the methods of ragging in our elite colleges and universities."

In this backdrop of little discernible change in the status of women in India, one of the major issue of concern is that there is increasing marginalisation and violence against women. The women's movement and organisations working on women's issues will have to dwell on these aspects with greater emphasis.

Voluntary organisations have an enormous task at hand in the new millennium. They not only have to work for the economic empowerment of women, but also address the issues of social, political and cultural empowerment.

For economic empowerment, voluntary organisations have a major role to play in training, skill building and in providing credit facilities. They have a role in bringing in attitudinal change in people on gender equality, education of girls, the menance of dowry, wife-beating etc.

Voluntary organisations and women's groups also have a role to force changes in policies, laws, rules and regulations on women. The overall focus has been to enhance the status of women.

CHILD

Child Rights—What do we know about them? There is a saying in Tamil which goes somewhat like this "what one has learned can be contained in one's palms and what one hasn't is as big as the universe" but we have to make a beginning somewhere. The concept of Human Rights is of course not new. However it is a fresh and alive topic, as long as there are people who have been denied access to rights. One can therefore, place the concept of Child Rights very much as part of Human Rights.

Why do we need something special like the Convention on the Rights of the Child (CRC) because even with it in the purview of human rights, there are groups and people whose concerns trail far behind and are left out. Children and women fall in this category. It is to make sure that Children's and Women's Rights are addressed on an equal footing that the CRC and the Convention on elimination of all forms of discriminations, against women (CEDAW) have emerged and found their rightful place.

The Convention on the Rights of the child was mooted in the

late Eighties. The general assembly of the United Nations adopted the Convention on November 20th, 1989 and the World Summit for Children was held in December, 1990. India acceded to the Convention on December 11, 1992. When a country has acceded to the Convention, all the provisions apply according to the International Law of Treaties and Conventions. Countries have to abide by it and periodically report on it. The CRC is divided into three sections and has 54 Articles.

For the purpose of common understanding one can divide the Right of the Child into four broad areas—the Right to Survival, Development, Protection and Participation. All the Articles of the Convention fall under these broad categories.

Let us examine now a few issues that have to be addressed both by the State and Civil Society, which includes NGOs:

1. The first and foremost is a good and acceptable definition of "Who is a Child". There are varying definitions and the law is unclear depending on what the issue is about; notions of the age at which one is a child or ceases to be one, differs. So we need to look at this and see that the provisions of all the Acts do not contravene each other.
2. We need a Unified Children's Code which is not exclusive but applies to all children.
3. Then we have the question of Implementation. In India we have very good legislation, but when it comes to implementation we fare very poorly. A time-bound agreed plan for implementing the CRC must be set by the Government and agreed to by all.
4. We need to systematically monitor violations of Child Rights and institute mechanism by which there will be widespread participation on monitoring the implementation of the CRC.
5. There need to be massive communication and Advocacy Campaigns to change the behaviours, attitudes, and practices of people, particularly of adults towards children. Attitudes have to change from one of Patronising the Participation.

Child Rights in Building Civil Society

Each aspect of the child rights' movement will need to be developed in different times according to the tactical needs of practical political activity with a firm belief in the human will, that can transcend historical and personal circumstances. Civil Society must raise the level of popular culture and popular understanding of child rights, especially convincing the liberal intellectuals of the need for the articulation of such rights. Spontaneous mass support for such a movement requires the fulfillment of these two conditions. Building a child right movement for an alternative politics signifies a break from the fetters of traditional politics—a change of political direction which must be absorbed in civil society as a social consensus if a new harmonious politics-economics historic block without internal contadictions is to be achieved. We now need the child rights movement to exercise its own hegemony within the system of traditional cultural and within the movement for an alternative politics.

For the child rights movements to exert a hegemony in civil society and upon the state, it will have to have tactical alliances and act in co-operation with other groups and will upto a point of time respect their interests and make concessions (e.g. Employers, parents, political parties, educational authorities, trade unions, agencies of the state). However the role of intellectuals will continue to be all important since the achievement and maintenance of hegemony for the child rights movement is largely a matter of education, and every relationship of hegemony is necessarily a pedagogic relationship. The degree of success of such an educational process for protecting the best interests of children will be proven by the extent to which a new consensus or a collective national will is formed. To create such a will we need to form a popular national bloc, which will enable a new politics to emerge for building a new society of which the rights movement will be an essential part.

The aim of the child rights movement should be to create the will and a collective consensus in civil society. The hegemony of the ruling classes that is primarily responsible for violation of children's rights must be replaced by the new political hegemony—a national will—formed out of a political alliance for an alternative politics.

The conventional theory of Human Rights presumes a homogeneous civil society and a strong and legitimate democratic state that will protect the rights of life, liberty and freedom of the individual. This is a very narrow perspective of human rights. Our ideology is based on a perspective and practice of human rights that is universal in its applicability but accommodates the specifics of our pluralistic society. It is based on the indivisibility of human rights rooted in the mandate laid down in the Universal Declaration of Human Rights (UDHR), the Indian Constitution, the two main UN Convents on Civil and Political Rights and Economic, Social and Cultural Rights and several International Treaties ratified by India. Human Rights are also collective rights of communities and peoples to the right to continuing sustainable development, eco-systems and livelihoods. The human rights mandate is heard in the voices of the oppressed and exploited, of indigenous people, fishing communities, women, dalits, children, workers, artisans and peasants; it is the voices from below of the resurgent civil society of sustainable livelihood and eco-systems, popular governance and equitable development.

Democracy, development and respect for human rights and fundamental freedoms are inter-dependent and mutually reinforcing. The right to sustainable development is universal, inalienable right and an integral part of fundamental human rights. Human rights is central to democratic development. Popular participation and transparent governance are essential pillars of sustainable development. Thus human rights for us is concerned with the creation and continuance of a decent standard of living and sustainable eco-systems in all regions, across class, caste, gender, ethnicity and nationality. It is concerned about an economic and cultural system that does not undermine the sustainability of ecology and livelihoods for the present and future generations, political systems which do not repress their own citizens and a system of international supervision which can prevent local and domestic national governments from infringing human standards.

The Programme of structural adjustment of the Indian economy and consequent realignment of decision making in the political and cultural domain advocated by the IMF-World Bank combine are being implemented vigorously by the Indian Government, resulting in extremely adverse effects on a wide cross-section of civil society. The new trading regime of WTO dominated by the leading trading partners and TNCs has now put a stranglehold on Indian trade and affected prices. Already visible is the escalating prices of life-saving drugs; essential food items, gifting the most profitable public sector units to Multi-national Corporations, the exit policy proposed for retrenching excess workers, restructuring the public distribution system to eliminate 50 per cent of the beneficiaries, privatising the power sector and numerous other industries, redefining the role of the state and dramatic changes being proposed in the Constitution of India and numerous welfare legislations. All these developments do not mostly affect adults but whole communities and children are the victims of this process. Parallely, we observe a whole new generation of human rights violation emerging. Increasingly we are witness to Corporate Crime for which, unlike in the industrialised countries we do not have mechanisms to monitor nor systems of accountability. The right to information and not just knowledge, is another right that is blatantly violated: what is needed is the right to informed consent. The attack on our bio-diversity is real and devastating. In the present global trading regime consumer rights protection becomes very significant. Workers' rights, hard won over decades of struggle are now being ruthlessly dismembered. The growth of the arms industry is unbelievable but real. All this again impacts adversely on thousands of poor families and their children.

After fifty-two years of Independence, India has the largest number of child workers in the world. It also has the distinction of having the largest number of children who never went to school or were pushed out of school. Inspite of many efforts children are not high on the political or administrative agenda notwithstanding promises in the election manifestos. In the present largely fluid, right-wing political environment, empowerment and rights of the poorest increasingly becomje non-issues. The capitalist-high technology path of development pursued by other countries including structural adjustment has not prevented these countries from ensuring basic needs for all children. Most theoreticians still don't believe that in a market run reality in India hybridly-engineered and propped up capitalism can co-exist with millions of empty and ill-fed stomachs. Hybrid parasitic capitalist development means a miserable livelihood for millions of children. The theory and politics that the movement or campaign for children's rights is fragmenting the broader social movement for social transformation, is untenable. Children's interests have been marginalised and pushed to the periphery by a crass adult world that would like to continue the same. A generation of upper class children continue to enjoy surplus, because of the emasculation of the children of the oppressed.

Similarly the great political theory that the emancipation of children can take place only after a revolution or the completion of social transformation to a social society, is mere reductionism. There is no doubt that the lives of children are intrinsically linked with the living conditions of adults. Yet there is a programme that is viable and possible, a programme to achieve the basic rights package even within the most exploitative and corrupt social order. It is this collective struggle from within on a daily basis which alone can democratise decision-making and place checks on the rate and character of exploitation of labour and the destruction of valuable eco-systems. Even after fifteen years the political establishment has not found it necessary to redraft the 1974 National Policy on the Child. The Report that the Government of India submitted in 1977 to the United Nations Committee on the rights of the Child, is a mere compilation of laws and programmes that the government has to implement. It does not have even promises for its 300 million children. This reveals the planned bankruptcy of the political establishment and the complacency of civil society. If there is no programme to protect and ensure fulfillment of children's rights there is no rationale for a government to govern.

What is the least information we can place on record about the status of children? Less than 4 per cent of GNP is spent on education, much less on school children. Per capita expenditure on education is systematically falling. In 1991,there was an estimated 8 million fewer girls than boys with the female to male ratio of 0.949. Sexual abuse of children is increasingly being reported especially in cities and in specific tourism areas; 15 per cent of 1,00,000 sex workers surveyed were children below 15 years of age at the time of entry into the profession and this would rise to 25 per cent if the age group 16-18 years is included. Nearly 5 lakh children live on pavements or in most inhabitable places either with or without their families; 60,000 children continue to go blind every year due to deficiency of Vitamin A. More than 40 million children are living with different forms of disabilities. Approximately 95 million children are out of school in different occupations and establishments. Two-third of our children suffer from one or another form of malnutrition leading to several diseases; 30 per cent of all infants born in India are of low birth weight. Child marriages constitute another gross denial of child rights and their full childhood development. There is a phenomenal increase in foeticide and infanticide. When it comes to custody, thousands are confined for unwarranted reasons in so-called juvenile/special homes. Everyday, the police continue to illegally detain children, torture and humiliate them; at times even murder them. Further there is an increasing body of evidence to prove that the impact of globalization processes and the structural adjustment package have had most adverse effects on children. Displacement from homes and lands, export oriented high-tech agriculture policies, deforestation, and ailenation of vast tracts of lands of children's families from their traditional source of livelihood. Cuts in food subsidies and fertilizer and power subsidies for farmers directed by the IMF and World Bank have affected the Public Distribution System (PDS). Increasingly, due to decreasing real wages and declining purchasing power, the poor are unable to take even their allotted share from the PDs. Prices of commodities are dramatically rising.

It is in this context that we consider, the present policy initiatives of the government are not just inadequate to the commitments made with regard to the Convention on the rights of the child and obligation to the Constitution, but most detrimental to the well-being and holistic development of children. Similarly several statutes require amendments for more democratic enforcement while several public institutions catering to child welfare need to be restructured. Budgetary allocations have to be reviewed and increased as part of the State's commitment to the First Call for Children. The promotion and protection of children's rights are central to human rights enforcement and standards. The United Nations Convention on the Rights of the Child combined with several other international human rights instruments, offers children the opportunity to realise their rights to a holistic development and a full childhood. It has set the minimum parameters, the world over for the promotion of children's rights. The enforcement of these rights for every child in a context of structural inequality, and eradication of poverty is the challenge. All the agencies of the state, the dominant interests in civil society and the middle classes are liable for neglect or acts of commission amounting to violations of child rights. This is a complex task when it comes to protecting the rights of children and women. A family likes to protect its own children but abuses other children. A trade unionist demands living wages for adults but believes that child labour is necessary till poverty continues. A teacher pays utmost attention to the education of his/her own child, often using no violence but for the 50 students in the classroom the teacher most often is a tyrant whenever he or she happens to be present. The I.A.S. officer, the famous journalist campaigns against child labour but has no problem in eating at catering establishments employing children or employing children as domestic workers at home. The social relations between children and adults is complex and varies across class. Hence the promotion and protection of children's rights is an emergency that can no longer be put off. The social relation of the production processes, that govern the lives of 80 per cent of the population, require the continuance of the system of exploitation especially the exploitation of the poor for super profits. The challenge for all child rights activists is no doubt to locate their struggles in the common struggle for social transformation for a more just, humane, equitable democratic order. Yet there is need for specificity: that the movement and campaign for children's rights while relating to and being part of the struggle of other social movements should have an ideology and programme of its own. The programme we believe in, a politically viable, is that even within this uneven, unjust, capitalist, exploitative order, the fundamental essential rights of children can be promoted and protected. This is possible because the Constitution, International law and substantive law does recognise and legally protect the special needs and rights of children. This has not yet become possible because the political-administrative establishment is not compelled to listening to the voices of children, especially oppressed children—or so they seem to think. This political combine, the state, has consciously subverted all efforts by all people to achieve a simple national aspiration—all children must be guaranteed the right to life, livelihood and holistic development. This is the crime of neglect in policy; nuclear power and nuclear bombs are priorities over the basic rights of children to a quality of life that ensures their childhood and development.

The state is aware that trade and commerce, the manufacturing industry, the information sector, merchants and landowners and the middle class require that atleast 100 million children are not in schools but engaged in the most dehumanising and menial jobs. The state also encourages the non-employment/non-payment of living wages to adults and oversees the destruction of all that goes to make up sustainable livelihood for the poor. This is necessary so that the poor children have no relevance for education, or play or childhood. For generations the poor were never allowed to enjoy a phase in their life called childhood or youth. Even as children, the oppressed only learn one lesson-survial against poverty and starvation, malnutrition and disease. It is for this reason that our efforts must recognise and priorities the urgency of building the broadest possible social alliance for a social consensus and collective action to stop the denial of the human rights of children and promote a new culture that thinks and lives by a simple value—"the first call for the child". Anything planned or done must be in best interest of the child.

YOUTH

The youth of the country are very precious human resource. They are the potential change agents of tomorrow. They possess not only fertile minds but an unique dynamism that requires to be nurtured. Their energies, if harnessed effectively, can contribute greatly in the nation's march towards progress and prosperity. However, today we find that they are victims of an educational and socialisation process that kills creativity, destroys initiatives and dehumanises.

As it is the youth who can play an important role in the rejuvenation of the country, a massive effort is needed to mobilise them into nation building. Swami Vivekanand's exhortation has assumed importance more than ever before, "My faith is in the younger generation, the modern generation out of them will come my workers. They will work out the whole problem, like lions... They will spread from centre to centre, until we have covered the whole of India."

Voluntary organisations have a major role to play in mobilising the youth in nation building. The development of the people and the community at large can be taken up by the youth. So voluntary organisations can help in encouraging youth to take to voluntary work.

Voluntary organisations can educate and sensitise the youth about the societal problems and encourage them to fight against injustice.

Presently there is no concrete youth policy. So voluntary organisations can play a major role in pressuring the Government to formulate an effective youth policy.

According to Dr. S. N. Subba Rao, Director, National Youth Project and reverently called Bhaiji, "organisations working on youth have been keeping in mind several issues while devising their strategies. These include concerns on health of the youth, increasing inequality in the society and also increasing corruption."

Dr. Subba Rao says both Swami Vivekanand and Mahatma Gandhi could influence a large number of youths into voluntary work. In fact after a call by Mahatma Gandhi to dedicate themselves for constructive social work, thousands of youth left their home and went to remote villages to work for the development of the society and people in distress. Later on many of them set up their own organisations.

Later on after Jai Prakash Narayan's 'Sampurna Andolan', a large number of youths, who were part of the movement set up voluntary organisations to do community development.

Talking about the National Youth Project, Dr. Subba Rao says a large number of youth camps are being organised in different parts of the country. On the routine, the NYP has been conducting about 10 camps in a year. They include, national integration camps, communal harmony camps, literacy camps, relief camps for victims of riots, earthquake, women's camps.

According to Dr. Subba Rao, on an average, there are 250 to 500 young men and women campers. He informs that the largest youth camp organised till date was in Kevadia, Gujarat where the National Youth Project collaborated with other youth organisations and the number of campers were 23,500.

Dr. Subba Rao had been instrumental in initiating the Sadbhavna Rail Yatra in collaboration with the Government of India. The yatra was aimed at bringing the youth of the country together and propagating the spirit of national integration. The mission was to spread the message of love, peace, friendship, communal harmony, brotherhood of man and world peace. About 2,500 young men and women from 26 states took part in the Yatra, toured the legnth and breadth of the country and lived for 12 months in the special train as members of one family, transcending all differences.

Talking about the Nehru Yuva Kendra (NYK), Mr. Chaudhry Mohammed Ateef says there are already 0.2 million youth club all over the country. "These youth clubs have developed into small voluntary organisations at their own level and are carrying out developmental work in their respective areas of activities. As many as 25 per cent of the youth club are self-sufficient," he underscores.

"Once the youth of a village realise their importance and are aware of their rights, they can act as the change agents in the development process," Mr. Ateef says, "The main focus of the Nehru Yuva Kendra is to empower the youth clubs. The Kendra cannot given employment to the youth but can help them give training to get jobs."

"One of the major advantage of the youth clubs are their acceptability amongst the villagers as the club members are themselves from the village," he continues, "When they start implementing various developmental schemes they become more sensitised to local problems as well as national problems."

Meanwhile another programme to mobilise the youth has been IGSS's Student Mobilisation Initiative for Learning through Exposure (SMILE). The programme was conceived in 1986. It is an alternate education programme that provides students and youth with multiple opportunities to critically reflect on society and on themselves thereby equipping them with the knowledge, attitudes, values skills and convictions necessary for a transformation of their lives and of larger society.

The SMILE programme comprises of three basic components including youth motivation, fellowships and exchange programmes. Youth motivation includes interventions where the focus is on sensitising youth to societal issues and struggle situations, encouraging them to question processes of marginalisation and helping them analyse societal structures and institutions.

The SMILE aims to promote several core values amongst the youth. These include social justice, gender equity, secularism, democracy, environmental sustainability, honesty and integrity and dignity of labour.

Youth have also been mobilised in a big way by voluntary organisations during calamities like earthquake, floods etc. Even for social development, lakhs of youth have been devoting their time to voluntary work.

As there is no proper youth policy, a large number of voluntary organisations have been campaigning on the issue to pressurise the Government to bring in a comprehensive youth policy.

According to Mr. Ateef, one of the major bottlenecks in mobilisation of youth is lack of convergence in youth programmes between government and voluntary organisations. "Probably if there is convergence of action, wonders can be done. All efforts are in actuality a piecemeal effort and also there is no co-ordination between the various departments. Through convergence, better training can be imparted to the youth and there could be increase in social mobilisation."

To produce better results, bring about convergence of action and cohesiveness in programmes, Mr. Ateef opines that there should be a confederation of voluntary organisations working on youth in the country. "Such a platform can co-ordinate better and mobilise a greater number of youth in the country," he emphasises.

Finally, according to Dr. Subba Rao, while addressing the increasing challenges before the youth like the drug habits etc., voluntary organisations will have to propagate what the ancient sages had said, "Those with small heart have small homes, those with large heart have the whole universe with them."

APPENDIX

SUMMARY OF DECLARATION AND PLAN OF ACTION OF THE WORLD SUMMIT FOR SOCIAL DEVELOPMENT

PART-I

Declaration

The Declaration of the World Summit for Social Development (held in Cophenhagen from March 6 to 12, 1995) begins with the words:

> For the first time in history, at the invitation of the United Nations, we gather as Heads of State and Government to recognise the significance of social development and human well-being for all and to give to these goals the highest priority both now and into the twenty-first century.

It emphasises the historic importance of the Summit and the urgency of addressing "profound social problems, especially poverty, unemployment and social exclusion, that affect every country"; and identifies the task as one of tackling "both their underlying and structural causes and their distressing consequences in order to reduce uncertainty and insecurity in the life of people." It acknowledges the fact that societies must respond more effectively to the material and spiritual needs of individuals, their families and the communities in which they live".

In a paragraph that was approved at the final stage of the negotiations, world leaders express their conviction that economic development, social development and environmental protection are inter-dependent and mutually reinforcing components of sustainable development, which is the framework for efforts to achieve a higher quality of life for all people. Equitable social development, which recognises empowering of the poor to utilise environmental resources sustainably, is a necessary foundation for sustainable development. World leaders also recognise that broad-based and sustained economic growth in the context of sustainable development is necessary to sustain social development and social justice.

The Declaration affirms that in both economic and social

terms, the most productive policies and investments are those which empower people to maximise their capacities, resources and opportunities. It also maintains that "social and economic development cannot be secured in a sustainable way without the full participation of women" and that "equality and equity between women and men is a priority for the international community and as such must be at the centre of economic and social development". The leaders express their determination to capture the unique possibilities offered by the end of the cold war to promote social development and to tackle its problems in a Summit of "hope, commitment and action".

Globalisation "opens new opportunities for sustained economic growth and development", the Declaration goes on. The challenge, however, is to manage the rapid processes of change and adjustment which engender intensified poverty, unemployment and social disintegration, in order to enhance their benefits and mitigate their negative effects upon people. Despite progress in some areas of social and economic development, the insecurity many people face about the future is intensifying. More than a billion people in the world live in abject poverty, a majority of whom are women, particularly in Africa and in the least developed countries. Over 120 million people worldwide are officially unemployed and many more are under-employed.

"We can continue to hold the trust of the people of the world only if we make their needs our priority," the Declaration states. Poverty, lack of productive employment and social disintegration "are an offence to human dignity" and "a manifestation of ineffectiveness in the functioning of markets and economic and social institutions and processes", it stresses. The challenge is to establish a people centred framework for social development and to build a culture of co-operation and partnership to respond to the immediate needs of those most affected by human distress. Among reasons for convening the Summit, world leaders acknowledge that there are "serious problems of a different nature and magnitude in countries with economies in transition and those experiencing fundamental political, economic and social transformations".

Summit participants declare "a political, economic, ethical and spiritual vision for social development". Such a vision forms the basis of a framework for action, covering several issues and components which are addressed in more specific terms in the action programme. The document stresses throughout that states have the primary responsibility to attain the goals of the Summit, but cannot do it alone, which is why a global effort is needed.

The final part of the draft declaration contains 10 commitments, which are the basis for launching a global drive for social progress and development, as follows:

> "Commitment 1" Concerns the creation of a conducive economic, political, social, cultural and legal environment that would enable people to achieve social development.

This commitment includes the following:

> "Commitment 2" addresses the goal of eradicating poverty in the world as an ethical, social, political and economic imperative of humankind.

This commitment includes the following:

> At the international level, we will focus attention on and support the special needs of countries and regions in which there are substantial concentrations of people living in poverty, in particular those in South Asia, and which therefore face serious difficulties in achieving social and economic development.
>
> "Commitment 3" urges the promotion of the goal of full employment as a basic priority of economic and social policies.

This commitment includes the following:

> "Commitment 4" calls for the promotion of social integration by fostering societies that are stable, safe and just, based on the protection of all human rights, non-discrimination, tolerance and respect for diversity.
>
> "Commitment 5" deals with the promotion of full respect for human dignity and the issue of achieving equality and equity between women and men.
>
> "Commitment 6" is on the promotion and attainment of the goals of universal and equitable access to quality education, the highest attainable standard of physical and mental health, and the access of all to primary health care, "making particular efforts to rectify inequalities relating to social conditions and without distinction as to race, national origin, gender, age or disability; and respecting

and promoting common and particular cultures".

"Commitment 7" pledges world leaders to accelerate the economic, social and human resource development of Africa and the least developed countries.

"Commitment 8" states that structural adjustment programmes should include social development goals.

This Commitment includes the following:

At the international level, we will work to ensure that multilateral development banks and other donors complement leading with enhanced targeted social development investment lending; strive to ensure that structural adjustment programmes respond to the economic and social conditions, concerns and needs of each country; enlist the support and co-operation of regional and international organisations and the United Nations system, in particular the Bretton Woods institutions, in the design, social management and assessment of structural adjustment policies, and in implementing social development goals and integrating them into their policies, programmes and operations.

"Commitment 9" calls for a significant increase and/or more efficient utilisation of the resources allocated to social development in order to achieve the goals of the Summit through national action and regional and international co-operation;

"Commitment 10" urges an improved and strengthened framework for all levels of co-operation for social development.

This commitment includes the following:

At the international level, we will refrain from any unilateral measure not in accordance with international law and the Charter of the United Nations that creates obstacles to trade relations among states.

The commitment ends with the stipulation that the UN General Assembly "should hold a special session in the year 2000 for an overall review and appraisal of the implementation of the outcome of the Summit and consider further actions and initiatives.

(*Source*, Mainstream, 1995, 25th March; pp. 31).

PART-II

Programme of Action

1. The present programme of Action outlines policies, actions and measures to implement the principles and fulfil the commitments enunciated in the Declaration adopted by the World Summit for Social Development.
2. Actions are recommended to create, in a sustained economic growth and sustainable development, a National and International environment favourable to social development, to eradicate poverty, to enhance productive employment and reduce unemployment, and foster social integration.
3. The Programme of Action takes into account the commitments, principles and recommendations of other world conferences; its importance is in its integrated approach and its attempt to combine many different actions for poverty eradication, employment creations and social integration in coherent national and international strategies for social development.

Chapter 1

An Enabling Environment for Social Development

Basis for Action

4. Social Development is inseparable from the cultural, ecological, economic, political and spiritual environment in which it takes place which is again linked with national and international development of peace, freedom, stability and security. Its promotion requires an orientation of values, objectives and priorities, towards well-being of all and the strengthening and promotion of conducive institutions and policies. Human dignity, all human rights and fundamental freedoms, equality, equity and social justice constitute the fundamental values of all societies. The pursuit, promotion and protection of these values among others, provides the basic legitimacy of all institutions and all exercise of

authority and promotes an environment in which human beings are at the centre of concern for sustainable development. They are entitled to a healthy and productive life in harmony with nature.

5. The economies and societies of the world are becoming increasingly inter-dependent globally. The global community is threatened by environmental degradation; severe food crisis, epidemics, racial discrimination, xenophobia, violence and risk of losing the richness of cultural diversity. Governments have recognised that sustainable development and social progress will require increased solidarity through international co-operation, benefiting especially the least developed countries, from the process of globalization.

6. Economic activities are a fundamental basis for social progress. Public policies are necessary to maintain social stability and to create a national and international economic environment that promotes sustainable growth, equity, social justice, tolerence, responsibility and involvement on a global scale.

7. The ultimate goal of social development is to improve and enhance the quality of life of one and all in the community, empowerment and participation are essential for democracy, harmony and social development. To create a new human world, gender equality, equity and full participation of women in all economic social and political activities is essential.

8. Promotion of an enabling environment based on a people—centred approach for sustainable development, like involvement of civil society in the formulation and implementation of decisions; integration of population into economic and development strategies; poverty eradication; equitable and non-discriminatory distribution of the benefits of growth; Strenghtened role for the family in accordance with the declaration of the World Summit for Social Development and those of the International Conference on Population and Development; access to acknowledge, technology education, health care services and information; protection and conservation of natural environment in the context of people centred sustainable development.

Action

(A) A Favourable National and International Economic Environment

9. The promotion of mutually reinforcing broad based sustained economic growth and sustainable development on a

global scale, as well as growth in production, a non-discriminatory and multilateral rule based international trading system, employment and incomes, as a basis for social development; implementing sound and stable macro-economic and sectoral policies; promoting enterprise and productive investment and expended access to open and dynamic markets, implementing the Final Act of the Uruguay Round of multilateral trade negotiations; to follow international law and the charter of the United Nations; ensuring that the special needs and vulnerabilities of small island developing states are adequately addressed by implementing the programme of action for the sustainable development of small Island Developing States.

10. To ensure that the benefits of global economic growth are equitably distributed among countries, efforts have been made to alleviate the onerous debt and debt service burdens connected with the various types of debt of many developing countries, strengthening and improving technical and financial assistance to developing countries; taking into account that the major cause of deterioration of the global environment is the unsustainable pattern of consumption and production, which is aggravating poverty and imbalances; the full implementation of the Final Act of the Uruguay Round of multilateral trade negotiations and assisting countries that are not currently in a position to benefit fully from the liberalization of the World Economy, supporting countries dependent on commodity exports to diversify their economies.

11. To support the developing countries at the national and international levels, implementation of effective policies and development strategies giving priority to human resource development, efforts to create an enabling environment that attracts foreign and domestic direct-investment in developing countries; supporting economic reforms through trade and partnerships; provide technical and financial support to developing countries for the preparatory phase of their commodity diversification projects and programmes; finding effective, development oriented and durable solutions to the external debt problems, through the immediate implementation of the terms of debt forgiveness agreed upon in the Paris Club priorities.

12. Making economic growth and the interaction of the market forces more conducive to social development requires implementation of open market opportunities for all; improving,

broading, and regulating the functioning of markets to promote sustained economic growth and sustainable development; establishing an open market policy; ensuring public and private investment in human resource development and for capacity building in health and education.

13. Ensuring that fiscal systems and other public policies are geared towards eradication of poverty and do not generate socially divisive disparities, calls for enacting rules and regulation that prevents all forms of corruption and exploitation of individuals familes and groups; enhancing co-operation between governments, the private sector and civil society; promoting international agreements addressing effectively issues of double taxation, as well as tax evasion.

(B) A Favourable National and International Political and Legal Environment

14. To ensure that the political framework supports the objectives of social development, it is essential that the government institution and agencies have the status, resources and information necessary to give high priority to social development in policy making; eliminating all forms of discrimination; encouraging decentralisation of public institution and services to local needs and facilitating local participation; strengthening the capacities and opportunities of all people especially, disadvantaged or vulnerable to enhance their own economic and social development; ensuring full involvement and participation of women at all levels in the decision making and implementation, process; resourcing all legal impedements to the ownership of all means of production and property by man and women; Taking measures in accordance with the charter of United Nations, the Universal Declaration of Human Rights and other international instruments to create political and legal environment to address the root cause of movements of refugees, to allow their voluntary return in safety and dignity.

15. It is essential for social development that all human rights and fundamental precedures including the right to development as an integral part of fundamental human rights, be promoted and protected through implementing the international human rights convention with ratifications where necessary, re-affirming and promoting all human rights and fundamental freedoms; ensuring

the participation of every human person in the development process; promoting and protecting the human rights of women, children, especially of the girl child and vulnerable and disadvantaged, in the society; prevent and eliminate all domestic discriminations and violence.

16. An open political and economic system requires access by all to knowledge, education and information by strengthening the education system at all levels, while removing economic and socio-cultural barries raising public awareness and promoting gender sensitivity education; enabling access of information on social development and gender issues.

17. International support for national efforts to promote a favourable political and legal environment, must be in confirmity with the Charter of the United Nations, principles of international law and the declaration on principles of international law concerning friendly relations and co-operation among states in accordance with the Charter of United Nations, making use of these to prevent and resolve armed conflicts and promote social progress; co-ordinating action and legal instruments and/or measures to combat terrorism and other activities contrary to human rights and human dignity; the right to development should be fulfilled so as to equitably meet the social, developmental and environmental needs of present and future generation; ensuring that human persons are at the centre of social development; elaborating policies that support the objectives of social development; strengthen the capacity of governments, the private sector and civil society to enable them to meet their specific and global responsibility.

Chapter II

Eradication of Poverty

Basis for Action and Objectives

18. Over 1 billion people in the world today live under unacceptable conditions of poverty, mostly in developing countries, and particularly in rural areas of low income Asia and the Pacific,

Africa, Latin America and the Caribbean, and the least developed countries.

19. Poverty has various manifestations, including lack of income and productive resources sufficient to ensure sustainable livelihoods; hunger and malnutrition; ill health; lack of access to education; increased morbidity and mortality; homelessness; unsafe environment; social discrimination and exclusion and lack of participation in decision-making and in civil, social and cultural life. Women and Children bear a disproportionate burden of poverty which not only depends on income but also on access of social services.

20. There is a general agreement that persistent widspread poverty, social and gender in-equities, have influences on, and are in turn influenced by demographic parameters, unsustainable consumption and production patterns.

21. Urban poverty is increasing with urbanization resulting in overcrowding, contaminated water and bad sanitation, unsafe shelter, crime and additional social problems. An increasing number of low-income urban households are female maintained.

22. Gender disparities are marked, especially in female maintained households. Increase in population will result in increased number of youth living in poverty. Hence, specific measures are needed to address the juvenilization and feminization of poverty.

23. Poverty has various causes, including structural ones, with origins in both the national and international domains. No uniform solution can be found for global application, it is in-separably linked to lack of control over resources, including land, skills, knowledge, capital and social connections. Eradication of poverty cannot be accomplished through anti-poverty programme alone, but will require democratic participation and changes in economic structures.

24. People living in poverty and vulnerable groups must be empowered through organisation and participation, in all aspects of political, economic and social life; and in the planning and implementation of policies that effect them; enable them to become genuine partners in development.

25. There is therefore an urgent need for, national strategies to reduce over-all-poverty; international support and co-operation to assist developing countries in their efforts to eradicate poverty; development of methods to measure absolute poverty; regular

national review of economic policies of national budgets; human resource development and improved infrastructural facilities; policies that strengthen family and contribute to its stability; mobilization of public and private sector to assist poverty striken areas.

Actions

(A) Formulation of Integrated Strategies

26. Government should give greater focus to public efforts to eradicate absolute poverty and to reduce overall poverty substantially by, promoting sustained economic growth; formulating national poverty eradication plans to address the structural causes of poverty; establishing policies, objectives measureable targets to enhance and broader women's economic opportunities; eliminating injustice and obstacles that women face; encouraging and supporting local community development projects to eradicate poverty.

27. Governments are urged to integrate goals and targets for combating poverty into overall economic and social policies and planning at the local, national and regional levels by analysing policies and programmes; redesigning public investment policies ensuring development policies that benefit low-income communities; establishing and strengthening, mechanisms for the co-ordination of efforts to combat poverty.

28. People living in poverty and their organisations should be empowered by, involving them fully in designning, implementing and monitoring of national strategies and programmes; placing special emphasis on capacity building; educating people about their rights; political system and the availability of programmes.

29. There is a need to periodically monitor, access and share information on the performance of poverty eradication plans, evaluate policies to combat poverty and promote an understanding and awareness of poverty and its causes and consequencies by developing, updating and disseminating specific and agreed gender disaggregated indicators of poverty and vulnerability, monitoring and assessing the achievement of goals and targets to international forums in the area of social development; facilitating exchange of knowledge and experience through sub-regional and regional organizations.

30. Members of the international community should bilaterally

or through multilateral organizations, foster an enabling environment for poverty eradication by co-ordinating policies and programmes in order to meet basic social development goals and targets; strengthen the capacity of countries with economies in transation to develop their social protection system, social policies, and eradication of poverty.

(B) Improved Access to Productive Resources and Infrastructure

31. The opportunities for income generation, diversification of activities and increase of productivity in low-income and poor communities should be enhanced by, improving the availability and accessibility of transportation, communication, power and energy services; promoting national and international assistance in providing economically viable alternatives for social groups; promoting comprehensive rural development; ensuring economic opportunities for rural women should be improved, through elimination of legal, social, cultural and practical obstacles.

32. Rural poverty should be addressed by, expanding and improving land ownership through land reform, security of land texure and ensuring equal rights of women and men in this respect; improving access to markets and market information; protecting traditional rights to land and other resources; promoting education, research and development on farming systems; and training for effective use of existing technologies and indigenous knowledge.

33. Access to credit by small rural or urban producers, landless farmers and other people with low or no income should be substantially improved, with special attention to the needs of women and dis-advantaged and vulnerable groups by receiving, national legal, regulatory and institutional framework to credit on reasonable terms; access to affordable credit.

34. Urban poverty should further be addressed by, strengthening micro-enterprises, facilitating the transition from the informal to the formal sector, educating and training the women, that youth, unemployed and the under-employed; strategies for shelter should give special attention to women and children; promote better employment opportunities.

(C) Meeting the Basic Human of All

35. Government in partnership with all other development actors in particular organisation of, and people living in poverty,

should co-operate to meet the basic human needs of all, by ensuring access to social services; recognising that improving peoples health is inseparably linked to sound environment.

36. Government should implement the commitments that have been made, to meet the basic needs of all by the year 2000, like basic education, life expectency, reduction of maternal mortality and malnutrition group children; attain food security and healthy living, control of major diseases; access of safe drinking water and affordable adequate shelter for all.

37. Access to social services for people living in poverty and vulnerable groups should be improved through facilitating and improving access of education, expanding pre-school education through new learning technologies; ensuring access to quality healthcare, especially in low income groups and rural areas.

(D) Enhanced Social Protection and Reduced Vulnerability

38. Social protection system should be based on legislation; in order to protect people who cannot work from poverty, sickness, disability, old age, maternity, etc., should be provided protection universally; should have social security programmes; ensure social safety nets associated with economic restructuring under structural adjustment programmes.

39. Particular efforts should be made to protect children and youth by promoting family stability and social support; taking legislative, administrative, social and educational measure to protect and promote rights of the child, particularly girl child; addressing special needs of, indigenous children and sing parent in the society.

40. Particular efforts should be made to protect older persons, by strengthening family support system; ensuring that they get the basic human needs; encourage cross generational participation in policies and programme development and in decision making bodies at all levels.

41. People and communities should be protected from improverishment and long term displacement and exclusion resulting from disaster through the following actions at the national and international levels, by designing effective mechanisms to reduce the impact and mitigate efforts of natural disaster, such as earthquake, cyclones and floods; planning the logistical mechanism to enable quick response in disaster situation.

Chapter III

The Expansion of Productive Employment and the Reduction of Unemployment

Basis for Action and Objectives

42. Productive work and employment are central elements of development as well as of human identity. National efforts need to be reinforced by international co-operation in achieving the goal of full employment.

43. Globalisation is leading to increasing labour mobility giving rise to new employment opportunities as well as new uncertainties. To meet the changing circumstances, human resource development need to be oriented towards enhancing the knowledge and skills of particularly women and youth to enable them to work productively.

44. The informal sector is the leading source of employment for those like women who have limited access to formal sector wage employment. Removal of obstacles to the expansion of this sector must be accompanied by protection of the basic rights, health and safety of workers and improvement of overall working conditions.

45. Particular efforts by the Public and Private Sectors have to be made in all spheres of employment policy to ensure gender equality, equal opportunity and non-discrimination on the basis of race/ethnic group, religion, age, health, disability and full respect for applicable international instruments so as to ensure their integration into productive activities.

46. Women the world over face the double burden of remunerated and unremunerated work. The social and economic importance of unremunerated work need to be acknowledged. The very conception of productive work need to be broadened and one way to promote this is to develop methods for reflecting the value of unremunerative work in quantitative term for possible reflection in accounts.

47. In order to promote sustained economic growth and sustainable development, there is an urgent need for placing the creation of employment at the Centre of National Strategies and Policies; expanding work opportunities and increasing productivity

in both rural and urban sectors; education and training that enable workers and entrepreneurs to adapt to changing technologies and economic conditions; quality jobs with full respect for the basic rights of workers as defined by ILO and other international instruments; special priority to the problems of structural, long-term unemployment and under-employment of youth, women, persons with disabilities and all other disadvantaged groups; empowerment of women, gender balance in decision-making processes; empowerment of members of vulnerable and disadvantaged groups through provisions including education and training.

Actions

(A) Centrality of Employment in Policy Formulation

48. Placing the expansion of productive employment at the centre of sustainable development strategies and economic and social policies requires policies for full, productive appropriately remunerated and freely chosen employment.

49. Minimising the negative impact on jobs of measures for macro-economic stability requires co-ordination of macro-economic policies so that they are mutually conducive to broad based and sustained economic growth and sustainable development; removing structural constraints to economic growth and employment creation; disseminating information on the impact of trade and investment liberalisation on the economy and employment; establishing social safety mechanisms to minimise adverse effect of structural adjustment or reform programmes through education and retraining.

50. Promoting patterns of economic growth that maximise employment creation, requires labour intensive investments in economic and social infrastructure and developing community assets in both rural and urban areas; giving developing countries the capacity to select specific and suitable technologies; providing technical assistance and expand transfer of technology to developing countries and strengthen national and local technology institutions; encouraging community economic development strategies involving governments and members of civil society; introducing policies for mobilising savings and stimulating investment in capital-short areas; conservation and management

of natural resources; promotion of alternative livelihoods in fragile eco-systems and rehabilitation of vulnerable land areas and natural resources; encouraging utilisation of renewable energy.

51. Enhancing opportunities for the creation and growth of private-sector enterprises that would generate additional employment; requires removing obstacles faced by small and medium-sized enterprises and easing regulations; facilitate access to small and medium-sized enterprises to credit and markets, training and technological information; improving opportunities and working conditions for women and youth entrepreneurs by eliminating discriminations in access to productive resources and by providing social security protection; promoting legal frameworks to foster development of co-operative enterprises; assisting informal sectors and local enterprises to progressively integrate into the formal economy.

(B) Education, Training and Labour Policies

52. Facilitating people's access to productive employment in the rapidly changing global environment and developing better quality jobs requires well-defined educational priorities and investing in education and training systems; revitalised partnership between education and other departments of government including labour and communications, and partnership between governments and non-governmental organisations; participation of youth and adult learners in the design of education and training programmes; training on a continuous basis and also securing access of women to training programmes; retraining of displaced and retrenched workers to facilitate their re-entry; encouraging national and international exchange of information of innovative models and best experiences.

53. Helping workers to adapt and to enhance their employment opportunities under changing economic conditions requires active labour policies to stimulate the demand for labour in order to ensure that the burden of indirect labour costs on employers does not constitute a disincentive to hiring workers and establishing institutions and processes that prevent all forms of discriminations and improve the employment opportunities of groups that are vulnerable and disadvantaged; promoting access of women and girls to traditionally male-dominated occupations, promoting labour mobility and maintenance of adequate levels of solid

protection to worker redeployment; integration of women into workforce by developing adequate child care, care for older persons and other support services; co-operation between employees and employers for the introduction of new technologies, while ensuring adequate protection; strengthening public and private employment services to assist workers to adapt to changing job markets and also strengthening labour market information systems. All data gathered in this process should be disaggregated by gender in order to monitor the status of women relative to men.

(C) Enhanced Quality of Work and Employment

54. Governments should enhance the quality of work and employment by observing and fully implementing the human rights obligations that they have assured; safeguarding and promoting respect for basic worker's rights including prohibition of forced labour and child labour, freedom of association and the right to organise and bargain collectively; using international labour standards for formulating national labour legislation and policies; promoting the role of the ILO for improving the level of employment and the quality of work; promoting co-operation between workers and employers in the decisions of enterprises.

55. Remove exploitation, abolish child labour, raise productivity and enhance the quality of life for safe and healthy working environment by developing and implementing progressive policies, promoting sound labour relations based on tripartite co-operation and full respect for the freedom of association and the right to organise and bargain collectively, setting specific target dates for eliminating all forms of child labour, designing policies and programmes to help eradication of family poverty, protecting workers especially women from sexual harassment and violence.

56. Full participation of women in the labour market and their equal access to employment opportunities requires promoting gender sensitivity training to eliminate prejudices against the employment of women improvement in access to technologies to women changing policies and attitude that reinforce the division of labour based on gender; providing affordable quality child-care facilities and paying attention to the needs of single parent households.

(D) *Enhance Employment Opportunities for Groups with Specific Needs*

57. Activity involving representatives of particular groups in planning, designing, management, monitoring, evaluating programmes by providing access to accurate information and sufficient resources.

58. Employment policies can better address the problem of short and long-term unemployment by incorporating, involving unemployed and/or their associations in employment planning, re-education and training, literacy, skill upgrading, counselling and job-search assistance.

59. Programmes for entry or re-entry into the labour market aimed at vulnerable and disadvantaged groups by increasing the level of skills, and also improving the ability of getting a job through improvements in housing, health and family life.

60. Policies should seek to guarantee all youth constructive options for their future by providing equal access to education, designing and carrying out comprehensive and co-ordinated programmes that stimulate the resourcefulness of youth.

61. Full participation of indigenous people in the labour market and their equal access to employment opportunities requires developing comprehensive employment, education and training programmes.

62. Employment opportunities for persons with disabilities requires non-discriminating laws and regulations, organising support services, devising incentive schemes, and small business, providing conducive work place and promoting public awareness.

63. For migrant workers and their family an intensified international co-operation and national attention is needed. Government of countries of origin, transit and destination are urged to safeguard their basic human rights and prevent them from exploitation and adopt effective sanctions against those countries who exploit or engage in trafficking. Governments are also urged to facilitate the return of migrants and their reintegration into their home communities.

(E) *A Broader Recognition and Understanding of Work and Employment*

64. Acknowledging the important contribution of unremunerated work to societal well-being and bringing respect,

dignity and value to societal perceptions of such work and the people, promoting socially useful volunteer work and allocating appropriate resources to support such work without diluting the objectives regarding employment expansion.

65. The development of additional socially useful new types of employment and work requires helping vulnerable and disadvantaged groups to integrate better into society and participate more effectively in economic and social development.

Chapter IV

Social Integration

Basis for Action and Objectives

66. The aim of Social Integration is to create "a society for all" which must be based upon respect for human rights and fundamental freedoms. However, the pluralistic nature of most societies has resulted in problems for the different groups to achieve and maintain harmony and co-operation.

67. Nevertheless, progress has been noted in the ongoing process of decolonisation and the wider spread of democracy, wider recognition of respect for human dignity and increasing recognition of the unique concern of indigenous people in the world, expanded economic and educational opportunities and globalisation of communication.

68. There are negative developments of social polarisation and fragmentation, wider disparities and inequalities of income and wealth within and among nations, degradation of the environment, marginalisation of people, migration and major dislocation of population.

69. Violence is a growing threat to the security of communities everywhere and the global social order. These are compelling and urgent reasons for action to foster social cohesion while recognising, protecting and valuing diversity.

70. There is therefore an urgent need for, transparent and accountable public institution, opportunity for all to participate and involve in civil society; publicly available objective data for decision making, maintainance of social stability, justice and progress; gender equality and equity and empowerment of women;

rights to highest attainable standard of physical and mental-health and to health as a factor of development; promoting addressing caring for each others well-being and mutual support; danger to society of armed conflict, violence, crime and trafficking of drugs, women and children.

Actions

(A) Responsive Government and Full Participation in Society

71. Government should promote and protect all human rights and fundamental freedoms and should make public institution more responsive to peoples needs, by ensuring decisions are based on accurate data and are taken with the participation of those who will be effected; review and allocate resources to promote community cohesion; simplify administrative regulations facilitating maximum access to information opening channels of communication to seek redress of grievances; production of relevent studies/researches and dissemination of information on innovative models and successful practices of global and technical changes on social integration; accountability of public services from all public officials; strengthening transparency and accountability of political groupings.

72. Encouraging the fullest participation in the society requires strengthening the capacities and opportunities for all people, especially the vulnerable and the disadvantaged; enabling institutions of civil society, especially those representing vulnerable and disadvantaged groups; giving community organisations greater involvement in the design and implementation of local projects; ensuring a legal framework that encourages contributions from community organisations and voluntary associations; establishing a universal and flexible social safety net, facilitating the access of disadvantaged and marginalised people to education as well as their participation in social and cultural life.

(B) Non-discrimination, Tolerance and Mutual Respect for and Value of Diversity

73. Eliminating discrimination and promoting tolerance for diversity requires enacting and implementing laws and regulation to combat all forms of discrimination; taking sepecific measures for the implementation of Nairobi Forward-Looking Strategy for

the advancement of women ensuring gender equality and equity; disseminating information in plain language about peoples rights and means for redressing complaints; respecting and protecting all language used in the world; protecting traditional and cultural heritage of all nation; encouraging independent communication media promoting peoples understanding of social integration.

(C) Equality and Social Justice

74. Government should promote equality and social justice by ensuring equality of all people before laws; regularly reviewing public policies and public spending from a social and gender equality, expanding and improving access to basic services, providing equal opportunity in employment, encouraging free formation of co-operatives; community and other grass-roots organisations that strengthen social integration; ensuring that structural adjustment programmes are designed to minimise their negative effects on vulnerable and disadvantaged groups; full access to preventive and curative health care for all; providing basic education accompained by improved quality for all, evaluating school system on regular basic and ensuring access to formal and non-formal learning activities, specifically to girls.

(D) Responses to Special Social Needs

75. Government responses to special needs of social groups should include identifing means to encourage institutions and services to adapt to the special needs of vulnerable and disadvantaged groups; recognising and promoting their abilities and experiences; ensuring access to work and social services to them; supporting by legislation incentives and other means of involving them in national decision making; improving their opportunities to seek position of public authority; promoting and protecting the rights of indigenous people; implementing the Plan of Action adopted by the World Summit for Children 1990, encouraging youth participation in designing and implementing policies and programmes; promoting the UN standardised rules of equalisation of opportunities for people with disability, older persons taking measures to enable persons belonging to minorities to participate in development of their society.

(E) Responses to Specific Social Needs of Refugees, Displaced Persons and Asylum Seekers, Documented Migrants and Undocumented Migrants Seekers

76. In order to address the specific needs of refugees, and asylum governments are urged to address the root causes of movement of refugees and displaced persons, strengthening their support for international protection and assistance activities for refugees and displaced persons; extend international support to countries of asylum to meet the basic needs of refugees; create comprehensive condition that allow for the voluntary re-patriation of refugees in safety and dignity; abide by international laws concerning refugees.

77. To promote the equitable, treatment and integration of documented migrants and their families government should ensure that they received fare and equal treatment and early integration, by giving them right to long-term residence, civil and political rights and responsibility and naturalisation; international exchange of information on educational and training institution to promote productive employment among them and encourage international harmony and cross-cultural understanding.

78. In order to address the concerns and basic human needs related to undocumented migrants government are urged to cooperate in reducing the causes of undocumented migration; countries of destination transit and origin should co-operate to manage their flows; international co-operation to reduce their effects on receiving countries; promote effective measures to protect them from all forms of discrimination.

(F) Violence, Crime the Problem of Illicit Drugs and Substance Abuse

79. Addressing the problems created by violence, crime, substance abuse and production, the use and trafficking of illicit drugs, and the rehabilitation of addicts requires introduction and implementation of specific policies and public health and social services programme; measures to eliminate all forms of exploitation abuse; harassment and violence against women; implement creative programmes channelising the energy of youths away from crime, violence, drugs abuse; improving mechanism for resolving conflict peacefully and reintegrating society; establishing partnership with

NGOs and community organisation for the rehabilitation and reintegration into society of offenders; strengthen international co-operation and co-ordination in measures for combating and violence and transnational organised crimes and terrorism; cambating drugs and substance abuse and trafficking through national and international co-ordination; combating trafficking in women and children through nationally and internationally co-ordinated measures.

(G) Social Integration and Family Responsibilities

80. The family should be strengthened and supported in all different cultural, political and social systems.

81. Helping the family in its contribution to social integration should involve encouraging social and economic policy that meet the needs of families; ensuring equal opportunities among its members; promoting mutual respect and equal partnership between women and men.

Chapter V

Implementation and Follow-up

82. Social development and the implementation of the Programme of Action of the Summit are primarily the responsibility of governments, although international co-operation and assistance are essential for their full implementation. At all levels of implementation, the crucial and essential requirements are promotion and protection of human rights, partnership with all actors especially voluntary organisations, recognising the diversity in the world, empowerment of people, efforts to mobilise new and additional financial resources and solidarity in mutual respect among individuals, community and nations.

Actions

(A) National Strategies, Evaluations and Reviews

83. At the National level an integrated approach to implementation of the Programme of Action requires analysing and reviewing policies and their impact on social development, effective co-ordination of all efforts of national and international

actors, assessing poverty, integrating social development goals into national development efforts, developing quantitative and qualitative indicators for social development and strengthening institutional capacities for co-ordination.

Countries to formulate and strengthen by 1996 strategies for implementing Summit outcome, defining time bound goals and targets, strengthening implementation and monitoring mechanisms and assessing regularly the progress in the form of consolidated reports.

UN should declare the Decade for the Eradication of Poverty starting 1996 which is the International Year for the Eradication of Poverty.

84. International support for national actions will require assistance in capacity building, co-ordinating assistance and disseminating information for facilitating policy analysis at the request of countries.

(B) Involvement of Civil Society

85. Effective implementation of POA requires strengthening community organisations and NGOs; establishing legislative and regulatory frameworks, institutional arrangements and consultative mechanisms for involving them at all stages; supporting capacity building; providing resources e.g. small grants and strengthening networking and exchange of expertise.

86. Contribution of civil society including the private sector can be enhanced by developing policies and procedures that facilitate government—civil society co-operation; encouraging and enabling business enterprises, trade unions and farmer's representative organization, co-operation, academic and research institutions and media to participate in social development programmes.

(C) Mobilisation of Financial Resources

87. Augmenting the availability of public resources for the social development requires at the national level greater domestic savings through effective taxes that are cognisant to social development and through cutting back on subsidies that do not benefit the poor; reducing excessive military expenditures consistent with national security requirements: ensuring predictable

funding for social development and that resources are available at the level of administration that is responsible for the same, increasing effective and transparent utilisation of funds, creating a supportive environment for resource mobilisation and developing innovative sources of funding.

88. Additional resource for Africa and other least developed countries require striving for the fulfilment of the agreed target of 0.7per cent of GNP for overall official development assistance as soon as possible and increasing share of funding of social development; agreeing on mutual commitment between interested parties to allocate 20 per cent of ODA and 20per cent of national budget to social development; providing assistance for social sector activities including in the form of grants of soft loans; implementation of the commitments to the special needs of small island and land-locked developing countries; giving preference to national experts, ensuring minimum project and programme overheads costs; expanding south co-operation, monitoring the impact of trade liberalisation and encouraging recipient governments to strengthen their national co-ordination mechanisms for international co-operation.

89. Continued international co-operation and assistance in terms of assessing the financial implications of the commitments of the summit, enhanced technical and financial assistance, support and encouragement of transformation of HRF will be required for economies in transition. Multi and bilateral donors will be invited to consult for effective co-ordination to achieve the objectives of the Summit.

90. Recognising the need for debt reduction, further progress can be made by inviting the international community including the financial institutions to continue to explore ways of implementing additional and innovative measures to alleviate debt burdens; encourage possibilities of debt swaps for social development, mobilising the resources of the ODA/debt reduction facility and inviting creditor countries, private banks and multilateral financial institutions to continue their initiatives to address the commercial debt problems.

91. In order to ensure that SAP include social development goals, governments should protect basic social programmes and expenditures, review the impact of SAP on social development, develop policies to reduce their negative effects and promote policies enabling small enterprises, co-operatives and other forms

of micro enterprises for generating employment.

92. International financial institutions should contribute to the mobilisation of resources for the implementation of the POA and are urged to integrate social development goals in their policies, programmes and operations including higher priority to social sector lending; should work together with concerned countries to improve policy dialogue and develop new initiatives to ensure that SAP promote sustained economic and social development with particular attention to people living in poverty. The UN should in co-operation with these agencies, study the impact of SAP and assist countries in creating the needed conditions for social development.

93. New and innovative ideas to generate funds should be considered by the relevant UN bodies.

94. A framework for international co-operation must be developed to integrate implementation, follow up and assessment of the outcome of UN conferences/Summits which have been held or proposed.

95. The General Assembly is the principal policy making and appraisal organ on matters relating to the follow up of the summit. The General Assembly should review the effectiveness of the steps taken to implement the outcome of the Summit in 1996 and call for a special session in 2000 A.D. for review and appraisal.

The Economic and Social Council would oversee system wide co-ordination in the implementation of the Summit outcome and made recommendations in this regard; review the reporting system in the area of social development. The Council should be invited to review the mandate, agenda and composition of the Commission for Social Development at its substantive session in 1995.

Regional Commissions, in co-operation with regional inter-governmental organisations and banks could convene meetings at a high political level to review progress and report through appropriate mechanism to the Council.

The role of the Committee on Economic, Social and Cultural Rights in monitoring those aspects relating to compliance with the International Covenant on Economic, Social and Cultural Rights is important.

96. There is a need to renew, reform and revitalise the various parts of the UN system to serve the objectives of the Summit. They should expand and improve their co-operation in the field of

social development to ensure that their efforts are complementary.

97. For economies in transition, UN should provide technical co-operation in designing, implementing and supporting social development programmes.

98. Implementation of the POA will involve strengthening of the UN system and inviting the WTO and ILO to contribute to the implementation of the POA. The Secretary-General will be requested to ensure effective co-ordination.

99. Operational activities of the UN to be strengthened in order to supplement the Summit outcome by capacity building at local, national and regional level, co-ordination at the country level, encouraging south-south co-operation, increasing resources for operational activities for development, strengthening their capacity for information gathering, analysis and developing indicators of social development; and providing policy and technical support.

100. Major groups identified in Agenda 21 to be involved in planning, elaboration, implementation and evaluation at both national and international levels. Mechanisms are needed to ensure this.

Bibliography

Aiach, Pierre and Sarah Curtis, 1990, *Social Inequalities in Self-Reported Morbidity: Interpretation and Comparison of Data from Britain and France*, Social Science and Medicine, Vol. 31, No. 3.

Ali, Almas and Jill Carr-Harris, 1991, *Assessing the Potential of Environmental Health Research in India*, New Delhi: South-South Solidarity.

Ali, Almas and N.C. Das, *Case Study of Chronically Drought-Affected Populations of Kalahandi, Orissa*, New Delhi: South-South Solidarity (mimeo).

Alok, S.K., 1988, *Indian Systems of Medicine and Homoeopathy: State and National Profile*, New Delhi: Ministry of Health and Family Welfare, pp. 42-47.

Anand, T.R., 1984, *Financing Through Health, Insurance and Co-operatives*, Health and Population, pp. 299-304.

Anubhav, 1966, *Urban Health*.

Attivale, Anand Danwdar (ed. with a commentary by Indu), 1980, *Astanga Sangraha*, Pune: Atreya Prakashan.

Banerjee, D., 1983, *National Health Policy and its Implementation*, Economic and Political Weekly, 22 January, pp. 105-08.

Banerjee, D., 1995, Foundation for Research in Community Health, Newsletter IX, No. 1, January-February.

Banerjee, D., 1995, *Serious Implications of the World Bank's Revised National Tuberculosis Control Programme for India*, New Delhi: Nucleus for Health Policies and Programmes and Voluntary Health Association of India.

Banga, Ved Prakash, 1996, *Quackery—Real Threat to Dignified Health Care*, New Delhi: Jaya Medical Publications.

Basu, Salil, 1992, *Urban Slums of Delhi*.

Bhadouria, B.P.S. and V.B. Dubey, 1989, *Panchayati Raj and Rural Development*, New Delhi: Commonwealth Publishers.

Bhat, Ramesh, 1993, *The Private/Public Mix in Health Care in India*, Health Policy and Planning, Vol. 8, No. 1, pp. 43-56.

Bose, Ashish, *Population Profile of the Elderly (60+yrs.) in India*, New Delhi: Under Publication, B.R. Publishing Corporation.

Carr-Harris, Jill, 1992, *New Dimensions of Eco-health*, New Delhi: South-South Solidarity.

Carr-Harris, Jill, 1994, *Urban Eco-health*, New Delhi: South-South-Solidarity.

Carr-Harris, Jill and Geeta Menon, 1994, *Tribal Eco-health*, New Delhi: South-South Solidarity.

Central Pollution Control Board (CPCB), 1991, *Control of Urban Pollution Studies (CUPS/30/1989-90), Status of Water Supply and Waste Water Collection: Treatment and Disposal in Class I Cities, 1988*, New Delhi: Control of Urban Pollution Series.

Chakraborty, A., 1990, *Social Stress and Mental Health: A Social-Psychiatric Field Study of Calcutta*, New Delhi: Sage Publications.

Chatterjee, K.K., *Where Survival is the Question*, New Delhi: South-South Solidarity (mimeo).

Chatterjee, M., 1993, *A Decade Towards Health for All—Recommendations of the ICSSR—ICMR Panel*, Social Science and Health, ICSSR, 2:4, January-March.

Crawford, D.G., 1914, *A History of the IMS, 1600-1913*, Calcutta: W. Thacker and Co., Vol. II.

Creese, A.L., 1990, *User Charges for Health Care: A Review of Recent Experiences*, Geneva: World Health Organization.

Datta, Abhijit, 1995, *Reforming Panchayat Bureaucracy*, New Delhi: Institute of Social Sciences.

Deodhar, N.S., 1990, *Health Sciences Information and Promotion of Health Status*, Journal of Education and Social Change, 4: pp. 84-89, October-December.

Deodhar, N.S., 1996, *Health Problems of Old-Age*.

Diderichsen, Finn, 1990, *Health and Social Inequities in Sweden*, Social Science and Medicine, Vol. 31, No. 3.

D'Silva, Allwyn, 1993, *Jerimeri Bombay*, Jagruti Kendra.

Duggal, Ravi, and Sucheta Amin, 1987, *Cost of Health Care*, Mumbai: Foundation for Research in Community Health.

Duggal, Ravi and Sucheta Amin, 1989, *Cost of Health Care—A Household Survey in an Indian District*, Mumbai: Foundation for Research in Community Health.

Duggal, Ravi, 1990, *State Health Financing and Health Care Services in India*, Health Financing in the Voluntary Sector, New Delhi: Voluntary Health Association of India.

Duggal, Ravi, 1995, *Health Expenditure Pattern in Selected Major States*, Radical Journal of Health, Vol. I, pp. 37-38.

Employee's State Insurance Corporation, 1996, *Annual Report 1995-96*, New Delhi.

Feldstein, Paul, J., 1991, *Health Care Economics*, Delmar Publishers.

Fernandes, Walter and Raj Anthony, 1992, *Development, Displacement and Rehabilitation in the Tribal Areas of Orissa*, New Delhi: Indian Social Institute.

Foundation for Research in Community Health (FRCH), 1994, *Health Care Resources and Investment in a District*, Draft Report, Pune: FRCH.

George, Alex *et al.*, 1992, *Household Health Expenditure in Madhya Pradesh*, Mumbai: FRCH.

George, Alex., I. Shah and S. Nandraj, 1993, *A Study of Household Health Expenditure in Madhya Pradesh*, Mumbai: FRCH.

Ghosh, Shanti, 1996, *Whither Health Care for Women and Children*, Paper prepared for ICHI.

Gill, Sonya ed., 1987, *Health Status of the Indian People*, New Delhi: FRCH-ICMR, December.

Gopalan, C., 1995, *Towards India's Food and Nutrition Security*, Keynote address at the National Symposium on Food Security for the Poor, organised by the FAO and the Indian Association for the Advancement of Science, 4 October.

Gopalan, C., 1995-96, *Nutrition Security for Optimal Health*, Paper prepared for the 83rd Session of the Indian Science Congress on Science and Technology for the Achievement of Food, Economic and Health Security.

Government of India, 1883, *Census of India, 1881*, New Delhi: Government of India, Vol. 3.

Government of India, 1946, *Report of the Health Survey and Development Committee (Bhore Committee)*, Vol. I.

Government of India, 1952, *First Five-Year Plan*, New Delhi: Planning Commission.

Government of India, 1962, *Health Survey and Planning Committee (Mudaliar Committee)*, New Delhi: Manager of Publications.

Government of India, 1980, *Sixth Five-Year Plan, 1980-85*, New Delhi: Planning Commission.

Government of India, 1982, *National Mental Health Programme for India*, New Delhi: Ministry of Health and Family Welfare.

Government of India, 1983, *National Health Policy*, New Delhi: Ministry of Health and Family Welfare.

Government of India, 1983, *Report of the Task Force on Housing and Urban Development*, New Delhi: Planning Commission, Vol. 4.

Government of India, 1984, *Occasional Paper No. 1, Sample Registration System*, New Delhi: Office of the Registrar General of India.

Government of India, 1984, *Census of India, 1981—Five Per cent Sample Report*, New Delhi: Government of India.

Government of India, 1986, *Indian Systems of Medicine and Homoeopathy—Statistics*, New Delhi: Ministry of Health and Family Welfare.

Government of India, 1991, *Census of India, 1991*, New Delhi: Government of India, Series 1, Part VII.

Government of India, 1992, *Health Information of India, 1992*, New Delhi: Central Bureau of Health Intelligence, Directorate General of Health Services, Ministry of Health and Family Welfare.

Government of India, 1993, *Health Information of India, 1993*, New Delhi: Central Bureau of Health Intelligence, Directorate General of Health Services, Ministry of Health and Family Welfare.

Government of India, 1994, *Annual Report 1993-94*, New Delhi: Ministry of Health and Family Welfare.

Government of India, 1994, *Health Information of India, 1994*, New Delhi: Central Bureau of Health Intelligence, Directorate General of Health Services, Ministry of Health and Family Welfare.

Government of India, 1994, *Centrally Sponsored Schemes for Urban Development*, New Delhi: Ministry of Urban Development.

Government of India, 1994a, *Census of India, 1991, Occasional Paper No. 5*, New Delhi: Home Ministry.

Government of India, 1994b, *Fertility and Mortality Indicators, 1992, Sample Registration Bulletin*, New Delhi: Office of the Registrar General of India.

Government of India, 1995, *Economic Survey (1994-95)*, New Delhi: Ministry of Finance, Economic Division.

Government of India, 1995, *Sample Registration Bulletin*, New Delhi: Office of the Registrar General of India, Vol. 29, No. 2.

Government of India, 1995, *Panchayat Swasthya Sewa Scheme: Expert Committee Recommendations*, New Delhi: Directorate General of Health Services, Ministry of Health and Family Welfare.

Government of India, 1995, *National Family Health Survey, 1992-94*, Mumbai: International Institute of Population Studies.

Government of India, 1996, *Annual Report, 1995-96*, New Delhi: Ministry of Health and Family Welfare.

Government of India, 1996, *Report of the Sub-Group on Urban Planning*, New Delhi: Planning Commission.

Graig and A. Laurence, 1992, *Health of the Nations*.

Gupta, Gowri, 1992, *Unit Cost of Health Programmes at the Micro-level in India*, New Delhi: Faculty of Management Studies, University of Delhi.

Gupta, J.P. and V.P. Gupta, 1986, *Study of the Systematic Analysis and Functioning of Health Teams at the District and Block Levels*, New Delhi: National Institute of Health and Family Welfare.

Hardoy, J. and D. Satherwaite, 1989, *Squatter Citizens*, London: Earthscan.

Harpham. T., T. Lusty and P. Vaughan, 1988, *In the Shadow of the City*, Oxford: Oxford University Press.

HelpAge India, 1994, *Nationwide Survey Report* (Unpublished).

Heston, A., 1982, *National Income*, The Cambridge Economic History of India, Hyderabad: Orient Longman Limited, Vol. II.

Hsiao, C. William and P. Dave-Sen, 1996, *Co-operative Financing for Health Care in Rural India*, Foundation for Research in Community Health (FRCH) Newsletter, March-April 1996.

Indian Council for Medical Research (ICMR), 1989, *Utilization of Health and Family Planning Services in Bihar, Gujarat and Kerala*, New Delhi: ICMR.

Indian Council for Medical Research (ICMR), 1990, *Evaluation of the Quality of Family Welfare Services at the Primary Health Centre Level*, New Delhi: ICMR.

Indian Institute of Management (IIM), 1985, *Study of Facility Utilization and Programme Management in Family Welfare in Uttar Pradesh, Madhya Pradesh and Bihar*, Ahmedabad: Public Systems Group.

Indian Institute of Management (IIM), 1991, *Time Utilization and Productivity of Health Manpower*, Bangalore: IIM.

Indian Psychiatric Society (IPS), 1971, *Workshop Report on Mental Health Care in a Rural Population*, Nagpur, IPS.

Indrakant, S., 1996, *Food Security and Public Distribution System in Andhra Pradesh—A Case Study*, Hyderabad: Centre for Social and Economic Studies.

International Institute of Population Studies (IIPS), 1994, *National Family Health Survey 1992-93*, Mumbai: IIPS.

International Labour Office (ILO), 1973, *Minimum Age for Admission to Employment*, Convention 138, Geneva: ILO, 26 June.

Irudaya Rajan, S., 1995, *An Agenda for National Policies on Ageing*, Research and Development Journal, Vol. 1, No. 2, February.

Jaggi, O.P., 1979, *Western Medicine in India—Public Health and its Administration*, History of Science, Technology and Medicine in India, New Delhi: Atma Ram and Sons, Vol. 14.

Jain, L.C., 1993, *Panchayats—Window to a Million Possibilities*, New Delhi: People's Action, Vol. 8, No. 2.

Jamison, Dean, T., *et al.*, 1983, *Disease Control Priorities in Developing Countries*, Oxford: Published for the World Bank, Oxford University Press.

Jamuna, D., 1995, *Ageing Women in India: A Profile*, Research and Development Journal, Vol. 1, No. 3, June.

Jeffery, Roger, 1988, *The Politics of Health in India*, Berkeley: University of California Press.

Jessani, Amar and S. Anantharam, 1989, *Private Sector and Privatisation in the Health Care Services*, Mumbai: Foundation for Research in Community Health.

Jessani, Amar and S. Anantharam, 1993, *Private Sector and Privatization in Health Care Services*, Mumbai: Foundation for Research in Community Health.

Jolly, K.G., 1986, *Family Planning in India, 1964-1984: A District Level Study*, Delhi: Hindustan Publishing Corporation.

Juyal, B.N., 1992, *Environment and Existence in the Taungya Squatments in the Terai*, New Delhi: South-South Solidarity.

Kanan, K.P., K.R., Thankappan, Raman Kutty and K.P. Aravindan, 1991, *Health and Development in Rural Kerala*, Thiruvananthapuram: KSSP.

Kannapiran, Chandra, Christina De Sa and Indu Prakash Singh, 1996, *The Power of Partnership: Leprosy Workers and the Community: A Report*, New Delhi: Voluntary Health Association of India.

Khan, M.E. and C.V.S. Prasad, 1985, *Health Financing in India—A Case Study of Gujarat and Maharashtra*, Baroda: Operations Research Group.

Kosambi, D.D., 1975, *An Introduction to the Study of Indian History*, Mumbai: Popular Prakashan.

Kundu, A., 1993, *In the Name of the Urban Poor: Access to Basic Amenities*, New Delhi: Sage Publications.

Kurien, C.T., 1978, *Poverty, Planning and Social Transformation, Mumbai,* Allied Publishers.

Lagasse, Raphael, *et al.*, 1990, *Health and Social Inequities in Belgium,* Social Science and Medicine, Vol. 31, No. 3.

Lahelma, Eero, and Tapani Valkonen, 1990, *Health and Social Inequities in Finland and Elsewhere,* Social Science and Medicine, Vol. 31, No. 3.

Mathew, George and Ramesh C. Nayak, 1996, *Panchayats at Work: What it Means for the Oppressed,* Economic and Political Weekly.

Mathur, O.P., 1993, *The Impact of Urbanization on Children,* Urban Child Issues and Strategies, New Delhi: NIUA in Collaboration with the Planning Commission, Ministry of Urban Development, UNICEF.

Menon, Geeta, 1994, *New Dimensions of Tribal Ecohealth,* Unpublished.

Milton, T., 1985, *The Distinction between Public Health and Community/ Social/Preventive Medicine,* Journal of Public Health Policy.

Minhas, B.S., L.R. Jain and S.D. Tendulkar, 1991, *Declining Incidence of Poverty in the 1980s: Evidence versus Artifacts,* Economic and Political Weekly, Vol. 26, Nos. 27, 28.

Ministry of Finance, 1995, *Indian Public Finance Statistics, 1994,* New Delhi: Department of Economic Affairs.

Ministry of Health and Family Welfare, 1981, *Health for All by 2000 A.D. Report of the Sub-Group on Health Services Organisation to Achieve Health for All by 2000 A.D.,* New Delhi: Government of India, pp. 89-117.

Ministry of Works and Housing, 1993, *Government of India, National Master Plan for Water Supply and Sanitation (1981-91),* Government of India, July.

Mukherjee, Anindita, 1995, *Review of Trends Since 1980 in Relation to Rural Poverty,* National Conference on Poverty and Employment, New Delhi: Institute of Applied Manpower Research.

Nabarro, D. and McConnell, 1989, *The Impact of AIDS on Socio-Economic Development.*

National Council for Applied Economic Research (NCAER), 1992, *Rural Household Health Care Needs and Availability,* New Delhi: NCAER.

National Council for Applied Economic Research (NCAER), 1992, *Household Survey of Medical Care, New Delhi:* NCAER.

National Institute of Public Finance and Policy (NIPFP), 1994, *NIPFP Data Bank: Government Expenditure on Health Sector (1985-86 to 1989-90)*, New Delhi: National Institute of Public Finance and Policy.

National Institute of Rural Development (NIRD), 1989, *Health Care Delivery System in Rural Areas—A Study of a MPW Scheme*, Hyderabad: NIRD.

NMEP Directorate, 1995, *Strengthening Malaria Control in India*, Delhi: NMEP Directorate, Unpublished document.

NMEP Directorate, 1995, *Operational Manual for Malaria Action Programme*, Delhi: NMEP Directorate.

National Nutrition Monitoring Bureau (NNMB), 1989-90, *Report for the Years 1989-1990*, Hyderabad: National Institute of Nutrition, Indian Council of Medical Research.

National Nutrition Monitoring Bureau (NNMB), 1993, *Report for the Year 1993*, Hyderabad, National Institute of Nutrition, Indian Council of Medical Research.

National Sample Survey Organization (NSSO), 1987, *Morbidity and the Utilization of Medical Services*, New Delhi: Government of India, Report No. 364.

National Sample Survey Organization (NSSO), 1989, *Morbidity and the Utilization of Medical Services* NSS 42nd Round, New Delhi: Government of India.

National Sample Survey Organization (NSSO), 1992, *Morbidity and the Utilization of Medical Services*, NSS 42nd Round (1986-87), Sarvekshana, New Delhi: Government of India, 51st Issue, Vol. XV, No. 4, April-June.

National Sample Survey Organization (NSSO), 1992, NSSS 43rd Round (1987-1988), New Delhi: Government of India.

National Tuberculosis Institute (NTI), 1988, *Report of the Baseline Survey*, DANIDA Health Care Project, Bangalore: NTI.

Oommen, M.A. and Abhijit Datta, 1995, *Panchayats and their Finance*, New Delhi: Institute of Social Sciences, Concept Publishing Company.

Paradkar, Harisastri ed. (with a commentary by Arundatta and Aemadu), 1982, *Astanga Hrdayam*, Varanasi: Chaukhamba Sanskrit Series Office.

Payne, Katrina (ed.), 1993, *Adding Health to Years*, New Delhi: Help Age International.

Phadke, Anant *et al.*, 1994, *A Study of the Supply and Use of*

Pharmaceuticals in the Rural Districts, Pune: Foundation for Research in Community Health.

Planning Commission, 1996, *Working Group on Health Care Delivery in Urban and Rural Areas, Including Public Health Systems, Health Surveillance, HMIS, Health Legislations*, New Delhi.

Prabhu. K. Seeta and Somnath Chatterjee, 1993, *Social Sector Expenditures and Human Development*, Mumbai: Department of Economic Analysis and Policy, Reserve Bank of India.

Purohit, *Socio-Economic Correlates of Household Health Care Behaviour: A Factor Analytic Approach*, Asian Economic Review.

Rajkumar, S., 1995, *The Tragedy of Alzheimer Disease*, Research and Development Journal, Vol. 1, No. 3, June.

Rao, E.K., 1993, *PDS: Regional Variations*, Alternate Economic Survey 1992-93, New Delhi: Public Interest Research Group.

Rao, M. Govinda, and Tapas Sen, 1993, *Government Expenditure in India: Level, Growth and Composition*, New Delhi: National Institute of Public Finance and Policy.

Reddy, K.N., 1992, *Health Expenditures in India*, Working Paper No. 14, New Delhi: National Institute of Public Finance and Policy.

Reddy, K.N. and V. Selvaraju, 1994, *Health Care Expenditures by Government in India: 1974-75 to 1990-91*, New Delhi: Seven Hills Publications.

Report of the Technical Group on Population Projection, 1986, August.

Rhode, John and H. Vishwanathan, 1994, *The Rural Private Practitioner*, Health for the Millions, New Delhi: Voluntary Health Association of India, Vol. 2, No. 1, February.

Rossi-Espagnet, A., 1984, *Primary Health Care in Urban Areas: Reaching the Urban Poor in Developing Countries: A State of the Art Report by UNICEF* and *WHO*, Geneva: World Health Organisation.

Roy, Burman, J.J., 1990, *Shifting Cultivation: An Aspect of Tribal Exploitation*, Indian Journal of Social Work, Mumbai: Tata Institute of Social Sciences, Vol. 51, No. 1.

Sahani, A., 1990, *Leadership Styles for Effective Health Care, Leadership and Human Resources Development for Health Care*, ISHA Professional Development Series-III, Bangalore: Indian Society of Health Administrators, pp. 61-63.

Sastri, Pdt. Paramemar (ed.) (with a commentary by Adhamalla and Kasirama), 1983, *Samgadhara Samhita*, Varanasi: Chaukhamba Orientalia.

Sanyal, S.K., 1996, *Household Financing of Health Care*, Economic and Political Weekly, 18 May.

Seetaprabhu, K. and S. Chatterjee, 1993, *Social Sector Expenditures and Human Development*, Mumbai Development Research Group, Study 6, Department of Economic Analysis and Policy, Reserve Bank of India.

Sehgal, P.N. and K. Singh, 1992, *Knowledge, Attitude, Beliefs and Practices (KAPB): A Study Related to AIDS in Manipur and Intervention Strategies*, New Delhi: Voluntary Health Association of India.

Sen, Rahul, 1995, *Ecohealth: A Paradigm of People's Development*, New Delhi: South-South Solidarity.

Sen, Rahul, 1995, *Study on the North-Eastern Districts of Uttar Pradesh with Special Reference to Waterlogging*, New Delhi: South-South Solidarity.

Sethi, B.B., S.C. Gupta, R.K. Mahendru, and P. Kumari, 1972, *Migration and Mental Health*, Indian Journal of Psychiatry, Vol. 14, pp. 115-32.

Shah, P.M., 1984, *Specific Health Problems of Working Children: Alternative Approaches to Health Care*, Child Labour and Health, Mumbai: Tata Institute of Social Sciences.

Shankar, Darshan, 1992, *Indigenous Health Services—State of the Art*, State of India's Health, New Delhi: Voluntary Health Association of India.

Sharma, B.L. *et al.*, 1993, *Bibliographic View of Health Insurance Studies*, New Delhi: National Institute of Health and Family Welfare.

Sharma, P.V. (ed.), 1983, *Charaka Samhita (Mula)*, Varanasi: Chaukhamba Orientalia.

Sharma, P.V., 1992, *History of Medicine in India*, New Delhi: Indian National Science Academy, pp. 180-199.

Sivaramakrishnan K.C., 1993, *Managing the Urban Environment in India: Towards an Agenda for Action*, Calcutta: The Times Research Foundation, Vol. 1.

South-South Solidarity, 1996, *Freshwater Case Study in Garhwal Himalayas*, New Delhi: Draft Report prepared for UNICEF.

Tabibzadeh, I. A., Rossi-Espagnet and R. Maxwell, 1989, *Spotlight on the Cities: Improving Urban Health in the Cities*, Geneva: World Health Organization.

Tarimo, E. and A. Creese, 1990, *Achieving Health for All by the Year 2000, Midway Reports of Country Experiences*, Geneva: World Health Organization.

Thankappan, K.R. *et. al.*, 1987, *Health and Development in Rural Kerala*, Thiruvananthapuram: KSSP.

Thapar, Romila, 1973, *Ashoka and the Decline of the Mauryas*, New Delhi: Oxford University Press.

Trikamji, Yadaiya and Narayan Ram Acharya (ed.) (with a commentary by Dalhona), 1992, *Susruta Samhita*, Varanasi: Chaukhamba Orientalia.

Tulasidhar, V.B., 1993, *Expenditure Compression and Health Sector Outlays*, Economic and Political Weekly, 6 November 1996, pp. 2473-2477.

Upadhyay, Jayanta and Jill Carr-Harris, 1994, *Eco-systems Health in Industrial Settings: A Case Study of Coal Mining Operations in India*, New Delhi: South-South Solidarity.

Upadhyay, Jayanta and Jill Carr-Harris, 1994, *Eco-systems Health in Industrial Settings: A Case of Leather Tanneries in India*, New Delhi: South-South Solidarity.

United Nations Development Programme (UNDP), 1994, *Human Development Report*, 1994, New York: UNDP.

UNICEF, 1996, *The Progress of Indian States, 1995*, New Delhi, UNICEF.

Verma, R.K. and Anupama Verma, 1994, *Evaluation and Impact of Jawahar Rojgar Yojna*, New Delhi: Mohit Publications.

Webster, Neil, 1992, *Panchayati Raj and the Decentralization of Development Planning in West Bengal*, Calcutta: K.P. Bagchi & Company.

Weil and Cooper, *et al.*, 1990, *The Impact of Development Policies on Health, A Review of Literature*, Geneva: World Health Organization.

World Bank, 1993, *World Development Report 1993*, New Delhi: Oxford University Press.

World Bank, 1994, *India: Policy and Finance Strategies for Strengthening Primary Health Care Services*, Mimeo Report, Washington DC.

World Health Organization (WHO) 1991, *The Public/Private Mix in National Health Systems and the Role of Ministries of Health*, Geneva, WHO.

WHO-SEARO, 1992, *AIDS in South East Asia: No Time for Complacency*, New Delhi: WHO.

World Health Organization (WHO), 1993a, *Implementation of the Global Strategy for Health for All by the Year 2000, Second Evaluation*, New Delhi: WHO, Regional Office for South-East Asia.

Index